Leaderless
Jihad

Leaderless
Jihad

Terror Networks In the Twenty-First Century

Marc Sageman

UNIVERSITY OF PENNSYLVANIA PRESS | PHILADELPHIA

Published by
University of Pennsylvania Press
Philadelphia, Pennsylvania 19104-4112

Printed in the United States of America on acid-free paper
10 9 8 7 6 5 4 3 2 1

Library of Congress Cataloging-in-Publication Data

Sageman, Marc.
    Leaderless Jihad : terror networks in the twenty-first
    century / Marc Sageman.
    p. cm.   Includes bibliographical references and index.
    ISBN-13: 978-0-8122-4065-8 (hardcover : alk. paper)
    ISBN-10: 0-8122-4065-0 (hardcover : alk. paper)
    1. Terrorists—Social networks. 2. Terrorism. 3. Jihad.
    I. Title.
HV6431.S227   2008
363.325—dc22

                                    2007038323

CONTENTS

The threat from al Qaeda and its local affiliates is rapidly changing. The Islamist terror networks of the twenty-first century are becoming more fluid, independent, and unpredictable entities than their more structured forebears, who carried out the atrocities of 9/11. The present threat has evolved from a structured group of al Qaeda masterminds, controlling vast resources and issuing commands, to a multitude of informal local groups trying to emulate their predecessors by conceiving and executing operations from the bottom up. These "homegrown" wannabes form a scattered global network, a leaderless jihad. Although physically unconnected, these terrorist hopefuls form a virtual yet violent social movement as they drift to Internet chat rooms that connect them and provide them with inspiration and guidance. As the threat has migrated from outside to inside Western countries, the challenge for governments lies in detecting and neutralizing these groups before they become violent. The key to successful eradication of this threat, which is real but unlikely to endanger the existence of the nation, is to understand the dynamics of this process, which has serious implications for how Western governments should proceed to contain this menace.

This book, like its predecessor *Understanding Terror Networks*,[1] brings the scientific method to the study of terrorism, taking into account how it has changed in recent years. Reports that al Qaeda is regaining strength and mustering resources for another assault do not reflect the full picture (see Chapter 7). The threat to the West has evolved from infiltration by outside trained terrorists against whom international liaison cooperation and border protection are effective to inside homegrown, self-financed, self-trained terrorists against whom the most effective countermeasure would be to stop the process of radicalization before it reaches its violent end. Chapter 1 outlines how to study terrorism, consistent with the rules of scientific inquiry. Chapters 2 and 3 provide the necessary historical, religious, and socioeconomic background for the main argument in the book, showing how a very few young Muslims change to the point where they murder innocent people and sometimes give up their lives in the process. I use the term *radicalization* to express this process of transforming individuals from rather unexceptional and ordinary beginnings into terrorists with the willingness to use violence for political ends. In Chapter 4 I argue that this radicalization includes four prongs. A sense of *moral outrage* at apparent crimes against Muslims both globally and locally is a common theme among the terrorists. This outrage is *interpreted in a specific way*, namely that this moral violation is part of a larger war against Islam. This ideology appeals to certain people because it *resonates with their own personal experience* of discrimination, making them feel that they are also victims of this wider war. A few individuals are then *mobilized through networks*, both face to face and now more and more commonly online, to become terrorists. Chapter 5 concerns the differences in conditions for radicalization between Europe and the United States.

Chapter 6 examines the role of the Internet in this process of radicalization and the global structure of this movement. Chapter 7 shows that this bottom-up process of small local groups joining a violent global social movement, connected virtually via the Internet, results in a fluid, rapidly adaptive, and difficult to eradicate network of terrorists: the leaderless jihad. In Chapter 8 I present practical policy recommendations on how to counter this specific threat.

Leaderless
Jihad

Understanding the Path to Radicalism

The radicalization of Ahmed Omar Saeed Sheikh—the man convicted of kidnapping *Wall Street Journal* reporter Daniel Pearl, who was later beheaded—highlights the issues facing those who wish to neutralize global Islamist terrorists in the twenty-first century.

The parents of Omar Sheikh once expected the Queen of England to knight their son.[1] They had emigrated from Pakistan in 1968, opening up a clothing business in London. Omar, as he was called, was born in London on December 23, 1973. He had two younger siblings and the family moved to an upscale neighborhood when he was four.

His parents described his early life as idyllic. His brother Awais described him as "the kindest, most gentle person you could meet."[2] Omar grew up in an upper-middle-class environment and attended expensive elite private schools. He studied at the Forest School in England until 1987, when his family returned to Pakistan to try a new business venture. He then was enrolled in prestigious Aitchison College in Lahore. When the business venture failed, his family returned to England in 1990 and Omar once again attended the Forest School. He chose chess and arm wrestling as hobbies, and won tournaments in each. Some of his fellow students and teachers also shared his parents' memory of him as "the model of a London public schoolboy, a keen, courteous student heading for university." He was "popular and bright, a pupil who enjoyed chess and excelled at mathematics and computers." His economics tutor recalled him as "willing and capable, a jolly good brain. . . . He was in the premier league of students."[3] He continued, "Omar was a bright boy, popular with his peers and very personable."[4] A spokesperson from the Forest School went as far to say, "The chap we knew was a good all-around, solid and very supportive pupil; a nice bloke and very respectful. I never recall him being particularly religious or politically motivated."[5] Omar even received a bravery commendation from the London Underground after jumping on the track in front of an oncoming train to rescue a fallen commuter.

When the people who paint this version of Omar's childhood learned that he was arrested as a suspected terrorist, they could not believe it. "This is not our son. He is incapable of being involved in anything like this. He has never given us a moment's concern," his father said.[6] His economics tutor echoed his parents' assessment. "We are absolutely stunned that he might be involved in these activities. The chap we knew was a good all-around, solid and very supportive pupil . . . there was absolutely no sign whatsoever of all this."[7]

The reaction from Omar's family and friends—"He was such a nice boy" —betrays our attempt to make sense of and categorize people. A terrorist, by cultural definition, is a bad guy. How can it square with one's cherished memory of a loved one? Our memory remains frozen in time and we assume that people stay essentially the same. Parents, who remember their children in better times, greet with complete disbelief the announcement that their grown child is a terrorist. This response is more common than we suspect—parents are usually the last to suspect that their beloved child has become a drug addict, for example. Nevertheless, the "nice guy turned terrorist" story, whether flawed or true, still has not dented the conventional wisdom about terrorists— namely, that they were bad from the beginning, or were the product of their social conditions, or were simply naïve young people brainwashed by sinister characters at a vulnerable moment.

Some of Omar's former classmates challenge the portrait of a well-integrated and nice young Englishman. One recalled that Omar always wanted to show his size and strength. "When he was eight, he punched a teacher called Mr. Burns and knocked him to the floor. He was a full-grown man, and this was an eight-year-old boy."[8] Another recalled an incident when Omar was ten. "He [Omar] emerged from a church service to declare: 'Well, that was crap.' When a fellow pupil retaliated and said: 'Your religion is crap,' the little Pakistani boy embarked on his first violent defense of Islam and chased his

4

foes around the cricket field."[9] While everyone recalled his fascination with strength, some coupled it with an aggressive streak. "He was sufficiently inspired by the release of *Over the Top*, a dismal Sylvester Stallone film about a professional arm-wrestler, to take up the sport, but despite his bulk and superior strength, he still liked to cheat. He would lie about his age and then challenge younger pupils. At one point he won a local competition and insisted the headmaster present his award during assembly to a catcall of boos."[10] Another said, "He had a number of tussles and when he was in the junior school he had a fight with someone who was three or four years older than him; he knocked another guy out in the first year and split his lip open."[11] A few recall that he had been expelled from Aitchison College for beating up fellow pupils.[12] "He was a violent person, into boxing," recalled a classmate from Lahore.[13] Upon his return to the Forest School in London, Omar glossed over the incident by either claiming that he had been to military school or failed his higher secondary exam.[14]

Interestingly, none of the journalists reporting on this alternative version of Omar's youth bothered to record their informants' reaction to the news that Omar was arrested for terrorist activities. The implication is that his later terrorist career is a logical consequence of his essential character. Inbred evil requires no explanation.

A third version of Omar's childhood comes from Omar himself, as told to Peter Gee, who had been arrested in India for possession of marijuana and spent more than a year in prison (from 1998 to 1999) with Omar due to the proximity of the first letters of their first names. Peter also shared a British university education with Omar. Peter said that Omar had admitted to him that he had been radicalized because of bullying he was subjected to during his East London childhood. "Omar spoke of his childhood and of racism in the playground, of being rejected by his peer group, who used to call him a 'Paki bastard.' It may seem strange to people to think of Omar as a deeply sensitive person, but these taunts hurt him deeply. Most sensitive people quickly withdraw from rejection, while others rage against it. Omar eventually chose the latter course."[15]

We should be careful about invoking the "racism made me do it" explanation for Omar's later terrorism. Millions of second-generation children of immigrants are subjected to prejudice throughout the West, but very few become terrorists. What is significant is that Omar later talked about it. Had he really felt discrimination when he was young, or did it become an after-the-fact justification for his later career? This is one of the issues I focus on in this book.

Another insight provided by Peter Gee was Omar's sense of alienation, of being caught between two cultures, Pakistani and British. Peter theorized that this lack of belonging anywhere led to "a need to belong and to be liked." Peter recalled that Omar had told him he had been excited about coming to Pakistan at the age of thirteen. "It was one of the first steps in a search for a sense of belonging that he had not found in England." Finally, it seems that he did not fit in Lahore either and his family returned to London three years later.[16] This need to belong might have contributed to his cultivation of charm and the fact that he was, as Gee noted, "not averse to playing to the gallery. Quite a lot of it with Omar is macho bravado."

Since Omar's crimes were committed in the name of religion, a key question is, when did he become religious? As we saw earlier, the version of his childhood as idyllic and well integrated denies that he had been "particularly religious" before his university days. As his economics tutor recalled, "There was no hint of political or religious extremism" at the time.[17] Yet, there are some signs of religious devotion elsewhere. To Peter Gee, Omar had said that he had been radicalized years before coming to college because of the bullying he had been subjected to as a child. Before he went to Pakistan, "though not 'ultra-religious,' Sheikh would 'find it personally insulting if you said anything he didn't like about Islam.'"[18] One journalist reports that he had began to develop "an unhealthy interest in the idea of jihad, a holy war in defense of Islam" while he was still in Pakistan at Aitchison College.[19] When he returned to the Forest School in London, he began to discuss the worsening situation in the Balkans with friends. A former classmate recalled him as saying, "Muslims were being persecuted and he wanted to do something. Omar took religion very seriously."[20] Other classmates recall his twin obsessions about Islam and body-building. "He was obsessed about his physique. He boasted about how in Pakistan he had hijacked a bus, and was a kickboxing champion—which we took to be just fantasy."[21]

All versions agree that Omar was handsome, tall and muscular, very bright and charming when he wanted to be. He did well in school and gained acceptance at the London School of Economics (LSE). He continued his arm-wrestling career in London pubs and earned a place on the English national team. He competed for his country in two international championships in

Spain and Switzerland in late 1992. Every version of Omar's life agrees that his commitment to Islam deepened dramatically at LSE. We can reconstruct his life following his entrance to LSE from a diary of his activities he later wrote when he was in an Indian prison.

Omar began his studies at LSE in October 1992 and took courses in applied mathematics, statistical theory, economics, and social psychology. He immediately joined the school Islamic society. He apparently socialized with this new set of friends and participated in "Bosnia Week" in November 1992. His diary reported, "various documentaries on Bosnia were shown. One such film, *The Destruction of a Nation*, shook my heart. The reason being Bosnian Muslims were shown being butchered by the Serbs."[22] Another source elaborates that this forty-five-minute film depicted the castration of Muslim prisoners in Serb detention camps.[23] Afterward, Omar became more involved in various activities on behalf of Bosnia, such as fund collections, talks, demonstrations. In December 1992 he was part of a team of representatives from London colleges that organized a Bosnia conference in January 1993. The result seemed disappointing. From his diary: "January 93: The Bosnia Conference. Good conference but no follow up."[24] In February 1993, Omar accompanied his father on a week-long business trip to Pakistan, taking with him propaganda videotapes on the war on Bosnia and hoping to spread the message in Pakistan by way of local militants. "Meet Ameer-ul Aseem, secretary of information, Jamaat-i-Islami. Spread tapes."

In March, Omar attended a talk on the refugee crisis in Bosnia given by Asad Khan, a trustee of a London-based Muslim charity, Convoy of Mercy. "After the talk, two or three students came up and said they wanted to go, and he was one of them," Khan later reported.[25] "He was very moved and volunteered to come on one of our aid convoys. He was a beautiful boy, soft spoken, upright, religious, not at all aggressive. He was the sort of boy you would want your sister to marry."[26] Omar immediately started working with Convoy of Mercy. During his Easter vacation, in April 1993, he accompanied Khan's next convoy of six trucks taking relief material to Bosnia, which also provided clandestine support for Muslim fighters there.[27] However, Omar became sick and never made it to Bosnia. Khan recalled that "by the time we got to Croatia, he was sick as a puppy."[28] He was left behind in the town of Split, Croatia, near the Bosnian border.

While recuperating in Split, Omar met Abdur Rauf, a Pakistani veteran of the war in Afghanistan who had come to join the Muslim militia. Rauf belonged to the Harakut-ul Mujahedin (HUM), one of the many small Islamic guerilla groups that proliferated in Pakistan and Afghanistan during this period. Rauf counseled Omar not to waste his time as an aid worker in Bosnia and recommended training for jihad in Afghanistan first. Rauf provided him with a letter of recommendation for HUM and the name of a London imam who was a HUM sympathizer and could help Omar get his father's permission to take up jihad.[29]

Recovered from his "indisposition and fatigue," Omar returned to school. In his diary he wrote, "Try to get back into academic to prepare for exams. Still attending talks by various groups. Can't settle down." Omar also continued to work for Asad Khan and Convoy of Mercy. However, the appeal of jihad was becoming overwhelming. He gradually dropped out of his classes and lost his enthusiasm for the charity. Khan recalled that "After two or three months, he disappeared and we never heard from him again."[30] Friends and family remarked on his growing obsession about world events. "'To some people he was too intense,' said a cousin and fellow LSE student. 'He would only want to talk about God or Islam or politics.'"[31] Omar flew to Pakistan later that spring.

Asad Khan of Convoy of Mercy elaborated on the widespread sense of anger and injustice felt over the treatment of Muslims in Bosnia, Kashmir, the Palestinian territories, and elsewhere. "There are people going to all these places because they believe their fellow Muslims are suffering. The young men, who left Oxford and Cambridge in the 1930s to fight the Franco regime in Spain, were they terrorists? There are many things happening in the world that make Muslims angry. Some of us choose to put our energies into humanitarian relief work, others choose to fight. I do not condone it for one moment, but I do understand why it happens."[32] Khan elaborated, "Muslims look around the world and they see themselves being persecuted everywhere. All of us come to the same conclusion, but we do different things."[33]

Omar arrived in Lahore "with zeal and intention to undergo arms training and joining the mujaheddin," according to his diary.[34] He shopped around for the best group for his need. The diary continued, "Decide HUM best option. Leave for Afghanistan via Islamabad." In August 1993, he arrived at the Khalid bin Waleed training camp, which was associated with al Qaeda but used by many of the myriad Islamist guerilla groups. He was supposed to take the forty-day basic training course in small and medium firearms. The diary stated, "After two weeks in Afghanistan very ill. Have to leave for Lahore, where relations are shocked to see my state and put up great resistance." His uncle in Lahore "tried to persuade me to quit arms training and go back to the UK. But I remained adamant and resumed training after a hiatus of 10 days."[35]

Omar returned to Afghanistan in September 1993 to take the advanced four-month training course, "given to those dedicating their lives to jihad."[36] From a separate interrogation conducted by Indian authorities, who might have influenced its content, Omar stated that this course included special instruction of a "sort of city warfare training" provided by some active duty Pakistani military officers.[37] During the training, the students were visited by senior HUM officers, including Maulana Masood Azhar. When asked where he wanted to go, Omar mentioned Bosnia. He was asked to go to India first, but he realized that his British passport was about to expire. Omar then suggested that he should return to England to renew his passport and encourage people to come for training.[38] After a short stay with his relatives in Lahore, he returned to England in January 1994.

Back in London, Omar started martial arts classes for a group of Muslims and tried to interest his old friends and classmates in joining the jihad in Afghanistan. He collected some camping gear that was difficult to find in Pakistan and received funds from people without even soliciting for them. He noted in his diary: "Also have problem with convincing my family that I'm leaving again. Renew passport and get India and Pak visa." In May 1994, he returned to Afghanistan and after a two-week refresher course he started as an instructor for the forty-day basic training course. Meanwhile, some of the HUM leaders had been captured in India. In June, Omar was asked to help free them. He was told that HUM had kidnapped five Westerners in order to exchange them for the leaders. His diary stated, "due to weak planning they had to be released unconditionally."[39] But this was not true: the kidnapped Westerners had been murdered and their bodies have never been recovered.

Omar's mission was to carry out a plan to free the HUM prisoners by kidnapping another group of tourists and exchanging them for the HUM members. He accepted the mission and arrived in New Delhi on July 26, 1994. He made contact with his accomplices and started searching for potential victims. The plan was to befriend them and then take them to an isolated village and hold them hostage there.

Omar met his first victim, Rhys Partridge, a twenty-seven-year-old backpacker, on September 27. He talked to his new acquaintance and took him to dinner that evening. The next evening, they met again to play chess, and Omar invited him to his village. The following day Partridge was made prisoner. On October 16, two other hostages were taken and joined Partridge. On October 20, a fourth victim was kidnapped but held at a different site. The victims said that they were terrified every day because they had guns pointed at them and they were chained to the ground or to a wall. At one time, they thought they would die as they were forced to dig a pit, which turned out to be a latrine.

The captors were outraged when no one noticed that the victims were missing and decided to force the issue. They took pictures of the hostages. On October 31, Omar brought the photos to an Indian newspaper and the BBC with a threat that the hostages would be beheaded one by one if the HUM leaders were not released. When one of the recipients started to open the envelope containing the letter and photos in front of Omar, he ran away. Later that evening, the police managed to find one of the hostages. After interrogating one of his captors, they found out where the other victims were located. The next day, November 1, the captors freed the prisoners in an exchange of gunfire that wounded Omar; he was then taken prisoner.[40]

During his imprisonment, Omar wrote a diary of his experience and also penned a confession. Omar's diary is remarkable for the complete disconnect between his perception and that of his victims. His acquaintance with Partridge lasted two days from the time he first met him to the time he took him hostage, yet he called his relationship with Partridge a friendship. "But the strongest friendship by far was with Rhys Partridge. . . . We had many common interests like chess, traveling and writing. . . . In a short time it was probably the strongest friendship I had made for a long time (there is a great difference between comradeship and friendship) and all of a sudden the reality hit me."[41]

Contrast this affection for Partridge with the latter's reaction upon hearing that Omar had been released. "You can't let people like that out—especially when they are a bunch of madmen. . . . If we are going to let this guy out we might as well free Charles Manson. . . . You go through life and you meet good people and bad people, and I never believed in evil until I met that guy. He would take joy in killing anybody in the firm belief that it is right to do so. . . . Letting this guy loose is an act of insanity. He is just a murderer and he takes joy in it."[42] Partridge remembered his last days of captivity. Omar had told him, "We've just told the press we're going to behead you." Partridge remembered, "He was laughing. The prospect excited him."

Omar is a complex character. For five years he stayed in prison, where he met Peter Gee. At times he showed charm and a capacity to make friends, as he did with Gee. He also revealed a ruthlessness bordering on fanaticism. Yet he could be remorseful, too. Peter Gee remembered that Omar asked him to visit the victims and apologize to them on his behalf, since he expected Gee to get out of prison before he did. However, the reverse happened, and Omar never did anything to express this remorse to his victims himself. In prison, he seemed to flourish and became the natural leader: he lived like a mafia don among the prisoners. He could also show compassion for non-Muslims, taking the cause of others treated unfairly in prison. Omar also seemed genuinely religious and strongly believed in heaven. In the year and a half he knew Omar, Peter Gee never saw him read anything but the Quran or commentaries on it.[43] Even his Indian wardens held a grudging admiration for him. One of his interrogators said to a British journalist when Omar was first captured, "You are producing charming terrorists for India in England."[44]

Omar was released in December 1999 along with HUM leader Maulana Masood Azhar in exchange for 154 passengers onboard an Indian Airlines plane hijacked by fellow members of the progeny of HUM. After his liberation Omar stayed in Pakistan. He moved to Lahore, where he married and had a child. He continued to be active in militant Islamist politics, but his name did not reappear in the media until after the September 11, 2001 attacks as an example of the kind of person attracted to violent Islamist factions. It resurfaced again on February 12, 2002, when he was accused of kidnapping U.S. journalist Daniel Pearl on January 23. The incident was similar to the kidnappings in India. It later became known that he had been arrested on February 5, and on February 18, *The News* reported that he had confessed about his role in the kidnapping and eventual beheading of Pearl.[45] Omar was tried in Pakistan. It is difficult to comment on his role in the kidnapping because he challenged his alleged confession in court, and later evidence seems to undermine the government's case. He was convicted and condemned to death on July 15, 2002, and was awaiting execution at the time of this writing.

Omar Sheikh's story demonstrates the centrality of the radicalization process in the formation of a global Islamist terrorist. Those who would aim to neutralize this threat need to understand this radicalization process and devise ways to interrupt it. My goal in this book is to develop insights to this process with clear and direct practical implications. The final chapter consists of explicit policy recommendations—in this case for national security. At a more concrete level, this discussion should help concerned citizens and law enforcement personnel to understand the problems that they are facing, and help them protect ordinary citizens from political violence.

ONE

How to Study Terrorism in the Twenty-First Century

How should we study terrorism? The story of Ahmed Omar Saeed Sheikh illustrates the biographical approach, which focuses on the individual and examines his background to explain how he became a terrorist. Another popular approach searches for "root causes" in the social conditions that lead people to become terrorists. A third approach is a middle way, concentrating on how people in groups influence each other to become terrorists. Each approach has its benefits and drawbacks, but whichever path is taken, it can and must be studied scientifically. I will argue that the third approach offers the most fruitful way to understanding the process of radicalization.

Science is not a set of beliefs, but a methodology to choose among competing hypotheses. What distinguishes science from faith is that science allows factual evidence to adjudicate competing claims.[1] Many authors of books about terrorism offer case studies, such as the activities of Osama bin Laden, the first World Trade bombing of 1993, or the Bali bombing of 2002. Investigators are naturally attracted by the unusual cases and are ready to generalize from them. But basing conclusions on a single event or individual often leads them astray. Other writers opine based on selective information, choosing facts to support their arguments and neglecting anything that might contradict them. These are often nothing more than arguments made for the sake of scoring political points and have no role in a scientific study. This book takes as its starting point that the scientific method is essential in the study of terrorism.

A scientific approach should encompass all the available data, and not a biased selective sample. Scientific research on terrorism must specify or generate a set of data, which should be representative of the terrorist universe. Since all samples are inevitably slanted, it is important to understand the biases underlying the data (often due to the process of collection itself) and take that into account when making statements.

Far too many experts on terrorism misunderstand the scientific method and say that their work is "evidence-based" because they have found some facts to support their argument. Often such evidence comes from mysterious sources—anonymous tips from the "intelligence community"—that cannot be verified. Another claim to expertise in terrorism is based on the ability to speak Arabic. Being able to understand the language is important, but it is a mistake to think that all Arabic speakers are terrorism experts. We would not argue that knowledge of English makes one an expert in physics just because many books on the subject are written in English.

The key to unlocking the mysteries surrounding terrorism is found in social science methods—statistics, sampling theory, survey techniques, measurement, data analysis—as the basis for investigation. It is not found in privileged access to "secret information," which often turns out to be a rehash of unverifiable rumors, or in knowledge of relevant languages (important though they may be). Yet most terrorism experts come from the fields of journalism or intelligence analysis, have never taken an introductory course in social science methodology, and lack a basic understanding of the scientific method. One authority once said to me that he deeply distrusted statistics and trusted only the telling anecdote. I could not disagree more, because data is not the plural of anecdote. Anecdotes can be used to vividly illustrate a point, as I have done throughout this book, but they cannot be the basis of general statements about terrorism.

The importance of using the scientific method is underscored by the fact that our common sense sometimes leads us astray. We all think that we are experts in human behavior based on our observations of how people act. In a sense, we are. We constantly interact with other people around us and do a pretty good job of judging their strengths and weaknesses. But when dealing with extremes of behavior such as mental illness or suicide bombings, our common sense fails us.

It is often assumed that, because terrorists act in such extreme ways, what we understand about people does not apply. When confronted with apparently incomprehensible acts, we are all too willing to suspend our general sense of how people interact. It is easy to view terrorists as alien creatures who exist outside normal patterns of social interaction. To protect the understanding we have about ordinary people, we are eager to believe anything exceptional about terrorists: they are essentially bad; they are just mad; they are driven by sexual frustration; they are brainwashed or are simply robots following orders; they are thoughtless religious fanatics. We do not know any people like that in our daily lives, but this does not bother us because we do not know any terrorists, either. So it is easy to believe that those who carry out terrorist acts might not be "normal" human beings. But in order to understand terrorism, we must study those who carry out these acts through the scientific method without any preconceived notion of their essence.

Until recently, a large part of the literature on terrorism concentrated on definitions of terrorism, but without reaching consensus on what that definition is.[2] Thus we have the common refrain that one man's freedom fighter is another man's terrorist, and the suspicion that, if the word had existed at the time, the British authorities would probably have branded our founding fathers terrorists. Of course, most people know what they mean by terrorism, but it is a little like obscenity: people believe they know it when they see it, but cannot define it. Even the United Nations does not have a definition for terrorism.

Rather than spending time searching for a definition that will satisfy everyone, let us simply identify the subjects of this study. They are the men responsible for the September 11, 2001, attacks and all those who, like them, threaten the United States and the West on behalf of a larger community, the vanguard trying to establish a certain version of an Islamist utopia. What drives them? What do they want? How do they accomplish their murderous tasks? The United States faces many potential threats, but this study is limited to these specific terrorists. The focus on this group does not imply that all terrorists are Muslim. This is far from the truth. However, because the work is limited to these specific terrorists, its findings may not be relevant to other types of terrorism.

This work is an attempt to develop an understanding of this form of terrorism in order to help contain it and prevent further atrocities on the scale of the East Africa embassy bombings in 1998, the September 11 attacks, and the bombings that took place in Bali in 2002, in Casablanca, Riyadh, and Istanbul in 2003, and in Madrid in 2004 and London in 2005. Each of these atrocities left dozens to thousands dead and was claimed by or carried out on behalf of al Qaeda.

The Individual Terrorist: A Micro-Level Analysis

Three levels of analysis have been used to study terrorism: the micro-level, the macro-level, and a middle-range analysis.

The most common approach is a micro-level analysis. This method is based on the assumption that there is something different about terrorists that makes them do what they do—especially when they kill themselves in the process. The first impulse is to turn to clinical psychologists or psychiatrists and ask, "What is wrong with these people?" Clinicians, however, are trained to dig into the backgrounds of their patients to discover an explanation for their behavior. Reliance on these experts introduces two assumptions: that there is something personally wrong with the terrorists and that the explanation is to be found in their backgrounds. Since mental health providers are trained to look at patients one at a time, they collect case histories. They then try to generalize from these histories to other potential terrorists. A good story is mesmerizing, as the case of Ahmed Omar Saeed Sheikh in the Introduction illustrates, and his history seems to explain his later behavior. But precisely because such stories are so compelling, they can undermine good social science by taking attention away from comprehensive research and statistical analysis.

The work of some psychologists is nevertheless useful because they have actually spoken to or extensively studied terrorists, either in prison or after the terrorists have given up violence.[3] But others do not even go this far. They instead generalize from disputed theories and select items from the popular press to provide partial support for their arguments.[4]

Many problems crop up with this individualistic approach. The first is that we can never tell how significant or widespread the problem of terrorism is by simply looking at individual terrorists. It does not address questions such as: What is the proportion of terrorists in the general population? Is it one in one hundred people, one in a thousand, or one in a million? For the kind of terrorism carried out by al Qaeda, this is an especially important question. What is the size of the network of people who commit terrorist acts on behalf of al Qaeda? As many people ask, are we winning or losing the war on terror?

Are there more terrorists now or are there fewer? Establishing a baseline is critical not only in gauging how well we are combating this phenomenon, but also in knowing whether we are underestimating the problem of terrorism or blowing it out of proportion.

A second problem with the individual perspective is the assumption that terrorists are fundamentally different from the rest of us. This, in scientific terms, is called the rejection of the null hypothesis. The null hypothesis states that the sample under study is representative of the population at large—in other words, there is no difference between the sample studied and the larger population. For scientific explanation, researchers try to detect a difference between the people they study and the rest of the population, and weave this difference into an explanation of what they are trying to study. In the field of terrorism, it has been assumed that terrorists are psychologically different from "normal" people. For forty years psychologists throughout the world have tried to find this difference, and no "terrorist personality" has emerged. There have been some claims of such discoveries, which received wide media exposure, but none of these claims has survived further examination. Some believe that the failure to detect any difference from "normal" people is not proof that such abnormality does not exist. This may be true, but the failure to find a "terrorist personality" after extensive efforts argues that either such a personality does not exist or it is so subtle as to defy identification. At present, the consensus in the field of terrorism is that there is no terrorist personality.

We have come full circle in the last half-century. After prematurely rejecting the null hypothesis—by assuming that terrorists were different from the general population—we have failed to explain terrorism as a function of an abnormal personality. This means that mental health professionals, whose expertise lies in understanding illness or abnormality, do not have a better grasp of terrorism than nonclinicians. Therefore, their insights on terrorism should not be accorded any special significance.

A third problem with the micro-level of analysis is that it focuses too much on the individual and neglects situational factors. It limits the field of inquiry to the individual's background, which allegedly predisposes someone to acts of terrorism. A strong version of this argument would postulate that there is an innate predisposition—that we could, if we looked for it, discover a "T" gene for terrorism. It would be nice if we could devise a blood test to detect potential terrorists before they fulfill their destiny. Unfortunately, this is not possible.

The strong version of the belief that there is a background predisposition to terrorism carries the implication that people have some essence that eventually matures and results in violent behavior. In other words, terrorists are born with a kernel of evil that manifests itself in the terrorist act. This is often how people talk about terrorism, the unstated assumption being that people do not change. This comforting thought means that we, the rest of us nonterrorists, could never become terrorists. This is not true. No one is born a terrorist: people become terrorists. There is nothing inevitable about a terrorist life trajectory.

A weaker version of this argument holds that there is something in each terrorist's background—some kind of traumatic event, for example—that exerts an influence so strong as to predispose him or her to eventually become a terrorist. As mentioned earlier, there is no evidence that terrorists have personal flaws that inevitably lead them to terrorism. This is, however, what some psychiatrists argue,[5] and this evidence is discussed in Chapter 3.

It is difficult to give up the idea that terrorists are essentially different from the rest of us. This is part of our general tendency to explain other people's bad behavior by their personal qualities. Thus, if we find that people disappoint us, it is because they are untrustworthy. If they overeat, it is because they are gluttons. When we explain ourselves to others, however, we tend to blame circumstances. So, if we disappoint loved ones, we cannot help it—circumstances forced this one slip. If we overeat, it is because the food was irresistible. This near-universal tendency to attribute explanations for other people's bad behavior to personal disposition while blaming our own on external situations is what social psychologists call the fundamental error of attribution. The search for a specific predisposition for terrorism is likely just another example of this inclination, which leads us to greatly underestimate the importance of situational factors in the process of radicalization.

A fourth problem with the individual, micro-level perspective is the assumption that people know why they are doing what they are doing. Psychologists like to interview people to discover their motivation and intent, but sometimes their self-explanations are inaccurate. Memories are not perfect, and people tend to tell stories in a manner that justifies their past behavior.

Social psychologists try to understand people's actions through experimental manipulation of their environment; the factors that seem to explain human behavior are often counterintuitive and surprising. In Stanley Milgram's famous experiment on obedience to authority, the vast majority of people gave innocent subjects what they believed to be painful and possibly fatal electric shocks. However, when Milgram asked behavioral experts to predict how many subjects would actually carry out this experiment to its end, the responses were unanimous that only the worst psychopaths would continue the experiments to the point that they would cause the death of the subjects.[6] Going back to the overeating example, a recent study showed that variation in such a behavioral outcome as obesity is better explained by membership in a network of friends and family than by genetic or environmental factors. Yet, none of the participants of the study were aware of this strong influence.[7]

Although interviewing terrorists is an important tool, it comprises only part of the data that contributes to our overall understanding of them, and may in some circumstances misguide us. Even if terrorists are completely honest with the interviewer, they may not really know what drove them to do what they did. People think of themselves as responsible for their good deeds. The story they tell about their past is usually one that shows how they controlled positive behavior; bad behavior is attributable to "circumstances." In addition, the stories we tell about ourselves also follow cultural templates. If one were to ask an American why he failed at something—why he lost his job, for example—he might answer, "I did not try hard enough." In the land of opportunity, failure is attributable to the individual's lack of resolve. However, if one asks the same question of a European Muslim, he would be more likely to answer, "I never got a chance because I'm Muslim." This answer is collectivist, pointing out the discrimination experienced. Both might be true, but in the first instance the answer obscures the role of circumstances and in the other it obscures one's own contribution to a negative outcome.

We cannot presume that people are always aware of their motivation or remember it perfectly years later. Psychiatrists often work with patients who are to some degree puzzled by their own behavior. Long-term psychotherapy patients often relate the same story, but from very different points of view as time goes on. This is because people interpret their past according to what is taking place in their lives at the time of the telling. Although their past actions do not change, their understanding and interpretations of these actions do evolve over time. This should caution us against generating an overly cognitive view of terrorists, meaning that they are fully aware of their intention and motivation and then deliberately carry them out. By and large, captured Islamist terrorists, like those indicted in Miami, New York, New Jersey, and Toronto and those who have undergone trial in London, the Netherlands, France, and Madrid are definitely not intellectuals who decide what to do after careful deliberation. Many times, people act without thinking and only afterward tell a story to glorify their success or excuse their failure. Self-serving, after-the-fact explanations may not reflect before-the-fact motivations. While interviews with terrorists are an important tool, the information gained in this manner must be viewed with these caveats in mind.

Finally, focusing exclusively on terrorists can never tell us how they are different from those who might have become terrorists but did not. To understand this distinction, we need a comparison between the terrorists and a meaningful control group. There are many possible control groups, including the larger society, or people who believe what the terrorists believe, people who have grown up with them, or people who have gone to school with them. It is crucial to study this control group, because it is otherwise impossible to discover and understand any specific traits terrorists may have.

Root Causes of Terrorism: The Macro-Social Level of Analysis

Broad, sociological explanations form the second most common type of explanation for terrorism. This is frequently referred to as understanding the "root causes" of terrorism. Explanations for terrorism are believed to lie in social, economic, political, cultural, and historical factors. This level of analysis has generated a host of explanations: poverty leads to terrorism; ignorance and naïveté contribute to terrorism; biased education, seductive preaching, or charismatic leaders brainwash people into terrorism; insufficient economic opportunities or relative deprivation causes terrorism; a surplus of young males without any responsibility inevitably results in terrorism; prohibitions against premarital sex lead to sexual frustration in young males and turn them into terrorists; restrictions on free political expression cause violence and terrorism.

Typical "commonsense" explanations of this kind include images of young boys sitting on a bare floor, swaying back and forth while shouting the verses of the Quran to better memorize it as part of the process of becoming fanatics whose only desire is to die as suicide bombers. Let's call this an example of the madrassa (religious Muslim school) theory, which we shall explore later.

Or take the image of the radical preacher in a mosque spouting invective that inspires naïve and vulnerable young men to run out, immediately build bombs, and become suicide terrorists. It's all due to the "preachers of hate," the thinking goes; eliminate them and you eliminate the problem.

This perspective continues to exert influence—especially among policy makers—because it is, like the micro-level analysis, a commonsense paradigm. While politicians cannot change human nature (which is the focus of the micro-level of analysis), they can try to affect social, economic, and political conditions. The macro-level focus on society is the external counterpart of the internal explanation at the micro-level. External factors drive individuals to become terrorists.

This type of top-down analysis sees society as a system. The view naturally leads to asking questions about what kind of structure facilitates or encourages terrorism, or what kind of function terrorism plays in society. This kind of analysis—the structural-functional—formed a central intellectual tradition in the social sciences in the 1950s and 1960s. It fell out of favor once researchers found that it was much too static: most of the structural factors do not change quickly but political phenomena such as violence vary considerably over time.

The major problem with the macro-social level of analysis is an inability to draw out the argument. If the same social, economic, political, or cultural factors are acting on millions of people, why do so very few become terrorists? To answer this we need to ask another question that raises the fundamental problem of specificity. What is specific about the few who become terrorists if the same forces that made them become terrorists act on the entire population?

The macro-level perspective fits well into a popular form of terrorism analysis that views terrorist organizations as formal, abstract entities that act because of strategic interests dictated by the demands of the specific situation.[8] This is a useful abstraction to analyze the ideology and strategy of an organization, which, according to this view, are located at the top of a terrorist pyramid, in the leadership. The leaders then transmit their desire to the rest through a command and control structure. The strategy of this organizational unit can be analyzed with respect to larger socioeconomic and political variables both locally in specific countries and more globally with respect to larger transnational trends.[9] It also puts this organization squarely within a specific cultural context, which influences its behavior.[10]

Any perspective has implicit assumptions embedded into it. Assumptions are like blinders: they prevent us from asking questions that later may turn out to be the most relevant. Treating a terrorist organization as an abstract unity ("al Qaeda") simplifies the inquiry, which for instance facilitates understanding of how its members are influenced by a particular historical situation. On the other hand, it gives the abstract entity a life of its own that prevents us from asking how it came to life in the first place. Of course, the social, economic, political, and cultural dimensions of terrorist organizations cannot be ignored. But these larger dimensions cannot tell us how people get together and what motivates them to carry out the work of the abstract terrorist organization. The collective dimension of terrorist behavior is taken for granted and is assumed to flow directly on orders from the leaders above. This shortcut helps analysts to concentrate only on what the leaders say to explain terrorist behavior.[11]

But all this begs the question. How do terrorists who carry out operations get together, create their collective identity—becoming a "we" hostile to their environment—and decide to carry out directives coming from above? These are the critical issues that should guide the policy process in order to understand the creation of specific terrorist organizations and eventually to establish measures to prevent young people from drifting into violence. This is the essential problem of radicalization. Terrorism is not the inevitable outcome of some iron law of historical forces. Nor is it the result of the beliefs and perceptions held by terrorists. These two poles lead to two common research traditions. One locates the root causes of terrorism in the socioeconomic, the political, and the cultural and explains it in terms of the interplay of historical factors. The other seeks to explain terrorism in terms of the beliefs held by the terrorists, which manifest themselves in shared values and objectives.

Both of these macro-explanations are too deterministic and static. Terrorism is not a constant threat. It comes and goes, even within a specific situation. In any given country, there appear to be campaigns of violence that start slowly, spike quickly, and then fade abruptly. This dynamic cannot be explained through slow-moving societal forces and cultural templates. Explanations based on structural conditions take for granted terrorists' ability to perceive and interpret how these conditions affect them, to become aware of what they have in common, and to decide what to do to influence them. These explanations ignore the important processes that enable terrorists to make sense of their environment and come together in their murderous activities. These perspectives imply an overly passive view of terrorists, who are the recipients of social forces or slaves to appealing ideas. This determinism is contrary to terrorists' own view of themselves as actively making choices to execute operations.

Likewise, the cultural determinists do not appreciate that the violent ideologies are not representative of Islam as a whole[12] or that there is a great diversity of sometimes conflicting ideologies within this terrorist movement.[13] How do terrorists come to select some ideas that are rejected by the community at large, and how do intimate groups of terrorists select among the variety of available ideologies and conflicting directives disseminated by their leaders? The problem for people trying to prevent terrorist atrocities is not that they do not know what the directives are, but that there are too many directives, and they do not know which pose the greatest threat.

Terrorists in Context: The Middle-Range Analysis

Both micro and macro approaches to the study of terrorism have severe limitations. Nor can we combine them to create a more comprehensive picture. The combination would assume that formal terrorist organizations, which respond to larger societal influences, are simply the aggregation of atomized individuals, neglecting their relationship to each other. In this scenario, the societal structural conditions and cultural appeals would affect these individuals the same way, resulting in their joining individually the formal terrorist organization and each responding individually to the commands of their leaders. This is exactly the way the law treats terrorist defendants, a practice that leads to major difficulties in their prosecution. This is a point that I will return to in Chapter 8, which offers recommendations on how to fight terrorism.

Clearly, a new approach is necessary, one that bridges the considerable gaps between the micro and macro approaches and examines the terrorists themselves, fully embedded in their environment. This new middle-range approach to analysis should focus precisely on how the terrorists act on the ground: how they evolve into terrorists; how they interact with others (terrorists and nonterrorists); how they join terrorist groups; how they become motivated to commit their atrocities; how they are influenced by ideas; and how they follow orders from far-away leaders. These questions call for a perspective from the bottom up to see exactly what is happening on the ground in the hope of explaining the larger phenomenon of terrorism.

Some might object that this focus is too narrow—that looking at the foot soldiers at the bottom of the terrorist pyramid cannot explain the overall strategic behavior and ideology of a terrorist organization. My aim is to convince the reader that by building our analysis from the ground up, we might be able to discern larger emergent characteristics of the entire terrorist social movement.

To answer the question "How do people become terrorists?" we need to look at processes, especially the relationships between individuals and their environment. The field of social psychology has tried to explore this to some degree, but many of its experiments rely on complete strangers put in a controlled environment and asked to carry out a rather trivial task. Terrorist groups are not formed by complete strangers who do not know each other. People who form terrorist groups know each other, often for a long time. They trust and, for the most part, have a great deal of affection for one another. They are often the extension of natural groups of friends and family. Yet, we do not know much about natural groups: their formation, their informal structure and dynamics, and, finally, their termination. There is no academic discipline that has conducted comprehensive studies of natural groups, as opposed to groups of strangers that can be manipulated experimentally. My suspicion is that natural groups of long-term friends and family behave differently from a group of total strangers that will never meet again after an experiment is completed. The middle-range perspective used in this book will study the relationships of terrorists in context: their relationship with each other, their relationship with ideas floating in their environment, and their relationship with people and organizations outside their group.

It is also important to study the terrorists in their environment. Many experts rely entirely on what they read on the Internet or on uncorroborated stories in the news. A serious researcher must at least visit the physical habitat of the terrorists. One quick look around might dispel some of the common myths about terrorism, namely that it is the product of poverty, enclaves breeding fanatics, or ghettos separated from the rest of society. Terrorist groups might simply be a natural extension of everyday interactions among neighbors hanging around the neighborhood.

The emphasis of this middle-range approach is on processes of interaction in context: radicalization, mobilization, motivation, and, perhaps, separation.

These processes frame the central questions in understanding terrorism. How can we prevent radicalization? How can we disrupt mobilization into a terrorist group? How can we diminish motivation to carry out terrorist operations? How can we facilitate separation from terrorist groups? This will provide a dynamic perspective with practical implications for both law enforcement and national security.

Building a Relevant Database

The application of the scientific method to terrorism research requires data. With this data we can generate hypotheses and test different hypotheses. The database should support the type of middle-range perspective just described, focusing on relationships and dynamic processes. It should collect information on people and their relationships with other terrorists, nonterrorists, ideas, and the social, political, economic, cultural, and technological context. It should trace the evolution of these relationships to see how they form, intensify, and fade so as to describe them over time.

When I began my research, there was no such existing database, and I found it necessary to build one from scratch. The existing open-source databases are incident-based. This kind of database provides information about various terrorist incidents: location, time, outcome, and claimed perpetrators. They can be useful in studying certain trends in terrorism, such as the frequency of terrorist operations, their geographical distribution, and their killing efficacy. Examples of incident-based databases include the Rand–St. Andrews University database on Terrorism and Low-Intensity Conflict, the Memorial Institute for the Prevention of Terrorism (MIPT) Terrorism Knowledge Database in Oklahoma City, the International Policy Institute for Counter-Terrorism (ICT) database located at the Interdisciplinary Center in Herzliya, Israel, the new Worldwide Incident Tracking System (WITS) database at the National Counterterrorism Center, and the START database at the University of Maryland. Despite their usefulness for large and long-term trends, incident-based databases do not help us answer questions about terrorism and its processes, such as radicalization, mobilization, recruitment, and motivation.

Other kinds of databases are held by the U.S. government. One of the most notorious is the mysterious "no-fly list," which is used to identify suspicious people if they try to board an airplane, or attempt to secure a visa to travel to the United States, or apply for a job. This type of database triggers further scrutiny at airports, in U.S. consulates around the world, or at the workplace. The database appears to be a name-based database, which might include the name of a person, its variations (they are many ways to transliterate from foreign languages like Arabic or Russian to English), date of birth, citizenship, residence, and, possibly, passport number. A rudimentary database like this might protect the United States by stopping people on the list from entering the United States, but such a large database is bound to contain errors and can lead to confusing mix-ups, such as preventing Senator Edward Kennedy from flying. More to the point for this study, such a database cannot answer the types of questions we have in mind.

Building a database poses considerable challenges. The database needs to be reliable and should be checked independently by other researchers. This eliminates working with classified databases because they are not independently checked. Openness to peer review and challenge is a cornerstone of scientific research, and so I have confined my research to open-source information. This type of friendly competitive checking of each other's facts can eliminate incorrect accounts, like the claim that September 11, 2001, plot leader Mohammed Atta met with an Iraqi intelligence officer in Prague in April 2001. Immediately after an incident or a wave of arrests, there is considerable speculation in the press about responsibility. As time goes on, original errors must be corrected. The investigation must be followed for years until trial, when the evidence compiled by an extensive investigation is presented in an open forum—that is, to a jury. Unfortunately, if this kind of due diligence is not followed, it can lead to the survival of known errors, which feed the wildest speculations.

In developing my database, I have used a simple gradient as a rule of thumb to judge the reliability of information. I usually collect data from all sources on a specific group that carried out a specific operation and organize it in chronological order according to when the data appeared in the public domain. This allows me to follow the investigation as it unfolded, with subsequent accounts often correcting earlier misconceptions. When the trial takes place, I pay close attention. A trial presents both sides of the story: the government's prosecution of the case and the defendant's explanation. Like a jury, I select the facts from these competing narratives according to what fragment on a specific point appears more compelling. The most reliable information comes from captured documents (especially the contents of hard drives of computers belonging to terrorists) and intercepted conversations, especially when the suspects are not aware they are being recorded. When trial transcripts are not regularly produced, I collect legal documents and notes on testimony. All of this information comes from a variety of countries, including the United States, Britain, France, Germany, the Netherlands, Canada, Spain, Australia, Indonesia, Egypt, Morocco, Turkey, and Pakistan.

Next in terms of reliability are media accounts. I have collected media reports on developing investigations and interviews with terrorists in the world press (French, British, German, Arabic, Spanish, Turkish, Dutch, Australian, Danish, Egyptian) that have been translated through the U.S. government's Open Source Center, which is an invaluable resource for scholars who have access to it. For media accounts, I try to find independent sources that can provide confirmation on each piece of data. Most of the data I am interested in—where and when was the person born, marital status, education and job— is not classified. This information comprises the "throwaway" details that people who know the suspected perpetrators readily provide to journalists who interview them. Investigative accounts in the local press where perpetrators have lived are especially useful. Some of this material is priceless because local reporters know and understand their environment far better than foreign correspondents.

Less reliable are academic publications, for they are only as good as the author's skill as a historian. Most academic experts on terrorism are experts in other fields who do not follow the literature on terrorism closely and therefore pick selectively only those facts that support their arguments. As a rule, they are good at generating hypotheses, but not in testing them.

Finally, information on the Internet sometimes proves useful. A considerable amount of the Internet-based data is worthless, but occasionally there are some real pearls, such as Albert Benschop's analysis of Mohamed Bouyeri's assassination of Dutch filmmaker Theo van Gogh, which correlated online statements by the perpetrator with his offline behavior.[14]

I started building my database with the nineteen September 11, 2001, perpetrators as my index sample of terrorists. I knew whom I wanted to study: the people who carried out September 11, and all those like them who pose a threat to the United States. I wanted to study this specific threat and did not know whether this group constituted a "new" form of terrorism or was similar to other terrorists. I did not want to analytically dilute my sample in a way that might have blinded me to some new insights by mixing in other types of terrorists. Thus, I included at first only people who had solid operational relationships with this index sample. After my sample grew to 172 individuals, which was the basis of my earlier book,[15] I discovered that they were linked to a network of terrorists associated with Osama bin Laden. After the bombings of the U.S. embassies in East Africa on August 7, 1988, this group began to be referred to as al Qaeda.

It is important to understand that I did not embark on a study of the phenomenon of terrorism in general. I suspect that there are many forms of terrorism, just as there are many forms of murder. Yes, terrorists and murderers all kill, but each kills in his or her own way. It is difficult to place them in the same category and compare them. My goal was to understand how September 11, 2001, became possible, which meant I was interested only in the perpetrators of the attacks and those similar to them. That focus means the results of this study may not be generalized to other forms of terrorism not covered in this volume.

The size of the sample allowed me to see what they had in common, namely that they were part of a violent Islamist born-again social movement, which then allowed me to expand the sample to over 500 members at the time of writing. By concentrating on this particular sample, I do not mean to imply that terrorism is unique to Islam or that all Muslims are potential terrorists. This social movement consists at most of a few thousand people and the worldwide Muslim population is almost 1.5 billion. The social movement thus represents only an infinitesimal proportion of Muslims. Islam, like all religions, advocates peace. However, like any religion, scattered groups of people have justified their murderous activities in its name. This does not mean that there is something specific about Islam that implies terrorism. In fact, Muslims seem to be latecomers to modern terrorism.[16]

The next chapter will outline the historical, social, and political context of this terrorist movement.

The Globalization of Jihadi Terror

Al Qaeda: The Organization and the Social Movement

There is considerable confusion about the term al Qaeda. In 2005, a general in the U.S. military asked me whether al Qaeda was a network or a social movement. Surprised at his uncertainty on this point, I answered that the term refers both to a social movement and to a specific organization. However, this did not satisfy him. The U.S. military has strict definitions that guide its deployment of resources. Certain resources can be deployed against a specific organization according to one set of rules, but a social movement would fall under another set of rules. To the general, the definition of al Qaeda had both strategic and practical implications.

Terms used in the language of social science—even in everyday language—do not always have neat definitions. Al Qaeda originated as a label for the organization founded by Osama bin Laden. Its members swore *bayah*—an individual oath of loyalty—to him or his designated lieutenants.[1] It is important to understand that people in al Qaeda did not refer to themselves as members of al Qaeda. In fact, they kept their actual oath to bin Laden a secret, referring to themselves simply as "brothers." Bin Laden and other senior members would refer to their followers, whether they swore bayah or not (that is, whether they were actual members of al Qaeda), as the "youth." The followers would refer to their leaders by an honorific title such as "sheikh" regardless of whether they

were religious scholars or not. These are terms that carry no universally accepted meanings and cannot be taken to indicate whether one formally belongs to
al Qaeda. Two of the four defendants convicted of the u.s. embassy bombings
in East Africa in 1998, Khalfan Mohamed and Mohamed al-Owhali, had never
sworn bayah to bin Laden. They admitted their roles in the bombings—al-
Owhali was even slated to be one of the suicide bombers. Al-Owhali boasted
that he had refused to swear bayah to bin Laden because he wanted to be part
of a suicide operation and was afraid that if he swore an oath of loyalty and
obedience to bin Laden, the latter might have sent him on logistics missions
and not grant him his wish to die for the cause. I included both men in my
database, even though they were not formal al Qaeda members.

These two terrorists were, by their own admission, actively involved in
an al Qaeda operation, but the men who bombed the World Trade Center in
February 1993 are a bit more difficult to classify. The person who inspired them,
Sheikh Omar Abdel Rahman—the "blind sheikh"—had met bin Laden in
Pakistan in the late 1980s. Theirs was a relationship of fellow travelers—people
who believe in similar ideology and support the same goals but who do not belong to the same organization. (The term fellow traveler itself arose in another
context and referred to "one who sympathizes with the Communist movement without actually being a Communist party member," according to the
Oxford English Dictionary.) Fellow traveler is a useful term because it shows
that a political organization is not isolated, but part of a larger community of
sympathizers that might feed the formal ranks of the organization.

In order to carry out his plan to bomb the World Trade Center, Abdel
Rahman called on a young man, Ramzi Yousef, who was an experienced bomb
maker. Yousef, who never belonged to al Qaeda, received money from his uncle, Khalid Sheikh Mohammed (generally known by his initials as KSM), who
had probably obtained his money from bin Laden but was also not a member
of al Qaeda. The two stayed at apartments owned or rented by bin Laden's organization. Yousef was arrested in 1995 before he had a chance to actually join
al Qaeda. KSM, in late 1998 or early 1999, did formally accept bin Laden's invitation to work directly with al Qaeda, although "he refused to swear a formal
oath of allegiance to bin Laden, thereby retaining a last vestige of his cherished
autonomy."[2] It would be absurd not to include KSM in the database sample,
given his role in the 9/11 attacks, just because he did not formally swear bayah
to bin Laden.

But we can no longer talk about al Qaeda in these confining terms. In the wake of the closure of the training camps in Afghanistan, the halt of financial transfers, and the detention or death of key personnel, al Qaeda Central has receded in importance. In its place, of no less concern to those trying to understand terrorists and their actions, is a looser social movement with its own strengths and vulnerabilities.

The al Qaeda social movement is composed of informal networks that mobilize people to resort to terrorism. These networks may become formal organizations, like al Qaeda or its Indonesian affiliate Jemaah Islamiyah, depending on shifting circumstances. Nonetheless, a single organization, even a very dominant one like al Qaeda, is not a social movement. There is no doubt that this social movement, which might be more properly called global Islamist terrorism, is heavily influenced by the organization al Qaeda Central. But at present the social movement has spread far beyond the original organization. I believe the term al Qaeda should not be used for the social movement, but I fear it is too late; in common usage, al Qaeda refers indiscriminately both to the organization and to the social movement. However, the distinction between the two is still important. Although the organization itself has been largely contained—but not completely eliminated and seems to consolidate in Pakistan's Waziristan region—the social movement has grown dramatically.

The confusion between the organization and the social movement has led to muddled thinking and erroneous analysis. All too often, when referring to it as a social movement, experts speak of the success or failure of al Qaeda's strategy, tactics, leadership, membership, recruitment, and division of labor (operators, communicators, financiers, supporters, logisticians). But these terms apply only to formal organizations with a coherent command and control structure, not to the informal groups of wannabes, copycats, or homegrown initiates who comprise the majority of the social movement. Social movements simply do not have this formal structure. They are fluid networks that do not have members but participants. These participants to some extent share a vision of the world and a collective identity that permits them to place their operations in the same wider perspective. Although not formal members of al Qaeda, they are terrorists with full responsibility for their actions despite the fact that they do not belong to a formal terrorist organization. Thus, the participants in the Madrid bombings of March 11, 2004, which killed 191 people, and the Dutch individuals who attempted to conduct terrorist operations in the Netherlands and succeeded in killing the film director Theo van Gogh in 2004—labeled by the press and the authorities the Hofstad Group—are not directly linked to al Qaeda the organization, but they are unquestionably terrorists. However, we should not make the mistake of viewing these events as unrelated. They are components of a larger terrorist campaign, and the terrorists who participated in them were linked by feelings of solidarity and a common general ideology and goals with other, similar terrorists.

Al Qaeda and the Trajectory of Modern Terrorism

Shared views and solidarity play a large role in the al Qaeda social movement. Placing it in a larger historical context also provides some clues as to the nature of the form of terrorism al Qaeda engages in.

David Rapoport has described four waves in the history of modern terrorism: anarchism, anti-colonialism, left-wing radicalism, and religious terrorism.[3] The anarchists believed that the state was the source of all evil, and that if one could eliminate the state there would be heaven on earth. The anarchists were probably the most influential of all terrorist social movements. They killed heads of state in Russia, France, Italy, the United States, and countless high government officials in a number of European countries. The murder of the Archduke Franz Ferdinand triggered World War I. The anarchists carried out these killings even though there was no central organization to coordinate their actions. Each incident, broadcast through a spreading world media, acted as "propaganda by the deed," which inspired an audience of mostly young people to carry out terrorist operations in their own countries. In the end, the excesses of the anarchists led to the movement's demise.

The anti-colonialists believed that independence from Western countries would lead to economic and political success in their homelands. The bloodbath of World War II catalyzed their movement; with the war's end, imperial constituencies in all the colonialist countries lost their appetite for military repression abroad. Within two decades they abandoned the fight and went home.

The leftist revolutionaries believed that capitalism formed the essence of evil in society. Their goal was to eliminate capitalism and bring about the state of communism, redistributing wealth from each according to his means and to each according to his needs. These movements were inspired and often supported by Communist countries, especially the Soviet Union, Cuba, and the People's Republic of China. However, with the collapse of the Soviet Union, the depression in Cuba and the turn to state capitalism in China, these dreams have lost their appeal.

We are now experiencing a fourth wave: religious terrorism built on the belief that the world has decayed into a morass of greed and moral depravity (especially failures in sexual purity, family values, and the rule of the Word of God). A revivalist faction blames Western influence for corrupting the descendants of a virtuous religious community, which originally lived in proximity to its prophet or God. Re-create this original community and paradise will come. The Islamic version of this revivalist ideology—so termed because it calls for a revival of what people believe the original community was like—is known as Salafism, from the Arabic word salaf, the ancient ones. The Salafis want to reconstruct the original Muslim community under the rule of shariah—that is, Islamic law based on the Quran, which is believed to be the actual Word of God.

This brief sketch of the various ideologies of modern terrorism shows that in this religious wave, and the al Qaeda social movement in particular, the young, who are willing to sacrifice themselves in pursuit of a utopia and eventually use terrorist tactics to accelerate its coming, are essentially romantic men and women chasing a dream. Like the terrorists in the first three waves, they see themselves as heroes, fighting for justice and fairness. Their respective movements often began as nonviolent movements trying to change society. Their sense of personal sacrifice can already be detected in the journals of Russian anarchists:

> Despite our absolute certainty of the masses' revolutionary mood and readiness to act, despite our belief in the proximity of a social revolution and in its ultimate victory over the entire existing order, we made a strange distinction between our own fates and the radiant prospects of the revolution. About ourselves, we were always pessimistic: we would all perish; they would persecute us, lock us up, send us into exile and hard labor (we didn't even think about capital punishment then!). I don't know how the others felt, but for me that contrast between a radiant future for the people and our own sad fate was ex-

tremely influential when I was considering how to apply my socialist beliefs in practice. This contrast was always an emotional undercurrent in the streams of ideas that flowed freely in Zurich.

If not for the persecution, I'm not at all certain that I would have become a socialist at that time.[4]

The young woman who wrote these lines, Vera Figner, became the leader of the most important and well-known Russian anarchist organization, the People's Will. She wrote these thoughts in Zurich in 1872. After the organization's turn to violence six years later, capital punishment became the usual sentence for captured anarchists. Figner was later arrested and condemned to death, although her sentence was eventually commuted to life imprisonment.

The actual turn to violence was inaugurated by another woman, Vera Zasulich, who was morally outraged when she heard that the governor of St. Petersburg, Fyodor Trepov, had ordered the illegal whipping of a political prisoner, who had failed to take off his hat again when the governor crossed the prison yard a second time. Zasulich waited in vain for the public outrage. "I resolved at that point, even if it cost my life, to prove that no one who abused a human being that way could be sure of getting away with it. I couldn't find any other way of drawing attention to what had happened. I saw no other way. . . . It's terrible to have to lift a hand against another person, but I felt it had to be done."[5]

Zasulich went to Trepov's office and fired a shot, wounding him. She dropped the gun and waited to be arrested. When later asked why she did not attempt to flee, she proclaimed that she was a "terrorist, not a killer."[6] At her trial, two months later, her self-sacrifice in bringing attention to the injustice done to a stranger won over the jury. She was found not guilty to the zealous applause of the jury, the courtroom spectators, and even members of the prosecution.[7]

The Zasulich incident marked a turning point in the history of modern terrorism. Until then, socialists and anarchists had tried to persuade others, especially peasants, to join their movements through propaganda and the distribution of pamphlets in the countryside. With the trial of Zasulich, they noticed that violence dramatically enhanced the dissemination of their message through the media and decided to pursue this strategy of "propaganda by the deed." Violence brought an added inspiration for young people seeking glory. Through terrorist acts, they could become famous—especially among their comrades—and even if they died in the process, their names would live on forever.[8] Along with self-sacrifice for the cause and comrades came the thrill of potential glory. Similarly today, among religious terrorists the most worthy act and ultimate thrill are to fight the most powerful military in the world, America's, even if death results. If death is the price of glory, so be it. The martyr dreams that his life will persist in the imagination of others and inspire them beyond his death.

Justice, not Democracy

The global Islamist terrorists follow in the footsteps of their Russian predecessors. My data shows that they are generally idealistic young people seeking dreams of glory fighting for justice and fairness. The Bush administration frames its counterterrorism strategy in terms of promoting democracy and freedom. This plays well to the administration's domestic audience, which counts because it wields electoral power. Americans understand democracy and freedom, because these form the foundation of the U.S. political system.

But democracy and freedom do not resonate with foreign Muslim audiences. For Muslims in the Middle East, democracy means leaders who "win" elections with nearly 100 percent of the vote. And when a Salafi party wins in relatively free elections, as the Islamic Salvation Front did in Algeria or Hamas in the Palestinian Authority, either the local officials cancel the electoral process (Algeria in 1992) or the rest of the world turns away from the winning party (the boycott against Hamas in 2006). When other Salafi parties threaten to become too popular—like the Muslim Brothers in Egypt, for example—they are banned from taking part in the elections. In those countries where an unpopular ruler maintains his power through the ubiquitous presence of internal security agencies, freedom is often a sad joke. Newspapers are carefully monitored and citizens can be imprisoned for simply criticizing the government.[9]

This disconnect between American and foreign audiences has created huge problems for U.S. public diplomacy as it tries to counter Islamist propaganda. Polling in the Middle East shows strong sympathy for Islamist propaganda and equally strong hostility to U.S. foreign policy. The U.S. invasion of Iraq, based on the false pretexts of the threat of weapons of mass destruction and the alleged link among al Qaeda, the 9/11 attacks, and Saddam Hussein, has caused the United States to lose nearly all credibility. As a result, any attempt at public diplomacy in the Middle East is met with deep skepticism.

The Bush administration claims that the global Islamist terrorists hate democracy and freedom. They certainly reject democracy, which they interpret as the domination of man over man, as opposed to the rule of shariah, which is an egalitarian society under the rule of God. In their view, there should be no intermediary between God and individuals. Democracy, according to the Salafis, creates injustice because it leads to men enslaving or exploiting other men. They see this Western notion of democracy as a harmful innovation undermining their theocratic utopia, which they regard as the only fair and just social system.

It is not democracy but the idea of justice that resonates with young Muslims. Most Muslim fundamentalist parties in the Middle East call themselves the party of *adl* ("justice" in Arabic). Justice and fairness are vague enough terms that enable anyone to project his favorite fantasy in his utopia. Salafis advocate structuring the ideal society on the model of the Salaf because they claim that it was the only time in world history when a fair and just community existed.

According to Salafis, only such a community would allow Muslims to regain their lost virtue and glory. The Salafis see Muslims' political and cultural decline in the past few centuries as evidence that they have strayed from the righteous path. By rebuilding their utopian society, the Salifis reason, Muslims will regain God's grace and again rule the world. Therefore, the Salafis see their world caught in a crisis of values: Muslims' lost virtue against the moral decadence of the West, including its greed, materialism, and sexual degradation of women.

The Quran, which is the highest authority for Muslims, says little about how the community of the Prophet was organized. For that, Muslims must consult the *hadiths* and *sunna*, the words and deeds of the Prophet and his companions, collected after his death. The Prophet and his companions were constantly engaged in fighting during this Golden Age, which spanned about forty years, from 622 to 662. This period covered the end of the life of the Prophet and the first four righteous caliphs, before the Muslim community split between the Sunnis and the Shi'as.[10] The hadiths and sunna describe this community, whereas the Quran is mostly silent about it.

This difference underscores an important point: not only is global Islamist terrorism utterly distinct from Islam, but the Quran contains far more verses supporting peace than the very few that support violence. These scriptures have been the crucial opening that some Muslim authorities have used to show the captured terrorists that their violent way is misguided. As will be discussed later, most of the global Islamist terrorists are not religious scholars. Traditional theologians have visited imprisoned terrorists and bring a Quran with them. They tell the prisoners that the holy book is the only arbiter of their dispute, and then engage the prisoners by saying that they will debate them about their violent path. If the terrorists succeed in convincing them, then the theologians say they will join the jihad. If the prisoners lose, then the terrorists are invited to abandon violence. As was noted, the Quran does not contain as many violent references as the hadiths, which draw on the decade of violence before the Prophet's death. The conversation between the theologians and the terrorists sometimes leads the terrorists, who do not have a deep understanding of their beliefs, to see that there is very little support in the Quran for their violent ideas.

The Evolution of Global Islamist Ideology

The ideologies calling for global jihadi terrorism evolved over time.[11] The overwhelming majority of Salafis advocate the peaceful transformation of society through face-to-face preaching. A few more politically minded Salafis call for the creation of a political party to take over the government through the ballot box. The idea is that, through control of the state, they can more rapidly transform society by implementing shariah to bring about a reign of virtue (this was the FIS's goal in Algeria before the "cancellation" of the party's electoral victory in 1992). Hassan al-Banna, the founder of the Egyptian Muslim Brothers, was the main advocate of this path. As the Muslim Brothers suffered ever greater persecution in Egypt, a splinter faction argued that the capture of the state could never take place through peaceful means. Instead, this faction advocated the violent overthrow of the government, which was declared infidel for abandoning the true Muslim way because of corruption by Western influence. This line was most eloquently advocated by Sayyid Qutb,[12] the forefather of Islamist terrorism, and his main disciple, Muhammad Abdel Salam Faraj, who argued that violent jihad was the neglected duty of each Muslim.[13]

An interesting debate took place during the dissemination of Faraj's pamphlet in the late 1970s. Asked whether the overthrow of the unjust ruler should not wait until the capture of Jerusalem, Faraj replied that the overthrow of the "near enemy" (the local ruler) was more important than fighting the "far enemy" (the Israeli state) because if an infidel ruler captured Jerusalem, it would still be infidel and nothing would have changed. Faraj thus was a strong advocate for targeting the "near enemy," but this discussion popularized the debate about targeting the near and far enemy.

By the mid-1990s, followers of Qutb and Faraj had not overthrown any of their governments. In the ensuing debates to understand the source of their failure, one faction argued that the "far enemy"—in this case the West, and especially the United States and France—was propping up the "near enemy." The terrorists would never succeed as long as this was true. A very small faction advocated a switch in strategy, namely to expel the "far enemy" from the Middle East, so they could then overthrow the "near enemy," their government. The vast majority of the Islamist terrorists rejected this approach, claiming that they needed to focus their energies on toppling their own governments without the extra burden of taking on a Western power.

The 9/11 perpetrators were part of the "far enemy" faction. The sample that constitutes the basis for this study is composed of "those terrorists that used violence against the 'far enemy'—non-Muslim governments or population—in order to establish a Salafi state in the Middle East." These groups of terrorists are the *global* Islamist terrorists. This means that simple Islamist terrorists, who go after the "near enemy," are not part of my sample. For example, the Egyptian Islamic Group, which rejected the "far enemy" argument, is not part of this sample, but its rival, the Egyptian Islamic Jihad, led by Ayman al-Zawahiri, is. Likewise, the Palestinian and Chechen terrorist groups are excluded because they focus their attacks on the Israeli and Russian governments respectively, whom they consider infidel invaders. The same rationale disqualifies the vast majority of Iraqi fighters in Iraq, who direct their attacks on foreign invading coalition troops. However, the foreign fighters in Iraq should be included because they are not fighting their own governments, but have traveled to Iraq to fight the "far enemy." These fighters are part of the al Qaeda social movement, which is a global, transnational terrorist movement.

Since the emergence of the "far enemy" argument, the global Islamist ideology has evolved into many variants, each with its own preacher.[14] Many of the far enemy ideologies allow the killing of infidel noncombatant civilians because they pay taxes to their governments and support the armed forces that kill Muslims. One of the most virulent forms of this family of ideologies is the doctrine of *takfir* (from the Arabic root *kufr*, infidel).

The *takfiris* view themselves as the only true Muslims and believe that only they understand Islam. They reject traditional imams, whom they view as lackeys paid by the state or a corrupted mosque. They also reject various traditional religious interpretations that evolved over fourteen centuries because they believe such commentaries have been corrupted by Greek philosophy. They therefore reject the legitimacy of traditional religious authorities. Their radicalism grows so rapidly that even their local and fairly radical imam is no longer radical enough for them. Often they issue threats toward him and he has no choice but to expel them from his congregation. The takfiris believe that they are the only true believers, the vanguard of the true Muslims. Those who do not belong to the global Islamist terrorist social movement do not deserve the label of Muslim for, the takfiris claim, they have degenerated to a state of barbaric unbelief (*jahiliyya*) that existed in the Arabian Peninsula at the time of the Prophet's revelations. Therefore, they "excommunicate" the vast majority of the Muslim community as apostates, and believe it is permissible to do anything to them as long as it is in pursuit of the jihad. This contradicts the Quran, which prohibits a Muslim from harming another Muslim. But the takfiri group morality trumps the traditional morality.

The aftermath of the 2004 Madrid bombings offers an example of this takfiri belief. The police arrested a suspect, Jamal Zougam, two days after the bombings and interrogated him for twelve hours straight. Zougam kept silent. At the end of the day, the police had pieced together a preliminary list of the victims of the tragedy. Some names on the list were obviously Muslim. The police showed the list to Zougam and said to him, "See, you killed some Muslims in the bombing." For the first time, Zougam broke his silence. "They're not Muslims," he said. "They're infidels." He was a takfiri.

In the West, we tend to believe that there is a single al Qaeda ideology. In fact, there is considerable disagreement among the terrorists about the limits and types of operations they can carry out. All seem to have strong national accents, as Saudis address Saudi concerns in their preaching, Moroccans Moroccan concerns, Jordanians Jordanian concerns, Indonesians Indonesian concerns, European expatriates expatriate concerns. Many of the disputes relate

39

to the legitimacy of killing civilians, Shi'a Muslims, and other Sunni Muslims. Disagreements also center on the size of the attacks that have provoked the West into wiping out large sanctuaries in Afghanistan. But we should not make too much of these doctrinal disputes, because the terrorists rarely execute their operations as a direct result of their doctrines. They are young people seeking thrills and chasing dreams of glory, but the dreams are not well worked out, allowing them to project whatever they want into their imagined utopia.

The Evolution of the al Qaeda Social Movement

Just as the ideology of global jihadi terrorism evolved over time, so did the social movement itself.[15] In the case of al Qaeda as a social movement, this was a process of self-selection: the most militant among very militant Muslims became al Qaeda.

The many Muslim militants who traveled to Afghanistan in the 1980s to participate in the jihad to expel the Soviets became organized under the leadership of Sheikh Abdallah Azzam and his Maktab al-Khadimat, the Services Bureau. Many, in retrospect, view these foreigners, who came to fight with the Afghan mujahedin, as the equivalent of al Qaeda terrorists. Actually, very few went on to become al Qaeda. When they traveled to Afghanistan to help their Afghan brothers defend their country against the infidel Soviet invaders, they were the equivalent of the Abraham Lincoln Brigade, the idealists who flocked to Spain in the late 1930s to defend that country against the forces of General Franco. These young people, many of whom were leftist militants and anarchists, were hailed throughout the world for their bravery. A similar response was seen in Afghanistan in the 1980s. The young Muslim militants who answered Azzam's call were celebrated throughout the Muslim world and actively encouraged in the Western world. After the Afghan victory over the Soviets, most returned to their home countries and were given a hero's welcome.

Others, however, could not go home because they would have faced certain imprisonment. Azzam wanted to use this group of forced expatriates to continue the jihad abroad to liberate former Muslim lands occupied by non-Muslim governments, such as Kashmir, Palestine, and the southern Philippines. He frowned on any Muslim-on-Muslim fighting and urged his followers not to become involved in the new civil war in Afghanistan among various mujahedin factions. Some of the most militant foreign fighters wanted to continue their jihad in their home countries against the "near enemy," as advocated by Qutb and Faraj. Azzam opposed them. In August 1988 this group of ultramilitants formed a new group, in explicit opposition to Azzam, and led by his deputy and fund-raiser, Osama bin Laden.[16] Azzam was assassinated a year later by a car bomb. No one took responsibility for his murder and the crime is still unsolved. Many suspect it was the work of members of al Qaeda.

The withdrawal of Soviet forces from Afghanistan on February 15, 1989, ended the legitimacy of a jihad to expel infidel invaders of a Muslim land. Most young mujahedin who had come to defend Afghanistan went home. A very small faction of the most militant, who could not return, went on to form a new military organization, called al Qaeda ("the base" in Arabic, and which I will refer to as al Qaeda Central to distinguish it from al Qaeda the social movement). The members swore bayah to bin Laden or one of his senior representatives. Meanwhile, the home governments of these Muslim militants, who had stayed behind, complained to the government of Pakistan that it was harboring terrorists. In response, the Pakistani government expelled the unwanted militants, many of whom responded to the invitation to come to Khartoum issued by Hassan al-Turabi, the head of the National Islamic Front in the Sudan. So the most militant of the Peshawar expatriates moved their base of operations to Sudan.

Turabi had helped overthrow the former government in a military coup in 1989. He was, in a sense, the power behind the throne of General Omar al-Bashir. Turabi wanted to be a Muslim superstar. He organized the Popular Arab Islamic Conference (PAIC) and issued an invitation to Islamist terrorists, including bin Laden and his followers, to come to Khartoum. In a sense, al Qaeda the social movement is very much consistent with Turabi's grand vision. He wanted to unite all Muslim terrorist organizations under one umbrella, including the Shi'a, who at the time had a far greater reputation as terrorists than their Sunni counterparts. To this end he also invited representatives from Hezbollah, the best-known Shi'a terrorist organization, which had succeeded in expelling the French and Americans from Beirut in 1983 through the bombing of the French embassy and a U.S. marine barracks. The success of these Lebanese operations became a model for other terrorists.

In Khartoum the Muslim terrorist organizations were able to exchange information and techniques. Hezbollah taught the others their successful truck bomb techniques, which later became a staple of Islamist terrorist opera-tions. These early operations include the National Guard building bombing in Riyadh in 1995 carried out by a group of Saudis with some allegiance to bin Laden; the Egyptian embassy bombing in Islamabad in 1995 carried out by members of Zawahiri's Egyptian Islamic Jihad, and the Khobar Towers bomb-ings in Saudi Arabia in 1996 carried out by a group that called itself the Saudi Hezbollah. Their congregation in one place led to discussions about strategy, especially after noon prayers on Friday at the mosque. During the Khartoum exile, it became clear to the groups pursuing the near enemy that, despite a quarter-century of effort, they had failed to come any closer to their goal of overthrowing their home governments.[17]

These discussions occurred at a time and place when the role of the far enemy seemed prominent. The first Gulf War in 1991 established the contin-ued presence of U.S. troops in Saudi Arabia. The Somali humanitarian crisis in 1993 led to the dispatch of U.S. troops to Somalia to avert widespread starva-tion among the population. Those with a more paranoid conspiratorial view of history saw in this twin presence the beginning of a full-scale U.S. invasion of the Middle East through a pincer movement from the north in Saudi Arabia and from the south in Somalia. At the same time, the Algerian government cancelled the second round of elections in January 1992 when it became clear that the FIS was going to win by a landslide. The hand of the French govern-ment, another far enemy, was assumed to be behind this move. In the former Yugoslavia, Serb military forces were carrying out ethnic cleansing against an unarmed Muslim Bosnian population. To prevent the situation from escalat-ing, Western powers established an arms embargo on the region. Muslims de-cried the embargo, saying it favored the Serb forces, who had access to their own weapons from the remnants of the former Yugoslav army. In 1994, the conflict between Muslim forces in Chechnya and predominantly Christian Russian forces escalated into a full-blown civil war.

Given this global situation, the far enemy argument gained prominence among a small group centered around Osama bin Laden. Some of his lieuten-ants advocated going after the "head of the snake," arguing that it was necessary to carry the battle to America and France. In 1995, al Qaeda Central began to plot against far enemy targets.[18]

The vast majority of Sunni terrorist groups rejected this new strategy. They argued that they did not need to create additional enemies while attempting to eradicate the near enemy. The largest of these groups was the Egyptian Islamic Group, which had assassinated Egyptian President Anwar al-Sadat in 1981. It strongly advocated keeping the focus on Sadat's successor, President Hosni Mubarak. The group carried out a near-miss assassination attempt against Mubarak in Addis Ababa in June 1995 and plotted another attack for the fall of that year in New York during the annual meeting of the United Nations General Assembly. The Sudanese foreign ministry was discovered to have helped the Egyptian Islamic Group smuggle weapons into Ethiopia and the United States for the attacks. The United Nations imposed sanctions against the Sudanese government for its complicity in international terrorist acts. The Sudanese government, in anticipation of the exploitation of its newly discovered oil reserve, chose to make amends with the international community and reversed its policy of helping international terrorists. It put their champion, Turabi, under house arrest, collaborated with foreign countries in extraditing terrorists like Carlos the Jackal under international warrants, and expelled other terrorists, including bin Laden and al Qaeda.

Bin Laden and his close associates, who advocated the switch in strategy to attacking the far enemy, returned to Afghanistan in May 1996 on an invitation issued by local warlords. This was the third major self-selection. The most militant "internationalists" from the Khartoum militants, about 150 people, followed bin Laden to Afghanistan.

Within three months of his arrival, bin Laden issued his *Declaration of War Against the Americans Occupying the Land of the Two Holy Places.*[19] Some hailed this as a fatwa, or religious opinion, but bin Laden has no religious legitimacy despite his honorific title as "sheikh"; he was trained as a civil engineer and not a religious scholar. Regardless of its legitimacy, with the publication of the declaration, al Qaeda Central had matured into a perpetrator of global Islamist terrorism.

Al Qaeda's Golden Age

The five years between the declaration of war against the United States and 9/11 constitute the "golden age" of al Qaeda. Despite the financial setback he suffered with the Sudanese government's expropriation of his property in that country, bin Laden, the most popular advocate and face of global Islamist jihad, had become the personal recipient of donations from Islamic charities. With Muslims perceived as besieged across the globe—in Chechnya, Bosnia, the Philippines, Kashmir, Algeria, and Central Asia—Muslims from around the world gave generously to their charities to defend their brothers in danger. These charities had become efficient at forwarding the funds to bin Laden by the time he arrived in Afghanistan, and had established a central location for training young volunteers who wanted to defend their endangered coreligionists. This money flow was called the "Golden Chain."[20] In a sense, bin Laden became the financial nexus of support for international Islamist terrorism because the money came to him personally.

Shortly after bin Laden's publication of his declaration of war, the Taliban under Mullah Omar captured Kabul. Bin Laden, who had originally been invited to Afghanistan by a warlord friend from his Afghan days, chose to support Mullah Omar. In exchange for the latter's hospitality, bin Laden offered him gifts, money, and a brigade of foreign volunteers to fight against Mullah Omar's enemies—including Ahmad Shah Massoud, the Tajik commander of the Northern Alliance.

The Taliban is still generally misunderstood. They were a religious group, formerly composed of Mullah Omar's religious students (taliban means religious students) who wanted to establish the rule of God in Afghanistan. They believed that implementing shariah and creating a Committee to Command Virtue and Prohibit Vice would be sufficient to accomplish this goal, which was the government's central focus. The Taliban believed that people were essentially virtuous and would take care of themselves as long as they chose the right path. The government existed in name only. Mullah Omar did not delegate authority and issued orders in a haphazard fashion to his lieutenants over a radio from his home in Qandahar. In their view, there was no need for any effective central ministries, such as health or social services, as the virtuous did not require the mediation of government. Without a central government in Kabul, local committees were responsible for keeping the roads open. The country became relatively safe for travel because the punishments for infractions were harsh. However, the lack of a functional central government became apparent when Afghanistan suffered its worst drought in history during the Taliban's rule. Ironically, it was the U.S. government's largesse in the form of shipments of flour that kept the Afghan population from starving.

Meanwhile, Islamist militants heralded Afghanistan as the only true Muslim government and declared Mullah Omar as the Commander of the Faithful. Bin Laden played along and pledged his loyalty to Mullah Omar. In return, Omar and the Taliban leadership gave bin Laden considerable leeway to do as he pleased, as long as he did not embarrass them. This freedom of action was new; during his time in Khartoum, the Sudanese intelligence services had kept bin Laden on a very short leash. In reality, the Taliban and al Qaeda shared an uneasy relationship. The global terrorists looked down on their Afghan hosts, who resented the foreigners. Friction arose when bin Laden took advantage of his freedom to address the international media, proclaiming the formation of the "World Islamic Front" and declaring a jihad against "Jews and Crusaders" on February 23, 1998.[21] After that conference, the Taliban leadership banned bin Laden and his subordinates from holding similar media events in Afghanistan.

Bin Laden used the funds he controlled to set up multiple camps to train young Muslims who wanted to join the global fight. These camps were not under strict al Qaeda rule, but the funds supported a collection of instructors who taught their compatriots, often segregated according to country of origin.

Several levels of training were offered. The forty-day basic training course provided an overview of a guerilla tactics course. Ahmed Omar Sheikh's journey, described in the Introduction, shows what was involved in the more advanced four-month urban warfare course. Each camp had its emir, who had a large degree of independence. Bin Laden did not try to micromanage the camps he funded. Differences in emphasis arose among the camps even at that time, such as basic training in guerilla warfare, more advanced training in urban terrorism, and experiments in chemical and biological weapons.

Bin Laden provided housing for the families of global terrorists who had immigrated to the Land of the Faithful. Communities of global jihadi terrorists were established in Kabul, Qandahar, and Jalalabad. There, they developed contacts with each other and planned operations against their own countries and the West. Al Qaeda Central organized itself into a more formal organization, with committees for finance, religion, military affairs, and propaganda. The military committee staff vetted proposals suggested to them by local terrorists, who wanted their operations funded by al Qaeda. Typically, al Qaeda would provide seed money for the local terrorists. On very rare occasions, it would fund the proposed operation completely. These operations include the U.S. embassy bombings in Kenya and Tanzania in 1998 killing more than two hundred people; the USS *Cole* bombing in the port of Aden, Yemen, killing seventeen U.S. sailors, and the 9/11 operation. The committee was also able to help terrorists with the coordination of these transnational operations.

During its golden age, al Qaeda Central dominated the more nationalistic jihadi terrorist organizations and focused them on the far enemy, creating global Islamist terrorism, or the al Qaeda social movement. How young Muslims came to join that social movement in the years that followed is the subject of the next chapter.

THREE

The Jihadist's Profile

Why did a young man, who was neither poor nor oppressed, who had received a decent education, a man who had never had trouble making friends, who enjoyed smoking dope and drinking beer, why would such a man turn into a holy warrior whose only wish was to kill, and perhaps more mysteriously, to die? It was the same question people asked after the bombings in the London underground, set off by the similar young men, who played cricket, had girlfriends, went to the pub. All we know is they murdered in the name of Allah and his prophet. Quite *why* they did it is harder to explain.

—Ian Buruma, *Murder in Amsterdam*

The sense of bewilderment conveyed in Ian Buruma's questions about Mohamed Bouyeri, the young Muslim man who killed Dutch filmmaker Theo van Gogh in 2004, reflects the conventional wisdom that terrorists have something innately wrong with them. Now that we have the data, we can look at this view, which suggests that one or several individual characteristics drive people to terrorism. It is presumed that terrorists are poor, that they are brainwashed by either their cultures or their schools, that they are naïve young people who do not know any better, that they lack responsibilities such as a job or family, which leaves them open to join terrorist organizations, or that they are so sexually frustrated that they turn to terrorism to seek their reward of seventy-two virgins in paradise. Or they are just criminals, or simply crazy.

Vicarious Poverty

Poverty is one of the most popular explanations of terrorism. The theory is that economic deprivation breeds resentment, which in turn leads to terrorism. Despite all the empirical evidence to the contrary, this explanation persists. For example, at the Club de Madrid Conference commemorating the first anniversary of the March 11, 2004, train bombings in Madrid, the invited expert panels explicitly rejected this explanation, showing that there was little relationship between terrorism and poverty.[1] Nevertheless, the keynote speaker, the Crown Prince of Morocco, specifically mentioned poverty as a breeding ground for terrorism. (He probably had in mind the Casablanca bombings committed the year before, in which all the fifteen suicide bombers came from the poorest shantytowns surrounding Casablanca.) This misconception also lies at the root of the public astonishment in the aftermath of the plot to blow up parts of the West End of London and Glasgow Airport in June 2007, that physicians from elite family backgrounds could become terrorists.

The data shows a different picture. In terms of socioeconomic background of the family of origin, the vast majority of the terrorists in the sample came from the middle class. It is not poverty that causes terrorism, even though terrorists claim to carry out their acts on behalf of their poor brethren—it is instead vicarious poverty. Terrorists justify their acts in terms of justice and fairness and on behalf of the less fortunate—not from their own destitution.

The composition of the al Qaeda social movement is solidly middle class. This is true of just about every other political movement, which are also middle-class phenomena. We must look beyond the self-justification of terrorists and look at the facts rather than their claims.

There are some minor differences in this socioeconomic composition over time. We can divide the global Islamist terrorists according to waves. The first wave consists of the old guard; those who fought against the Soviets in the 1980s became the companions-in-arms of bin Laden and still form the core of al Qaeda Central. They developed a strong bond under fire and the group evolved together. They have intense loyalty to one another, even when they disagree ideologically. This old guard generally came from a higher socio-economic status, almost equally divided between upper class and middle class. An example of the upper class is of course Osama bin Laden himself, the very wealthy scion of a construction empire who grew up with the royal princes of Saudi Arabia. A second is his deputy, Ayman al-Zawahiri, who comes from one of the most prominent families in Egypt, with a grandfather who held prestigious diplomatic and academic positions and an uncle who was the founding Secretary General of the Arab League. Many first-wave al Qaeda leaders were Egyptian and had been student Salafi activists who fled Egypt when the government cracked down on their activities. Indeed, two-thirds of the leadership of the early al Qaeda Central were Egyptians. There is some evidence that bin Laden has not established the same bonds of trust with later generations that he did with the old guard. This means that as this old guard vanishes, either through death or capture, bin Laden may have trouble replacing the fallen leaders with new personnel.

The second wave comprises those who joined the global Islamist terrorist social movement in the 1990s. These young people come mainly from the middle class. They were motivated by the suffering of Muslims in Bosnia, Chechnya, Kashmir, and the Philippines and inspired by the alleged heroics of the first wave. Many found their way to Afghanistan for training, especially after bin Laden's return to that country from Sudan. A number of this wave's cohort volunteered to fight in the hot spots of the 1990s: Bosnia, Chechnya, and Kashmir. Egyptians were not as prominent in the second wave because the Egyptian Islamic Group, the largest Egyptian terrorist organization, elected not to follow bin Laden's internationalists and remained focused on Egypt, the near enemy. Saudis inspired by the alleged exploits of the first wave and Muslim expatriates in Europe instead became the most important members of the second wave. This second wave ended with the allied military invasion of Afghanistan after 9/11, which destroyed the training camps and eliminated the shelter for terrorists there. Governments turned off funding for global Islamist terrorists, hardened international borders to decrease their mobility and monitored communications. There was a worldwide open season on global Islamist terrorists.

The third wave is the post–Iraqi invasion generation. Between the second and third waves, there is a transition of about a year and a half, during which members of different waves would mix with each other in their home countries. With the destruction of the training camps in Afghanistan, aspiring terrorists no longer had the opportunity to link up with al Qaeda Central there. Although a few went abroad in search of training, most stayed at home. Members of the third wave in the West are the second generation, or children of Muslim immigrants, or were infant immigrants themselves. Because their parents formed part of the unskilled labor pool in Europe, this portion of the third wave tends to have middle to lower social class roots.[2] Little is known about the third wave that comes from the Middle East, but I suspect that they look more like the second-wave elite expatriates, as exemplified by the members of the bombing plots in Britain in June 2007.[3]

The Myth of Brainwashing

Another popular idea holds that the global jihadi terrorists were brainwashed—either by their religion, or by their families, cultures, or schools. The notion of brainwashing first became familiar in the United States when it was discovered that nearly two dozen American soldiers had refused repatriation to the United States after the Korean War. This caused a national scandal: How could Americans refuse to come back to their country? A mysterious Chinese process of mind control, brainwashing—coming from the Chinese characters for brain and washing—that used Pavlovian techniques and coercion, was blamed.

In fact, more than 22,600 Communist prisoners declined repatriation (22 percent of the total number of Communists captured), while twenty-three Americans and one Briton also refused and voluntarily decided to stay with the Communists (0.6 percent of those captured). Critics said the "betrayal" of country by the 0.6 percent of Americans resulted from brainwashing; whereas those Communist prisoners who refused to return simply rejected totalitarianism. The discrepancy in the numbers already cast some suspicion on the mysterious concept, for which there is no scientific evidence. Brainwashing now refers to the process of adopting an ideology that the labeler rejects.

But the concept of brainwashing is alive and well as an explanation of why people become Islamist terrorists: a charismatic leader "brainwashes" vulnerable youths and leads them astray. This argument is the Saudi government's main explanation for this type of terrorism. At first, the Saudis had denied they had a problem, but could no longer do so with the waves of bombings in the country in 2003. They blamed the attacks not on local grievances against the state, but on misguided religious brainwashing.

Religion

People assume that the jihadis are well educated in religion. That is not the case. A few religious scholars exist in their midst, but theirs is a very untraditional interpretation of the scriptures. The majority of terrorists come to their religious beliefs through self-instruction. Their religious understanding is limited; they know about as much as any secular person, which is to say, very little. Often, they have not started reading the Quran seriously until they are in prison, because then it is provided to them and they have lots of time to read it.

My data show that about a fourth of my sample was deeply religious when they were young and about two-thirds were secular. The rest were Christian converts. Since the data were too thin to tease apart the individual devotion of the child from the devotion of his family, I pooled these two concerns together when I had any information on either the family of origin or a child's life. In a sense, this is the "green diaper" theory of Islamist terrorism: young people become terrorists because they were born into it (their family was supportive of its aims). But there is considerable variation among terrorists in terms of devotion to Islam as a young person. The first wave, which provided the leadership of al Qaeda Central, was quite pious—about two-thirds came from religious families. Approximately a third of the second wave came from such a background, but only a very small minority of the third wave did.

Childhood devotion to Islam also varied widely according to geography. Those in my sample who came from Europe and North Africa had completely secular childhoods; in fact, they were from deeply secular countries, where wearing the veil is sometimes prohibited. There was more connection to Islam in the Middle East, especially in the Arabian Peninsula. However, the greatest percentage showing devotion came from Southeast Asia, where my sample from Indonesia and Malaysia indicated that the vast majority of later terrorists were religious as young people. These countries stand out in the sample because Abdullah Sungkar and Abu Bakar Baasyir, the headmasters of the Pondok Ngruki and Lukmanul Hakiem religious boarding schools, recruited their best students to become the backbone of Jamaah Islamiyah, the al Qaeda affiliate in Malaysia and Indonesia.

We can conclude that the vast majority of children who later became global Islamist terrorists grew up secular, in secular environments. They were not "brainwashed" into terrorism by their families or cultures. Nor, of course, were the 7 percent of the sample who were Christian converts to Islam.

A second version of the brainwashing argument holds that the terrorists were brainwashed by their schools. Visions of young children swaying to the rhythmic recitations of the Quran in madrassas (Islamic religious schools) suggest the idea that rote memorization of a text in a language that they do not understand invariably leads the young to fanaticism. It is easy to visualize these children as robots who could be persuaded to blow themselves up.

The data on the educational background of my sample show that only 13 percent attended madrassas. Of this group, most were students of Abdullah Sungkar and Abu Bakar Baasyir. This means that 87 percent did not go to madrassas.

A madrassa education concentrates on teaching the Quran to the exclusion of more secular subjects—such as science, which could be useful for making bombs. In fact, madrassa students generally do not become international terrorists, but tend to stay at home. Because of their relative lack of sophistication, madrassa students do not travel well (the Taliban recruited exclusively from madrassas in the tribal areas of Pakistan, but only because that is where most of the Afghan refugees were located). It is true that religious education also varies according to the country. Students in Saudi Arabia, for example, receive an especially large measure of religious instruction in their public schools. I did not count Saudi students as attending madrassas, and perhaps the influence of religious education might be greater than the figures show. However, the size of the additional Saudi sample was not large enough to affect my conclusions.

At first glance, the best example of brainwashing would be the "thirteen-year-old" Moroccan twin sisters who wanted to blow themselves up in Rabat in 2003. But a full account of their radicalization, including their own version of the influences from their environment, reveals the difficulties in such an argument.

The Path of the Laghriss Twins

Imane and Sanae Laghriss were arrested in Rabat in mid-August 2003 for plotting to kidnap Moroccan officials for ransom and to carry out suicide bombings of the Moroccan parliament and a supermarket that sold liquor. Five young girls as well as about two dozen men were also arrested for aiding the twins in the plot. The evidence came from the confessions of Imane and Sanae Laghriss and their best friend, Hakima Rojlane. The three girls later retracted their confessions, but the twins were sentenced to five years in prison and the men to more severe penalties; Rojlane was acquitted.

The press reported the case as a clear example of two young girls suffering a combination of poverty and ignorance and being preyed upon by cynical Islamist recruiters, who "brainwashed" them into wanting to commit suicide bombing attacks. The twins had been born to a poor single mother. She first sent them to live with relatives, who used the girls as maids. When they were a little older, the girls worked as maids in other homes. The family was reunited in 2001 and lived in a room rented from Rojlane's mother. The twins became more religious and eventually were arrested in 2003 for their plot after Imane asked a local radical imam, Rachid Nafae, whether it was lawful to become a martyr. The imam alerted the police.

In press accounts, the alleged Rabat Salafia Jihadia cell—composed of Mustapha Echater, Hassan Chaouni (known as Kichk, the name of the famous Egyptian preacher) and Fouad al-Gaz—brainwashed the innocent twins.[4] Even the girls' defense attorney portrayed them as innocent victims of society exploited by fundamentalists.[5] Their mother agreed. "Imane and Sanae were manipulated. They were so young. They were intoxicated by the Islamists' lies. It is as if they were brainwashed. They suddenly started wearing the veil around 12–13 years, praying constantly and the only words out of their mouth were halal and haram [religiously allowed and forbidden]. They refused to go to school."[6] El Pais noted that "all 17 adults who manipulated the two girls were given long sentences. They had converted them into radical Islamists and had convinced them to blow themselves up in the alcoholic drinks section of the Label supermarket in Rabat. . . . Daughters of a single mother who survives by begging and selling second-hand goods, they tended to skip school and hang out in the run-down suburb of Duar al Hajja 13 hours a day. They were easy prey for a brainwashing that still has an effect on them."[7]

Some investigative journalists from La Gazette du Maroc, unsatisfied with these attempts to understand what happened, went to interview the family and friends of the accused. All the evidence of the plot came from Imane Laghriss's confession. Hakima Rojlane had supported her friend because she was afraid that she would have been beaten if she had denied there was a plot. The twins' mother also blamed Imane, who had been separated from her, mistreated by her relatives, suffered a head injury, and transformed when she returned to live with her sister and her mother. In popular understanding, her "weak mind" made her a perfect scapegoat. A girl from the neighborhood allegedly influenced Imane to wear the veil, and she in turn convinced her sister and best friends to follow suit. The twins and Rojlane stopped going to school because they were forced to reveal their legs in physical education classes. They started going to the Al Wahda mosque to listen to Rachid Nafae's sermons. The mother claimed that her daughters were brainwashed at the mosque. Rojlane's mother, in contrast, denied that her daughter had anything to do with the plot.[8]

The journalists visited the home of Hassan Chaouni, the alleged leader of the cell. His mother and sisters denied that he had anything to do with the plot. He was married, religious, and attended the Al Wahda mosque. He had been arrested just after 9/11 and after the May 2003 Casablanca bombings, but was released after two days in each instance. Chaouni's sister said that Imane Laghriss had asked that Chaouni take her as his second wife. Chaouni, who had trouble providing for his own family, refused, but Imane kept insisting. According to his mother, Imane claimed that Chaouni knew about the plot while Sanae and Hakima denied that he had anything to do with it. Sanae said that they used to visit Chaouni because he would give them small amounts of money knowing that they were orphans and that they begged in front of the mosque.[9] The journalists also visited Mustapha Echatar's family. He was still single and his sisters said that Imane wanted to marry him. He was not particularly religious and only rarely went to the Al Wahda mosque.[10] Apparently, Fouad al-Gaz would also come to the mosque and knew the girls, but he worked sixteen hours a day to feed his family.[11]

At trial, Imane and Sanae received five-year sentences, while Hakima Rojlane was acquitted. When journalists interviewed Rojlane shortly after her release, she said that at first Imane had implicated her in the plot, but she retracted her confession. She did not blame her friends Imane and Sanae because they had been intimidated by the police. "I forgive them because they did not know what they were doing and if Imane mentioned my name the first day, I know it was to plead with the adults that they should leave her alone. She was very scared. I remember that she warned me before my interview, 'say yes to everything, otherwise they'll hit you.'"[12]

In February 2007, just before their release on their eighteenth birthday, the Laghriss twins gave an interview to explain their odyssey.[13] They were born on February 22, 1989, in Rabat. Their mother, who was not married, had been thrown out of her house when she showed signs of pregnancy. She thought about abandoning her daughters at the hospital, but her parents agreed to take them in. The twins lived there happily for the first five years until their grandmother died. Imane was sent to live with a cousin near Fez, while Sanae rejoined her mother as a beggar before being sent to another relative in Casablanca. Sanae moved to a new household on a yearly basis. She showed an aptitude for languages, especially Arabic. She loved to read the newspapers that her uncle brought home because they allowed her, she said, to dream of faraway lands: "It was the only way to escape the misery where I lived." She watched television with the family and became intensely interested in the Palestinian issue, especially after she witnessed the death of Mohamed al Dura, a young Palestinian boy killed by Israeli army bullets in a gun battle with Palestinian militants. She was so obsessed by the issue that she became the laughing stock of the family. "It seems that you feel it's your duty to liberate Palestine, they would tell me. They did not take me seriously. This assassination definitely upset me because I felt that this child was like me. We were suffering from the same type of injustice."[14]

On September 11, 2001, Sanae discovered a new hero: Osama bin Laden. "A man who fights for justice and sacrificed everything for a large cause," she wrote in her diary. Shortly thereafter, she was reunited with her mother and sister and they rented a room together. Although it was not as comfortable as when she was with her aunt, they had a home.

Sanae was the leader of the twins. Now about thirteen, they socialized with people their own age and even flirted with boys. They became impressed with the young religious men in the neighborhood, who grew beards and dressed like Afghans. The sisters started wearing the veil, began to pray, and became more integrated in the local religious community. Their mother did not suspect anything because she left home at eight in the morning and came back around ten at night. After they decided to veil, the twins stopped going to school because their physical education teacher tried to force them to wear shorts. Their mother tried to place them in homes as maids, but nobody wanted to hire veiled girls.

Finally, someone came to their home to ask for Sanae in marriage. He was twenty-seven and she was thirteen. The mother refused. Imane accused her mother of wanting to make her and her sister prostitutes like she was. The mother threw her out of the house. Imane went to the mosque, where she was welcomed by Abdelkader Labsir. He sheltered her at his home and introduced her to his wife and two children. A plumber by trade, he was also a takfiri and had spent five years in prison in the 1990s for his beliefs. This of course made him a hero in her eyes. Although she returned home to her mother three days later, she now began to take her sister Sanae to Labsir's house, where they spent hours reading jihadi literature and listening to radical preachers' cassettes. Labsir became their idol, the father they never had. They were angry at the world, and the ideas they read gave them an interpretation of the world and suggestions about what to do in life. The two girls admired the courage of mujahedin in Chechnya and the virtue of the Taliban regime.

Their reading and listening inspired them to want to act. They talked to Hassan Chaouni and a former soldier, Said Fafa, about their plans to blow up the liquor section in a large department store in Rabat. After the May 16, 2003, Casablanca bombings, the twins and the "brothers" were ecstatic and tried to firm up their project. They visited the Saudi cultural center in Rabat, where they read about jihad. They revealed their plan to Labsir, who suggested to them that they should instead attack Parliament, the symbol of evil in the state. The twins grew excited and wrote pamphlets criticizing the king and Moroccan society and showed them to other "brothers." The girls believed they could make bombs out of firecrackers, while Labsir tried to temper their enthusiasm by promising them some real weapons. In her excitement, Imane wrote an anonymous letter to the imam of the Al Wahda mosque to ask him his opinion about their plan. He denounced it publicly during a sermon and called the police, who easily unraveled the plot and arrested the twins.

At the police station, the twins were slapped a few times, and confessed when they heard the cries of people being tortured in the next room. At their arraignment, the two girls discovered that they enjoyed being the center of attention. The cameras focused on them and even the judges seemed deferential. At their trial, they proudly admitted that they were plotting to blow up Parliament and kill the king. They smiled when they were sentenced to five years because the conviction showed that the authorities were taking them seriously. They were no longer children, but important people. In prison, they became a curiosity for the other female prisoners, who protected and spoiled them. They also discovered they were celebrities, and other religious prisoners

respected them. The twins loved the attention and even wrote a new pamphlet criticizing the king, which earned them two more years in prison. They
were transferred to a different prison, where the warden offered them minia-
ture Qurans.

In the summer of 2005 they received a royal pardon and were transferred
to a reform school in Casablanca. At the reform school they were given their
own rooms. They did not mix with the rest of the inmates, who were there for
minor infractions, such as begging or vagrancy. At first, they still commanded
the attention of media and civil rights advocates, who regularly visited their
"private quarters." After two months, the novelty wore off, and they sank back
into anonymity. The twins became depressed, and ran away from the school.
They went to their grandfather in Rabat and after twenty days returned to the
reform school. They found work, but Sanae ran away again for nearly another
twenty days. She spent time with militant sisters in Meknes and Rabat. She
finally returned to the school, where she and Imane lost their privileges and
were assigned to the collective dormitory. They were allowed only one visitor,
their mother, once a week. Sanae started writing her memoirs in a notebook.
The twins ran away a third time and were once again returned.

At the time of their release, Imane, who got a henna tattoo praising bin
Laden, hoped to work to help her mother and also find a husband. She intended to stay in Casablanca. Sanae was more reflective about her experience.
She said, "The brothers really disappointed me. At the trial, they yelled 'Long
live the King' when the judge was asking them questions. They are all cow-
ards. I don't have anything against the King, and I am not ready to change
anything."[15] She intended to go to Rabat and edit her memoirs. She dreamt of
going to Egypt and spending the rest of her life working in a bookstore.

The Laghriss twins' account shows that far from being passive recipients
of brainwashing, they were active advocates of terrorism. They tried to prod
the men around them to support them in their goal. They dreamed about becoming heroines and loved the attention they received because they were seen
as serious adults. Their radicalization seemed to follow a familiar path. Their
trajectory started with a strong sense of moral outrage at the death of young
Mohamed al-Dura, which resonated with their own life experiences. They
connected with a network of takfiris, who educated them in an ideology that
framed their moral outrage with their personal life. It is hard to see them as
victims when they were shaping their lives even in prison.

Immature and Ignorant?

Although Imane and Sanae Laghriss do not fit the usual picture of Islamist terrorism, they share some characteristics with many terrorists. But their age is not one of them. A common misconception about terrorists related to the brainwashing theory holds that they are naïve young men with weak or vulnerable minds who are easily brainwashed by their elders. The image that comes to mind is a 2004 video of a fourteen-year-old Palestinian boy, draped in a vest filled with explosives and shaking uncontrollably, with his arms held high under the guns of Israeli soldiers, who carefully steer him away from other people at a roadblock in the Palestinian territories. One can easily imagine that this confused child obviously did not know any better and was involved in something that he probably did not understand.

To test this hypothesis of naïveté, I plotted the age distribution of my sample at the time each subject joined a terrorist organization. The average was about twenty-five years. Here again there was some generational variation. Members of the first wave were nearly thirty years old when they first joined al Qaeda Central. Most had taken part in more local militant activities before they went to Afghanistan. The average age of those in the second wave was around twenty-five when they became global Islamist terrorists. The third wave joined much younger; the average age of those arrested in Europe in the past two years is the early twenties. Although the age of terrorists seems to be ever younger, they are still not immature teenagers, acting out on a dare or from boredom.

The "ignorance" theory of terrorism (a variation of the "weak mind" theory) is based on the idea that young people join because they do not know any better. In my sample, however, I found, to my surprise, that the majority, 62 percent, had attended university. This contrasts sharply with the rest of their community of origin, in which fewer than 10 percent go on to college. In fact, it is even higher than in the United States, where just over half of the population has attended college.

Again, there are variations over time. The first wave is by far the best educated. Over 60 percent finished college and a sizable percentage has a doctoral degree. The second wave began college but many dropped out to join the movement. The third wave is too young to have gone to college and, as I will describe in the next chapter, a plurality has dropped out of high school.

People may object that the terrorists were highly educated in religious studies, which indoctrinated them into violence. This is not the case. The majority studied technical fields, such as engineering and medicine, as did the al Qaeda Central leadership. Osama bin Laden was a civil engineer; Zawahiri, a physician; Khalid Sheikh Mohammed, an engineer; Ramzi Yousef, an electrical engineer; Mohammed Atta, an architect; and Ziad Jarrah, an engineer. The physicians and engineer involved in the 2007 plots in Britain were more typical of the second wave than the third wave. Similarly, the Russian anarchists came from the faculties of engineering and medicine in Zurich before they returned to conduct their campaign of terror in Russia in the late 1870s.

For many observers, the prevalence of these careers is puzzling. Why the high numbers of engineers and physicians among Islamist terrorists? Engineering and medicine are the two most prestigious faculties in Middle Eastern countries like Egypt. The students, who are often from the middle class, idealistic, and want to serve their country, are trying to reach the highest ranks in their society. But as they reach the end of their formal education, they realize that the good jobs are available only through graft, corruption, or nepotism. If they are from the lower middle class or rural areas, they cannot afford to buy these positions. Although highly educated, they cannot find an outlet for their intellectual gifts. They become disillusioned and resentful and may turn against their government and society in general.

Engineers may also possess a specific frame of mind that draws them to Salafi ideas. Engineers, like mathematicians, try to build from elementary building blocks. They go back to the "drawing board" and construct their arguments from the foundations. The structure of the argument is similar for Salafis: "to build an ideal utopia, return to the purity of the first community, that of the Prophet." For the Salafis, everything that comes after is corrupted and polluted by Greek philosophy, and therefore is no longer the word of God. This quest for original principles is similar in both engineering and Salafism.

This parallel is convenient. Since they are engineers and not Islamic scholars, they do not know much about 1,400 years of Quranic commentaries. They turn to Islam in their mid-twenties without a strong religious background that might have put in context the new religious arguments they encounter. The turn to Salafi ideas, where the only legitimate authorities are the Quran and the hadiths, allows them to ignore the commentary and interpret the original texts for themselves.

This analysis turns on its head the argument that madrassas are breeding grounds for future suicide bombers. The Islamist terrorists find religion fairly late in life, in their mid-twenties, and do not have an adequate background to evaluate the Salafi arguments and interpret the material they read. The new-found faith and devotion to a literal reading of early Islamic texts are not a result of brainwashing in madrassas; their fervor results from their lack of religious training, which prevents them from evaluating their new beliefs in context. Had they received such training, they might not have fallen prey to these seductive Manichaean arguments. It follows that more religious education for these young men might have been beneficial.

Lack of Responsibility?

Conventional wisdom suggests that people become terrorists because they do not have any responsibilities, such as a family or a job, which might steer them away from the criminality of terrorism.

The majority of the overall sample held professional or semi-professional positions. Again, there is some variation over time. The first wave has the highest percentage of professionals, commensurate with their education. Most of the second wave was also employed or attending university at the time they joined the jihad. The third wave is basically unskilled because its members did not go to college.

Although many employed future terrorists apparently had professional jobs, they did not have the top jobs in their fields and compared poorly with their school peers. They were not employed at the level of their skills or education.

In terms of family responsibility, three-fourths of the terrorists were married. Again, there is a variation over time. All the jihadis in the first wave were married. Most in the second wave were married, but fewer in the third wave are. Some terrorists married just before carrying out their deadly mission, including those who were embarking on suicide missions. There is also some geographical variation. All the terrorists from Southeast Asia were married. Moreover, they appear to have married into the jihad: they were not fully trusted unless their wives were daughters or sisters of other terrorists. Marriage was less common among the second-wave terrorists who were immigrants in the West, paralleling the findings of the third wave, composed mostly of second-generation immigrants.

Sexual Frustration?

Another popular theory explaining terrorism is the "sexual frustration" or "testosterone" theory of terrorism. The argument goes like this: Because the terrorists are religious Muslim young men, prohibited from having premarital sexual relations, they are so sexually frustrated that they go crazy and blow up themselves and people around them. A variant of this is that terrorism is a result of a surplus of young men, full of testosterone, who are unable to find any kind of work or meaningful employment. They turn to terrorism as an escape valve. A third variant is the "seventy-two virgins" theory of terrorism. These sexually frustrated young men welcome the opportunity to go to paradise and meet their reward: seventy-two virgins waiting to please their every desire, and a pass to paradise for their close relatives.

We have already seen from the previous section that the vast majority of global Islamist terrorists were married, which would seem to undermine the sexual frustration theory of terrorism. The vast majority of the first two waves were also employed, which refutes the testosterone "idle hands" theory. I already hear objections to these facts. Some might argue that many of these marriages are just rituals, consummated just before a suicide bomber embarks on his mission. It is true that a few are such marriages. But about two-thirds of the terrorists in my sample have children, and many have a large number of children—in order to continue the jihad after they are dead.

This line of reasoning, like most of the thinking debunked in this chapter, shows that once the word terrorism is mentioned, people seem willing to believe just about anything about the terrorists. Their deeds are so horrific that they are no longer considered human and what we know about humans no longer applies to them. But they are human. When I lecture on terrorism, I often ask my audiences whether they would die for sex. After an uncomfortable moment of silence, the women start smiling and the men do not know how to react. I point this out and joke, "Women know there is no sex to die for, while men are still hoping." This breaks the ice and people realize that it is nonsense to assume that terrorists are so different from themselves. Just as normal people will not kill themselves for even heavenly sex, neither would terrorists.

The sexual frustration theory is one of the easiest claims to refute, by examining the facts. Yet many believe that the story is too good to check, so why bother? The data indicate that the terrorists do not lack for sex. In view of their large families, one could as easily argue that the terrorists blow themselves up to get away from sex as the other way around.

The point is that the entire issue of sex and terrorism is a complete dead end. This is not why people turn to terrorism. But the issue of sex is a great illustration of our reaction to terrorism and rejection of the null hypothesis, the strong belief that "they" are so different from "us." We are so eager to believe that terrorists are different that we are willing to believe nearly anything about them.

Neither Bad nor Mad

We have seen that social conditions do not explain why people become terrorists. Another popular explanation finds that terrorists act as they do because there is something wrong about them personally. There are two versions of this argument: one is that they are simply bad—that is, they are all criminals; and the other is that they are simply mad—that is, they are psychologically abnormal.

In terms of the criminal theory of terrorism, I have tried to look into the past histories of those in my database to see whether there was any evidence of criminal activity. One way to do this is to look at arrest records prior to joining a terrorist organization. Overall, there was a very low rate of arrest in the sample. None of the nineteen people in the index sample had a criminal record anywhere in the world. But there are variations according to waves. The first wave, especially the Egyptians, did have a significant incarceration rate. Many had been caught in the dragnets preceding and following the assassination of Egyptian President Anwar al-Sadat in 1981. But their imprisonment was due not to criminal but to political activity. There is no indication of any criminal activity at the time.

The second wave is more complicated. As I will show in the next chapter, those terrorists who are second-generation North African immigrants to Western Europe were involved in some unlawful activity before turning to global

Islamist terrorism. In general, they were in the minority and their criminality was confined to petty misdeeds: false documents trafficking, credit card fraud, insurance fraud, car theft, and minor drug trafficking. Violent acts were generally not part of their criminal repertoire. Other members of the second wave had no criminal record.

The third wave is even more complicated. Many dedicated Islamist terrorists do turn to petty crime to fund their activities. I will later argue that they turn to crime to raise money for their operations because they are disconnected from al Qaeda Central.

Underlying the entire criminality issue is the commonly held belief that terrorists are simply psychopaths or sociopaths. This also turns out not to be so. The closest scientific definition of these popular terms is antisocial personality disorder (ASPD). One of the requirements for this diagnosis is that the antisocial behavior must take place over a long period of time; this is to help us distinguish someone with a true personality disorder from a common criminal. A person with ASPD has to have some antecedent in his past, such as a childhood conduct disorder. In my dataset, very few displayed such childhood behavior. One of the exceptions is Ahmed Fadl Nazzal al-Khalaylah, better known as Abu Musab al-Zarqawi, who headed al Qaeda in Iraq until he was killed by U.S. forces in 2006. Zarqawi appears to have been a thug from very early on, getting into trouble with the law even as a child.

Zarqawi's career illustrates the problem that an armed or clandestine organization has with people who have ASPD. These people are so self-centered that they have no consideration for others in the organization. They simply cannot be trusted, either because they might compromise security or act in ways that would embarrass the organization. The military or a police department will discharge someone with ASPD "for the good of the service" as soon as it is detected in boot camp or the police academy. A similar approach is taken by clandestine organizations, which cannot risk having undisciplined members. Furthermore, people with ASPD would quickly leave an organization that expects its members to sacrifice themselves for the greater good—which is the essence of suicide terrorism. People with ASPD are not known for their altruistic behavior. Rather than sacrifice themselves for others, they expect others to sacrifice for them. Indeed, Zarqawi was never part of al Qaeda Central until the very end of his life, when al Qaeda Central had to acknowledge his success in Iraq and invited him to join formally. This was a marriage of convenience, as demonstrated in letters to him from al Qaeda Central, which tried to rein in his enthusiasm for murdering other Muslims.[16] Up to the point when Zarqawi offered to swear allegiance to bin Laden in order to attract more recruits to Iraq in 2005, rivalry between Zarqawi and al Qaeda Central was very strong. To the end, neither party fully trusted the other.

At this point, it appears that most Islamist terrorists are not criminals, even though there is something about the group that leads them to entertain unlawful activities. In terms of criminality, it appears that under the right conditions, individuals very unlikely to do harm individually are easily able to do so collectively.

So, if terrorists are not bad, are they simply mad? As a psychiatrist, I have looked at my sample for any hint of major mental disorders, especially those that the public calls psychotic but are more scientifically labeled "thought disorders." In my sample of about five hundred, there were about four with hints that they experienced beliefs that were not based in reality. However, since these beliefs were culturally consistent, there was some question as to whether they could be considered true illusions. (In Ireland, for example, it is common for people to believe in and see ghosts, and nobody there would think it is crazy. It is a cultural phenomenon.) In any case, less than 1 percent of people in my sample had these beliefs. The worldwide base rate for these psychotic symptoms is about three percent. So, there is evidence that, as a group, global Islamist terrorists may be in better mental health than the rest of the population.

Likewise, I saw little evidence for any personality disorder.[17] Terrorists are not narcissistic, as has sometimes been claimed. As I have noted, they are willing to sacrifice themselves for comrades and the cause. This is opposite of what we would expect from a narcissistic person, who would expect others to sacrifice themselves for him.

Another version of the abnormal personality version of terrorism is to postulate some form of pathological hatred. Yes, there is some hatred for Israel and the United States, and Islamist terrorists seem to subscribe to conspiracy theories about Jews, the CIA, Zionist control of the world, and the like. But they are not any different in this regard from the rest of the world, which often holds conspiracy theories. It is actually difficult to convince people to sacrifice themselves just because they hate their target. This might be possible for a "hot situation," when in the heat of the moment people retaliate against what they have just witnessed. However, this type of emotion fades quickly and does not account for why people do things months or years after experiencing moral outrage. On the contrary, it appears that it is much more common to sacrifice oneself for a positive reason such as love, reputation, or glory. Those who do so hope that their sacrifices will advance their cause, as described in the diary of the anarchist Vera Figner.

Trauma is another popular explanation for terrorism. This perspective comes from research in refugee camps in Palestine and Chechnya. In my sample, I saw very little trauma in the background of the global Islamist terrorists. Many were from solid upper-class or middle-class backgrounds, with opportunities open to them. In fact, as a group, they seemed to have been slightly overprotected as children. Recall the widely reproduced photograph of Mohammed Atta, the field leader of the 9/11 operation, sitting on his mother's knees as a child. They appear to be looking lovingly at each other. This tender scene is typical of the childhood of global Islamist terrorists. Perhaps, because they were overprotected as children, they were not exposed to the harsh reality of their environment and went on to become dreamers or idealists. When they reached their mid-twenties and their childhood dreams were shattered by a perceived moral outrage, they may have become more receptive to violent Salafi messages that suggested a new worldview that could replace the original idealistic vision.

Out of the Diaspora

So far, this exploration of the social and psychological backgrounds of the global Islamist terrorists has yielded very little in terms of explanation. Let us then turn to the situational variables at the time my sample subjects joined a terrorist organization, which may provide insights into their motivations.

I looked at the circumstances under which people joined global Islamist terrorism. A frequent theme was that of being an expatriate; about 60 percent of my sample joined a terrorist organization while living in a country in which they did not grow up. An additional 20 percent were the sons (second generation) or grandsons (third generation) of Muslim immigrants to the West. So, the total of my sample that was part of the diaspora, expatriates, and second or third generation, was 84 percent. This finding is consistent with other studies on terrorism. The link between a diaspora and terrorism appears strong. The anarchists flourished in Zurich in the 1870s. The IRA began in a pub in Boston and crossed the ocean to Ireland during World War I. The Tamil Tigers terrorist organization in Sri Lanka is strongly supported by large Tamil diaspora communities in London and Toronto. ETA, the Basque separatist terrorist organization, finds sanctuary in France. This link between terrorism and diaspora has not been fully explored, but already, for global Islamist terrorism, it points to an interesting finding.

A majority of the sample joined global Islamist terrorism in a country where they did not grow up. They were from country A, living in country B (when they joined), and targeting country C. The group from Hamburg that provided the leadership for the 9/11 operation is typical. Middle Eastern students in Germany traveled to Afghanistan to join the fight against the Americans. This dynamic is unlike the traditional type of terrorism: people who were born in country A, living in their own country A, and going after their own government A. In the more national form of terrorism, local grievances may play a more important role in furthering terrorism. In the transnational form of terrorism, like the al Qaeda social movement, the dynamic of radicalization might be more complicated.

Friendship and Kinship

My original criterion as to who should be included in my sample was based on the relationship between a person and others with whom that person had an operational link. One major question is whether these potential recruits had any prior relationships with their future comrades before they joined the terrorist social movement. It turns out that joining the global Islamist terrorism social movement was based to a great degree on friendship and kinship.

About two-thirds of the people in the sample were friends with other people who joined together or already had some connection to terrorism. There were two major pathways. The first is a "bunch of guys" who collectively decided to join a terrorist organization. This was a collective decision, not an individual one. The typical example was the above-mentioned Hamburg group. They were Middle Eastern students in Germany who met at school, became friends and were radicalized together through discussions in collective apartments. Eight of them decided to join al Qaeda and traveled together, in two waves, to Afghanistan in the hope of being selected by al Qaeda Central. The first wave became the pilots and the second the support group. The four Montreal friends who included the so-called millennial bomber, Ahmed Ressam, also went to Afghanistan as part of a group. There are many other examples.

A second common pathway to becoming a terrorist was that of joining childhood friends. When people who grew up together in the old country emigrated as young adults to the West, they looked up their old friends in the new host country. Five of the seven Madrid bombers—who committed collective suicide on April 3, 2004, in their apartment in Leganes—played together on the streets of Tetouan, Morocco. If a former friend is part of a terrorist group, a latecomer will start to socialize with him, and soon his entire social circle will be people involved in terrorism. The odds are very strong that the latecomer will join his childhood friend in terrorism.

About a fifth of the people in the sample were close relatives—sons, brothers, first cousins—of people already in the global Islamist terrorism social movement. There are some families of terrorists, such as the al-Khadr family from Toronto, where the father, an al Qaeda leader, encouraged his four sons to join. The wife and daughter were also strongly supportive of their male family members. In the sample, which describes a largely diaspora community, many terrorists married the sisters of fellow terrorists. Kinship bonds cemented friendship bonds.

In Southeast Asia, students from two major madrassas formed the backbone of the Indonesian Jamaah Islamiyah, the al Qaeda affiliate in Southeast Asia. As mentioned earlier, Sungkar and Baasyir, the headmasters of two schools in Indonesia and Malaysia, recruited their best students for the jihad. But even in these cases, it was not simply the exposure to the ideology that brainwashed the students but the patterns of friendships that developed outside the classroom. It was not enough for children to be in class; it was also the relationships forged in recreational activities and study groups that prepared them to join Jamaah Islamiyah.

How did people actually join? There were two major trajectories. The first was the one of young Muslim expatriates who were sent to Europe from the Middle East to study. They came from the elite of the Levantine Middle East, where their families were part of the "best and the brightest" of their respective countries—Egypt, the United Arab Emirates, Lebanon, Jordan, Saudi Arabia. They came from mildly religious, caring upper-middle-class families. By the time the young men went to Europe to study, they were already true global citizens, able to speak three or four languages and skilled in computer technology. They were sent to the West to study because the best universities are located there. As they became separated from their families, friends, and culture, many started to feel homesick and lonely. They also felt marginalized and excluded from their immediate environment. Many decided to adopt a Western lifestyle by going to clubs, drinking, and dating, but this did not relieve their feeling of alienation. They sought out people like themselves. Traditionally, Muslims hang out at the local mosque. So, they drifted to the mosque, not out of religiousness—if there was a time that their religiosity dipped, it was at that time since they adopted a Western lifestyle—but for companionship.

They met in the vicinity of radical mosques, went out to eat together, and over dinner, they became friends. There seems to be a strong division according to food preferences in terrorist groups, since they socialized around meals at cheap local ethnic restaurants. This is the "halal" theory of terrorism. Since keeping halal is sometimes difficult, people get together to prepare and eat meals, or simply go to a halal restaurant. At dinner, they talk about shared interests and traditions and reinforce common values. To conform to conversational courtesy, they stress their commonality and in the process create a micro-culture and develop a collective identity. Over time, they become friends. If their friendship intensifies, they often move in together to save money and further enjoy each other's company. When they are at this stage, they form strong cliques that continue to radicalize over time. This trajectory is especially prominent in the second wave of global Islamist terrorism.

The second major trajectory is that of the second or third generation of immigrants. Their fathers came to Europe as unskilled labor to rebuild its infrastructure after World War II. There is now a third generation in the older immigrant communities. I have also included in this group immigrants who came to Europe as small children. Born in the old country and living with their mothers while their fathers worked in the West, they moved to their adopted countries in the 1980s and 1990s as young children and were essentially raised in Europe. They came from a completely secular background and attended secular state schools, but realized that they did not have the same opportunities as the host "native" children. Many dropped out of school as teenagers and formed youth gangs, turning to petty crime and drugs. They resented the host society, which excluded them. After about a decade of gang life, a few came to the conclusion that there had to be something better. They collectively drifted to religion to escape the hopelessness that permeated their lives. Their personal experiences resonated with the Salafi critiques of Western society and they became attracted to the global Islamist terrorist interpretation that they were excluded from the economy because the West was engaged in a war against Islam. This trajectory is more prominent in the third wave of global Islamist terrorists, who are referred to in the media as "homegrown" terrorists.

Not inconsequentially, the daughters of unskilled working immigrants did not follow a similar trajectory. The unemployment rate for fifteen- to thirty-year-old Muslim men in Europe is two or three times that of their non-Muslim peers. But the unemployment rate for young Muslim women is similar to comparable female populations in the West. This gender difference may be explained by the greater latitude boys are given among immigrant parents. If the girls were to quit school or unable to find a job, they would immediately be sent back to the "old country" to be married to their first cousins (and they would be very valuable to their potential husbands because their citizenship would allow their spouses to immigrate to the wife's Western country). But second- or third-generation immigrant girls do not want to get married to their cousins back home, and so they stay in school, especially during the period where they would be considered an excellent marriage prospect. They therefore become well educated and, on reaching adulthood, they are able to find decent jobs and are given their autonomy. They also take advantage of the rights women enjoy in the West to pursue their interests.

A Select Group

The global Islamist terrorist social movement forms through the spontaneous self-organization of informal "bunches of guys," trusted friends, from the bottom up. I refer to them as a "bunch of guys" because that is what the Royal Canadian Mounted Police called the group in Montreal associated with Ahmed Ressam. More to the point, it also describes the process of radicalization and recruitment into this social movement.

I was surprised by the lack of a top-down recruitment program into al Qaeda. There was no campaign drive for new members, no dedicated committee for recruitment, and no budget allocated specifically for this task. This is all the more surprising because al Qaeda Central was a splinter group from Maktab al-Khadimat, an organization devoted to the recruitment of young Muslim men for the jihad against the Soviets in the 1980s. It seems that al Qaeda had no need for a separate recruitment program. There were plenty of volunteers who traveled to Afghanistan in the hope of being selected to join al Qaeda. In a sense, getting into al Qaeda Central was like getting into an elite college. Like Harvard, al Qaeda did not have to recruit. People want to go to Harvard because of its reputation and the rewards a degree from the school brings. Likewise, some young Muslims want to join al Qaeda because of its reputation. The Hamburg group sought out al Qaeda in 1999. Al Qaeda did not seek them out. More recently, Mohamed Sidique Khan, the leader of the 7/7 London bombers, sought out al Qaeda and traveled to Pakistan to find it, not the other way around. During its golden age, Al Qaeda's acceptance rate was about 15 to 20 percent of the pool of young Muslims coming to Afghanistan for training, a selection rate similar to Harvard's 13 percent. Al Qaeda could select the most dedicated and smartest of the young candidates in the Afghan training camps. All the potential recruits, who came in groups of friends, were enthusiastic volunteers.

The groups who came to Afghan training camps were in search of thrills, fame, and glory. They believed in Salafi ideology, the revivalist brand of Islam. As new born-again novices, they constantly proselytized their beliefs and enthusiasm for the fight. They wanted to impress their friends. In a sense, it was a constant, mutual self-recruiting atmosphere, and there was no need for an outside recruiter.

Nor was there any evidence of brainwashing. As I have already described, the recruits simply took on the beliefs of their friends. In the camps, they forged a strong bond of esprit de corps from the multiple adversities encountered. Their ideology was also reinforced through lectures more sophisticated than those they had heard previously. But they had come to camp as true converts to the cause. The indoctrination of the camp was just polish.

The shared nature of this experience is consistent with the finding that social bonds came before any ideological commitment. The process of joining al Qaeda Central was a collective process. Theirs was not the path of a lone individual, as often portrayed in the press; it was a group adventure.

But knowing about their background does not tell us how global Islamist terrorists became transformed from normal young Muslims into fanatic terrorists. This is the subject of the next chapter.

FOUR

Radicalization in the Diaspora

September 11, 2001, and especially the invasion of Iraq, mark a watershed in the evolution of the threat to the West. Before these events, which demarcate the second and third waves of global Islamist terrorism, the threat had come from the outside in the form of terrorists who had been trained in Afghanistan and come to the West to carry out operations. Examples are the Hamburg-based 9/11 plotters and the Canada-based Los Angeles airport "millennium" bombing plotters. In the third wave, the threat comes from the inside, from "homegrown" terrorists, most of whom have never traveled abroad for training or indoctrination. The threat is no longer "foreign fanatics" but people who grew up in the West and became radicalized there. When the threat came from the outside, a reasonable defense against it was to harden national borders against the intruders. Now that the threat comes from inside, the only way to defend against it is to understand the process of radicalization and devise strategies to prevent its reaching the point of violence.

The story of Ahmed Omar Sheikh, the terrorist who allegedly kidnapped *Wall Street Journal* reporter Daniel Pearl, illustrates how this process takes place. As we saw in the Introduction, the suffering of Muslims in Bosnia outraged Omar Sheikh, leading him over time to believe that war was being waged on Islam. This worldview resonated with his childhood experiences of discrimination, which hardened his beliefs. And it was through his meeting with a member of the Harakut-ul Mujahedin, a Kashmir-based Islamist terrorist group, that he became an active participant in a terrorist organization.

In this chapter, I develop the dynamics of this radicalization process more fully. I do not wish to suggest that the four prongs of radicalization illustrated by Omar Sheikh's story are a linear progression. They do not have to occur in this order. For instance, it is possible that one can belong to a group of young people who want to become warriors for Islam. This may lead one of them to espouse the interpretation that the West is at war with Islam, which was reinforced by videos of the horrors experienced by Muslims around the world. (The brainwashing theory requires that indoctrination comes first.) What is most important is that each dimension of this process of radicalization can occur at its own pace, and often in parallel with other dimensions. There are many interactions among these dimensions. For instance, events depicting some injustice are discussed in informal networks, which provide an ideological frame to discuss them and in so doing amplify the significance of the injustice. One cannot simply draw a line, put markers on it and gauge where people are along this path to see whether they are close to committing atrocities. I will separate each aspect of the process of radicalization for the sake of analytical clarity, but it will be readily apparent that they feed on each other.

Moral Outrage

In many of their writings and speeches, terrorists refer to the strong motivational effects of hearing about or watching the suffering of fellow Muslims. One especially vivid image became the symbol of such suffering. This was the video showing Mohamed al-Dura, a twelve-year-old Palestinian boy, crouching in terror behind his father, both caught in the cross-fire between Palestinian snipers and Israeli Defense Forces in Gaza on September 30, 2000. The killing of Mohamed was one of the most viewed videos on the Internet and was the inspiration for Sanae Laghriss, as we saw in the previous chapter.

The death of Mohamed al-Dura was the type of act that triggers moral outrage. Not every form of suffering or misfortune elicits such an emotional response—it has to be brought about by human hands and seen as a major moral violation such as killing, injury, rape, or arrest—obvious physical injustice. Tsunamis, earthquakes, and volcanic eruptions can bring about far more human suffering, but do not trigger such hot emotion because they are caused by forces of nature. Corruption and discrimination, by themselves, do not have this power.

They are more likely to lead to resignation and apathy than to hot anger. But when people are seen as the cause of an outrageous tragedy, a moral judgment is triggered. The youth and implied innocence of Mohamed al-Dura increased the sense of moral outrage. This generates anger and provokes a strong desire to retaliate.

Many analysts see humiliation as a factor contributing to terrorism.[1] These arguments are not persuasive. Humiliation or perceived humiliation in various degrees is so ubiquitous in life that it dilutes any explanatory power. Personal humiliation leads to shame and the desire to hide as well as passivity. If experienced as intentional, disrespect can lead to immediate violence. Once that moment is past, the disrespect turns into humiliation and shame. The humiliation of friends can evoke strong anger. But in this case, someone coming to the help of a disrespected friend would do it out of anger rather than humiliation. Anger brings the desire to right a wrong, and this may lead to violence.

In looking at the background of the terrorists in the sample, I was not struck by any common theme of personal humiliation. Yes, terrorists talk about the humiliation of the Muslims in general, but it is not personal experience with it that drives them. If humiliation is a factor in their radicalization, it would be a form of vicarious humiliation. They do not feel humiliated themselves, but act on behalf of their humiliated brothers. Although plausible, this seems more like an after-the-fact justification for terrorism than a before-the-fact motivating factor.

The narrative the media uses to describe events fuels this moral outrage. A media account presents an abbreviated story that turns into a morality play about good and evil. The template of the story is that an evil-minded person caused a grave injury to an innocent victim, with little analysis of what larger societal factors might have contributed to this end result. The story starts with self-motivated and fully responsible people causing this major moral violation. On television, there is no "unfortunate collateral damage" (the neutered military label for unwanted consequences). The empathetic viewers see horrific dismembered bodies, and immediately impute maximum evil intent to the perpetrators. It is curious how military leaders the world over believe that labeling such killing "collateral damage" and arguing that the victims were not the intentional target of the action exonerates them. The bystanders who observe the consequences of an errant bomb definitely hold the perpetrators responsible. If there is a bond between the victims and the witnesses, there will be a great deal of anger at the perpetrators. No amount of aid—rebuilding schools, digging new wells, outfitting hospitals—can change the calculus; moral violations count far more than attempts at restitution and forgiveness.

Of course, the media bring vivid evidence of such moral violations from around the world. Television images and videotapes of the atrocities in Bosnia and Chechnya moved second-wave Muslims to join terrorist organizations to defend their communities. This impulse is celebrated when it is consistent with one's values. As we have noted, the volunteers who joined the Lincoln Brigade in Spain in the late 1930s were praised throughout the West. In fact, Asad Khan of the Muslim charity Convoy of Mercy made this comparison when explaining Omar Sheikh's desire to help the Muslim victims of the Bosnian war.

An analogy sheds some light on this behavior. In 1948, 1967, and 1973, when the existence of the young state of Israel was threatened by its neighbors, young Jews came to Israel to offer their services. They did this because they felt themselves to be Jewish even though they were not particularly religious. They reasoned, "I'm Jewish, and if Israel was gone, we'll have the Holocaust again, so it is really what keeps us safe." Jews in their twenties, who traveled to Israel to fight, were celebrated in the newspapers as young idealists who had answered the call. The reality is that the Israelis did not know what to do with these volunteers, who for the most part had no military training. They would have gotten in the way of a fairly well-trained and well-disciplined army that was indeed fighting for its survival. The volunteers could not be immediately integrated into fighting units so the Israelis moved them out of the way where they could do no harm. I suspect that many of them spent the war working on a kibbutz.

Nobody makes the argument that these young Jews were brainwashed, fanatics, or crazy. At the time, they were heroes. Many Muslims have answered a similar call in the last decade. They, too, believe that they are defending their fellow Muslims, whose only crime is that they are Muslim. The events in Afghanistan, Kashmir, Bosnia, Chechnya, and now especially Iraq have expanded this pool of potential recruits for global Islamist terrorism.

People will object that the young Jews who went to Israel did not intend to become suicide bombers, killing innocent victims. This is undoubtedly true. So we see that what bothers people is not the impulse to come to the aid of beleaguered people, but the acts of suicide and murder. In terms of suicide, I suspect that many Jews would have proudly jumped at the opportunity to detonate themselves during World War II if they had the chance to kill Adolf Hitler in the process. Indeed such instances of sacrificial heroism took place during the liquidation of the Warsaw Ghetto. I am not, of course, condoning suicide bombing. I am, however, drawing an analogy to make the Islamist terrorists' apparent behavior more understandable. Murder is more difficult to explain. Unfortunately, my experience with interviewing murderers is that they give little thought to their victims. Terrorists are probably no different. There is scarcely a mention of the victims of terrorist bombings on the jihadi Internet chat rooms. It is all about the glory of the Islamist martyrs. To most people, there is a big distinction between defending a country and killing innocent women and children; to the global Islamist terrorists, there is no difference, for they view their struggle as defensive. To them, Westerners are guilty because they are infidels and support the infidel enemy army, while the innocent victims will be rewarded in paradise.

War Against Islam

For many young Muslims, the sense of moral outrage is the start of a process. But by itself, it is not sufficient. This outrage has to fit into a moral universe, to resonate with one's own experience and to be amplified within a group for it to reach a level where it contributes to the formation of an Islamist terrorist. For that to happen, the person must make sense of the violation and put it into a context that affects him personally and leads to his personal involvement. This is the role of an enabling interpretation. Analysts often assume that only leaders generate ideas, interpretations, and ideology, and that followers are passive recipients, who automatically follow these guidelines in the actions they take.

This passive view of followers is reminiscent of the "brainwashing" argument in Chapter 3. This undervalues the active role that people play in making sense of their environment and their lives. Consciousness, like solidarity and collective identity, does not always precede action, but may arise in the process of carrying out an action. These are processes that develop simultaneously, mutually influencing and reinforcing each other. As we have seen, people generate beliefs, often from cultural templates available in their societies, and they are not always aware of the main reasons for their actions. The assumption that people are always aware of their motivation leads to an overly cognitive theory of terrorists. One needs only to go to the various courtrooms where terrorists are tried to see that they are not intellectuals who act after careful deliberations. The twenty-eight thugs who were on trial in Madrid for the March 11, 2004, bombings that murdered 191 people did not impress me as very thoughtful people. Likewise, the defendants at the trials in London for the failed attempts to bomb Heathrow airport in the spring of 2004 and the London tube on July 21, 2005, were not intellectuals.

There seems to be an assumption about terrorists that, once their minds are completely programmed by ideology, they cannot help but carry out their conscious program. As a psychiatrist, I am fully aware that people rationalize their past actions all the time. They are not always aware of their main motivation for doing things, but they do not lack for explanations. They often make them up on the fly or afterward when questioned about them. These post hoc justifications may not have much to do with the actual reasons for doing things. To evaluate the real role of ideology in terrorism, we need to see its use in the everyday life of terrorists, which is almost impossible to do. We would need to identify the future terrorists beforehand and witness their interaction. Even if this were possible, it would create difficult ethical dilemmas for social scientists.

Yet this is almost exactly what happened in the past, not for social scientists but for law enforcement officials. They had identified most of the global Islamist terrorist groups before they carried out their atrocities. Many agencies used wiretap surveillance on these groups—the 9/11 bombers when they lived in Hamburg, the Los Angeles airport millennium bomber Ahmed Ressam when he lived in Montreal, the Hofstad Group terrorists in the Netherlands, who killed film director Theo van Gogh in 2004, and some of the Madrid bombers. These conversations, captured without the knowledge of the perpetrators, are invaluable because they provide a window into the terrorists' minds and everyday behavior, unadorned with after-the-fact rationalizations. However, it is rare for this form of evidence to surface in the press, with the exception of the Italian media. One terrorist "ideologue" who was recorded gives us some insight into the role of ideology.

This is a wiretapped conversation between Ahmed al-Sayed Osman Rabei ("Mohammed the Egyptian"), implicated in the Madrid bombings, and Mahmoud, his nonterrorist Muslim Egyptian expatriate roommate. Mahmoud had just undergone a quick random identity check in Italy, about two months after the Madrid bombings. This raised Rabei's ire. The conversation is reproduced in full in order to reflect the men's reasoning.

[Rabei:] They attempt to carry out these checks, which in the end
 are senseless because they [terrorists] strike when they want to

do so. All the countries that follow the United States will end up like [former Spanish Prime Minister José María] Aznar. Madrid served as a lesson for Europe. France was very shrewd, and so is [Spanish Prime Minister José Luis Rodríguez] Zapatero. If something similar [to the Madrid bombings] happened in Italy, [Prime Minister Silvio] Berlusconi would be to blame, because those who follow that dog [U.S. President George Bush] only harm themselves. This one [Berlusconi] invites the dog son of dogs [Bush].

[Mahmoud:] You cannot say that; he can invite anyone he wants, this is his country.

[Rabei:] You have another view of things.

[Mahmoud:] No. When I lived in another country, before arriving here, I saw that the Americans had done this and that. Then, when I arrived here, I found that everything was different.

[Rabei:] You watch other television news broadcasts, you have to know that it is all propaganda.

[Mahmoud:] There are those who say we are wrong, and then there are others who say we are right.

[Rabei:] However, you must know that they are enemies of God.

[Mahmoud:] Listen to me, there is only one God. Frankly, I do not care if someone is Jewish, Orthodox, or Catholic; everyone is free to pray to the God he chooses, and it is neither up to me nor you to judge. We do not know what God wanted to do, nevertheless there is only one God, because all prayers are addressed to God.

[Rabei:] [These disbelievers] end up in hell: it is not I who says so, but the book of God.

[Mahmoud:] I only know one thing: praying to God. The important thing is for you to know God, to pray, and to not behave badly, and to not do things that are not right. All the rest is superficial, and it does not matter whether you are Jewish, Arab, or Orthodox.

[Rabei:] Why are you on the Jews' side? Do you like it when they kill our brothers?

[Mahmoud:] That is not how the issue stands; I am sorry you fail to understand me. It is because everyone claims he is right. The Jew says he is right, the Arab says he is right, the Christian says he is

right. I do not want to side with anyone. God and I; I do not mean
to sound disrespectful, but I want you to know that I absolutely do
not agree with your ideas.

[Rabei:] In my opinion, you do not see the blood that flows over the
land of the world.

[Mahmoud:] It flows over both parts, and not only in one.

[Rabei:] And what about the children who are dying?

[Mahmoud:] I can only tell one thing. In all the attacks that have
been carried out, there is always the hand of an Arab. I hope that
nothing dangerous happens in Italy, because otherwise things will
go ill for us, and we [who have official residence permits] will be
the ones to pay for them [terrorists]. I am very worried, because
we all came here to work, and thanks to this country our fellow
countrymen have managed to create something. Some have bought
a house, others have set up businesses, and there are some who have
made money.

[Rabei:] They are asses, disbelievers, they exploit you, and after you
have been here you have nothing, neither your honor nor dignity.

[Mahmoud:] I told you that everyone has his own ideas. Only God
knows my faith, and you need not come and judge me.

[Rabei:] We do not agree, so it is best that you and I not speak.[2]

The essence of this conversation is political, with Rabei trying to convince
Mahmoud of the rightfulness of his view. Rabei raves about unfair police checks
targeted at Muslims and refers to a conspiracy by Jews to kill Muslims and to
the blood of Muslims and the deaths of Muslim children. He tries to bring religion into his conversation, but Mahmoud will have none of it. Mahmoud is
the one that uses religious elaborations to refute Rabei's political ideas. One gets
the impression that Rabei cannot compete with his roommate on this ground
and quickly returns to the political. Rabei's ritualistic and superficial reference to
religion to support his views contrasts with the deep religious convictions of his
roommate, who rejects Rabei's views—on religious grounds, no less.

Rabei is not just one of the global jihadi terrorists. He was accused of being
the ideologue and one of the masterminds of the Madrid bombings. Some analysts have referred to him as a "recruiter" of the group, the "imam" who indoctrinated or brainwashed the eventual perpetrators, or perhaps the "sanctioner" who

authorized the attacks. Such members, who are older than the rest of the group and who speak Arabic, are suspected of having a strong influence on these groups of young people, especially in the third wave of terrorism, when "homegrown" wannabe terrorists did not have any religious background. These allegedly influential older members surface regularly in these groups. Other examples are Redouane al-Issa for the Hofstad Group and Qayyum Abdul Jamal in the case of those arrested in Toronto in 2006 for plotting to bomb targets in Ottawa. From the evidence presented at court or in the media, there is no doubt that these older men encouraged the eventual perpetrators to carry out a local operation. However, when authorities try to elevate their role within each group, the facts simply do not add up. All of these people were drifters, with no formal religious background. Rabei occasionally worked as a house painter but most of the time was living on welfare. He left Madrid over a year prior to the attack, in February 2003, and had only very rare telephone communications with the eventual perpetrators. None of the intercepted telephone conversations in the Madrid indictment mentions him. There is no evidence that most of the eventual perpetrators even knew or had heard of him. Al-Issa was a reformed drug dealer who had recently discovered religion late in life. He also left prior to any serious operation and the remaining members of the Hofstad Group rarely mentioned him. Like Rabei, al-Issa seemed to have simply disappeared from his group. Jamal was the janitor of a mosque. Although they were not Islamic scholars, based on the fact that they knew Arabic, these older men acquired reputations and were able to impress young people who knew even less than they did. As we saw in Chapter 3, global Islamist terrorists, especially in the third wave, know very little about Islam. They were not particularly religious and did not need the sanction of a religious man to carry out their atrocities.

So what was the role of these older men for the younger group? They certainly were not necessary for the formation of these groups or the execution of an operation. They were not necessary to sanction such operations either. They seemed to have more limited but still important roles as proselytizers, who inspired the younger wannabes with their stories. They served as role models through their alleged examples and claim of important links to the global jihad. Rabei boasted about his very close ties to al Qaeda Central deputy Ayman al-Zawahiri and his exploits as a celebrated jihadi veteran. Because of the breakup of the global terrorist network after 9/11, his admirers could not verify his claims. After his arrest, the investigation showed that he had made it all up.

Converts and young people without a background in Islam lack the context to evaluate the religious claims of people like Rabei, al-Issa, and Jamal. The previous chapter showed that, for the most part, the global Islamist terrorists lacked any religious education and turned to religion in early adulthood. Unlike Rabei's interlocutor, Mahmoud, these young men could not immediately spot the flaws in the religious arguments and accepted the legitimacy of the arguments of the self-taught religious experts. It does not take much religious knowledge to put extremist ideas in a proper context. Mahmoud was not a religious scholar himself. He was a young man from Cairo, with a diploma in tourism, who had come to Italy four months prior to the conversation. He was studying for a master's degree and supported himself with a cleaning job.[3] A simple traditional religious education like Mahmoud's might have inoculated the wannabes against the violent ideas. This may also explain the disproportionate representation of converts in this global terrorist movement. In their eagerness to demonstrate commitment to their new religion, they are all too willing to accept the words of any Arabic speaker who claims special expertise as a representative and legitimate voice for Islam.

The interpretation that the global Islamist terrorists adopt is political rather than religious. It is couched in religious vocabulary, which makes it appear to be religious in character, but its structure is very much built on the notion advocated by Jean-Jacques Rousseau that people are born virtuous but are corrupted as they grow older.[4] In making sense of their world, radical Islamists blame Western values of greed and moral decadence as sources of corruption. They see themselves as the last defenders of virtuous Islam against agents of the decadent West, who intentionally try to ruin it. These evil Western agents become the focus and target for a political movement. Rabei's question "Why are you on the Jews' side?" and bin Laden's declaration of war against "Jews and Crusaders" suggest the target of their ire and the role they should play to build a better world.

Global Islamist terrorists see themselves as warriors in pursuit of fame and glory. They are at war, not with the world, but against a small cabal of evil people that is manipulating the world. All global Islamist terrorist ideologies share a moral reductionism, which ascribes simple causes, and their implied remedies, to complex events. This simplicity makes them easy to grasp, explain, and accept. This vagueness of these ideas about the nature of man, God, society, and history mixes politics and morality in a clear appeal for young Muslims to join the fight. In a sense, imagery and emotion are more important than concepts. Islamist terrorism is more about how the terrorists feel than about how they think. Their worldview boils down to a morality play where human events are totally shaped by a constant fight between good and evil or virtue and corruption. To them, the West is actively engaged in an apocalyptic "War against Islam." In this war, human character, good or evil, must be the real engine of human history. "Character" is more important than weapons in this ultimate fight.

This worldview lends itself to global conspiracy theories. These theories are surprisingly ubiquitous in the world. Secret plots are not signs of mental illness or paranoia but in fact a constant in political life. This is especially true where governments are not accountable to their constituencies, as in authoritarian states. In the Middle East, the lack of transparency in government decisions invites credible conspiracy theories. A global conspiracy theory is different. It is comprehensive in nature and points to the existence of a vast, insidious, and effective international network designed to perpetrate acts of the most evil sort. In this view, this wicked cabal is the decisive factor in making history. A global conspiracy theory does not merely hint at a political conspiracy. It suggests that this collusion is the explanation for understanding history. To the global Islamist terrorists, a small cabal of evil men—Crusaders and Jews—manipulates the world. This theme appears in the bestselling *The Protocols of the Meetings of the Learned Elders of Zion*⁵ and is shared by many people around the world. Again, Rabei's question, "Why are you on the Jews' side?" This personification of evil in history not only makes world events easy to understand, but also provides a clear target for political action.

This global conspiracy provides the dramatic background for the self-appointed role of the global Islamist terrorists. They view themselves as warriors willing to sacrifice themselves for the sake of building a better world, and this gives meaning to their lives. They are part of an elite avant-garde devoted to absolute principles regardless of personal cost. Their enemies, who pursue their self-interest and give into temptation, are symbolic of the decadence of the present world. This "good fight" is at its base a crisis of values: the purity of absolute moral principles representing God's will against the decadence of the West, which has subverted God's will by promoting exclusive materialism and moral perversions such as pornography, homosexuality, women's equality, and usury. The global Islamist terrorists reject this depraved Western morality. Better a dead virtuous hero than a live happy sinner.

The jihadi warrior hero must prove himself in this fight. Easy victory has no glory. At this point, after a gradual escalation of the price of glory, the standard of heroism has become martyrdom. Suicide bombers are now the rock stars of militant Islam. In a sense, martyrdom is easy; it does not involve ethical compromise. However, their fight also implies moral challenges like the killing of apparently innocent bystanders. Unlike the portrait of absolute evil painted in the West, many terrorists are conscious of these distasteful dimensions. Wannabe terrorists discuss the legitimacy of various forms of killings in Internet forums. On the other hand, self-sacrifice or martyrdom is seldom discussed because it is taken for granted. Ayman al-Zawahiri described the unintentional killing of a young girl named Shayma during an assassination attempt against Egyptian Prime Minister Atif Sidqi. He noted that the girl was about the same age as his own daughter: "The unintended death of this innocent child pained us all, but we were helpless and we had to fight the government."[6] The implication here is that the true hero must carry on despite the potential revulsion at what they must do. The justification is that God will reward the righteous victims in paradise. Jihadi websites celebrate the nobility of the sacrifice of their heroes. For instance, the 9/11 perpetrators are usually referred to as "the magnificent 19 who did holy Tuesday."

Heroic sacrifice requires a personified villain—in this case the cabal of Crusaders and Jews. If these villains did not exist, they would have to be invented. The more formidable the enemy is, the more glorious the fight. Today the most formidable enemy is the remaining superpower, the United States. The war against Islam perspective is intertwined with strong anti-Americanism. The most glorious activity a global Islamist terrorist can perform is to confront U.S. military personnel in uniform. If Americans in uniform are not available, then symbols of American power such as U.S. embassies can be acceptable substitutes. Failing that, U.S. companies will do. Next on the list, according to bin Laden, are American civilians because they elect the U.S. government and support it by paying their taxes. Finally, if no American is available, any foreign partner of the United States will do.

Global Islamist terrorist ideology is not unified. There is a high level of disagreement among the various advocates.[7] The main areas of disagreement concern the killings of innocent civilians, the killing of other Muslims, overreach, and blowback resulting in the loss of sanctuary in Afghanistan. As mentioned in the last chapter, takfiris argue that traditional Muslims have sunk into a state of barbarism and are no longer Muslims. Therefore, they see themselves as the only true Muslims left. Obviously, Rabei is a takfiri because he called other Muslims "disbelievers" in the wiretapped conversation. Takfiris like Zarqawi extend the "War against Islam" to other Muslims and have no reservations about killing them.

Resonance with Personal Experiences

Many people are exposed to the jihadist interpretation, but most do not internalize it. It is more likely to be adopted if the idea that there is a war against Islam resonates with one's everyday experiences. If this is the case, then the overall perspective that there is a war against Islam bridges global moral violations perpetrated in foreign countries and local grievances. With this local link, global moral outrage acquires a new relevance and immediacy. Likewise, the interpretation gains strength from the indisputable evidence in one's own personal experience. Through this interpretive bridge, the moral outrages from the global and the local reinforce each other and are viewed as part of the same whole, namely a war against Islam, and make young Muslims feel personally involved in it. They are then more likely to try to join this fight.

An analysis of local grievances brings in the traditional analysis of the "root causes" of terrorism. Low-level local discrimination usually does not by itself become a direct cause of terrorism. It acquires significance as another manifestation of the war on Islam. As young Muslims try to make sense of their environment, they actively interpret what is happening to them in a global context. They are not passive recipients of any new message, but are more ready to accept one that fits with their past experiences.

Like most people, Muslims compare themselves to their peers. If they fall short, they become resentful and are willing to accept interpretations for their situation that make sense to them. In some Middle Eastern countries, the state educated the lower middle class eager to climb up the ranks of society. However, the provision of an education without a commensurate job opportunity is a recipe for disaster, as happened in Egypt after the 1970s when the state could no longer absorb the young graduates of the faculties of medicine and engineering. The economic paralysis due to widespread corruption played into the hands of the Salafists. Their message, that they needed to transform society on a more just and fair basis like the original Muslim community, resonated with much of the population.

Second-generation Muslims in the diaspora do not compare themselves with their cousins left back in the old home country. They compare themselves to host peers. In Europe, they do not fare as well as the host young men for a variety of reasons that will be analyzed in the next chapter. They interpret their perceived discrimination in the context of moral violations against Muslims

83

elsewhere, and the notion that their local grievances are part of a more general hostility against Islam appears more compelling to them. This is less the case in the United States.

An analysis of local grievances must be done with a finer level of granularity. Important factors will include acceptance by the host population, educational and economic opportunities, and use of leisure time. These issues will be discussed in the next chapter, where I compare the radicalization process in Europe and the United States and suggest that there are significant differences between these two continents.

Mobilized by Networks

If we stopped here in our analysis, we would have a lot of angry young Muslims, but no real terrorists. They would be in front of their computers, writing about their anger or talking to others about the iniquity of life. They would not know where to turn to remedy the situation as they see it. To take the next step, they need some guidance, someone to take them to the next level of violent radicalization. Only other people who share their outrage, beliefs, and experiences, but who are further along the path to violence or who are willing to explore it with them, can help them cross the line from venting their anger to becoming terrorists.

At the conclusion of the last chapter, we saw that joining global Islamist terrorism was a collective process, based on friendship or kinship. Close intimate networks have strong influence on their members. The networks that facilitated mobilization into the al Qaeda social movement were of two major kinds: face-to-face offline groups and virtual online groups. I will deal with virtual groups at greater length in Chapter 6. Here, I will consider only the offline groups.

The global Islamist terrorists who are the subject of this study emerged from informal groups of young Muslims. Living in the diaspora, the majority had been members of gangs, which reflected the segmental patterns of immigration to the West. In France, almost half of the people arrested for global Islamist terrorism in the 1990s had grown up together in Oran, Algeria. In Montreal, most of the members of the group that formed around Fateh Kamel, and included Ahmed Ressam, the millennium bomber, grew up together in the suburbs of Algiers. In Amsterdam, the backbone of the Hofstad Group came from the port of al-Hoceima in the Rif region of Morocco. Most of the perpetrators of the Madrid bombings came from the city of Tetouan, in Morocco. Many of the second-generation, homegrown terrorists arrested in Britain were children of people who came from the Mirpur district of Azad Kashmir.

This list shows that it is meaningless to look at the country of origin of these gangs. We need much greater granularity to our analysis. This is because emigration follows a pattern. One person goes, then brings a family member, then a friend, and so on. This creates in the host country small clusters of people, who were friends or family in the home country. New acquaintances from different cities in the same home country are not trusted like friends and relatives with whom one grew up. The British groups are mostly from Kashmir. This means that, back home, they may have a family member that might link and vouch for them with local terrorist groups that are loosely connected with al Qaeda Central. This gives the impression that al Qaeda Central might still be able to command and control different groups in the world. However, this process is specific to the British gangs that have family in Kashmir. If someone from Morocco traveled to Pakistan to try to make contact with these groups, he probably would not be able to make that connection because no one would trust him. So, the continued linkage from al Qaeda Central to parts of the al Qaeda social movement is specific to the British gangs whose parents came from Kashmir.

Other networks that mobilize young Muslims into terrorist groups are radical Muslim student associations. As mentioned before, many of the members of the terrorist social movement had come to the West to study. When they were lonely, they joined fellow Muslims in the local university student association. This was the case with the Hamburg group. These radical student associations played a role only in countries where there is a tradition of an active student social life, like Germany, Britain, and the United States. In many other countries, students commute and do not have an active student life on campus outside class. Some radical groups, such as al-Muhajiroun in Britain, targeted universities to increase their membership.[8] These associations were the vehicle for total strangers to form friendship bonds. Some continued their radicalization to the point where they collectively decided to join the violent social movement. These radical student associations provided an important pool of candidates for the expansion of global Islamist terrorism.

A third type of group was study groups that formed around radical mosques. Such study groups formed a network of ever more radicalized people, such as the study group around Mohammed Belfas at al Quds mosque in Hamburg, groups around the M-30 Mosque in Madrid, groups at the Finsbury Park mosque in London, and groups in the radical madrassas of Southeast Asia, like Lukmanul Hakiem.

All these networks could link up, which both expanded them and further radicalized them. A good example was the link between the radical Muslim student association at the Technical University of Hamburg-Harburg and Belfas study group at the al Quds Mosque.

The radicalization of these informal groups was an insidious process.[9] It could begin with low-risk participation—a soccer team, a youth gang, a student association. If they met in the vicinity of a radical mosque, the chance of radicalization was greater. As described in the previous chapter, most of them drifted to a mosque in search of companionship. However, if by chance they met in the vicinity of a radical mosque, the odds are that one of them went to that specific mosque because he liked the extreme message preached there. Since the environment was radical, this member of the nascent group would have a disproportionate influence on his friends because his views would be validated and supported by this specific environment. Little by little, the rest of the group would start to endorse these radical beliefs.

This argument is supported by the data. The global Islamist terrorist network is not evenly distributed. It is very spotty, according to the distribution of the radical mosques worldwide. In fact, twelve Islamic institutions worldwide generated about half of my sample. These friends became born-again Salafi Muslims, who tried to proselytize their new beliefs and drag their old friends to the mosque, becoming unbearable to them. These former friends and acquaintances progressively avoided them, leaving them to become ever more radical through a double process of outside social isolation and internal mutual reinforcement. This gradual isolation of the new converts or reverts intensified their loyalty to their new comrades and their beliefs that they were the true vanguard protecting the *ummah*, the Muslim community. They developed a collective identity that they were not just the vanguard of real Muslims that fight back, but that they might be the only true Muslims on earth. They started living in their own world, trying to imitate the heroism of the *Salaf*, who waged constant war against tribal enemies in the seventh century.

This experience of faith and commitment was grounded in intense group dynamics that completely transformed them in a process of in-group love. With the gradual intensity of interaction within the group and the progressive distance from former ties, they changed their values. From secular people, they became more religious. From material rewards, they began to value spiritual rewards, including eventually otherworldly rewards. From the pursuit of short-term opportunities, they turned to a long-term vision of the world. They abandoned their individual concerns for community concerns and became ready to sacrifice for comrades and the cause. Martyrdom, the ultimate sacrifice for the group and the cause, became their ultimate goal and the true path to glory and fame with respect to their friends. This is the true meaning of the videotapes they made before going on a suicide mission. They knew their friends would respect them, watch their videos for inspiration and celebrate their sacrifice. The mutual support of the group allowed them to transcend the apathy they felt in their situation of injustice and unfairness. If sacrifice leads to no change, what is the point of the effort? However, if sacrifice inspires others to join the fight and their friends to intensify the fight, then it is possible that together they might eventually achieve their goals. This belief encourages active engagement. The mutual group reinforcement also allows them to leave behind traditional societal morality for a more local morality, preached by the group.

The other side of the coin of in group love is out-group hate. Of course, this discrimination against the out-group is natural, but in this case, it turns to hate through the group dynamics blending moral outrage, personal experience of discrimination and economic exclusion, and a specific interpretation tying everything together in a dangerous mix. Here, the group acts as an interactive "echo chamber," encouraging escalation of grievances and beliefs in conspiracy to the point of hatred. A humorous illustration of this process of blaming the "enemy" for everything negative that happens was the time when the toilet got clogged at the apartment where Mohammed Atta and his friends were living in Hamburg. According to witnesses, they started screaming at the Jews for having intentionally done this to them. This belief that the world is in a conspiracy against the group is common where the group relies exclusively on its members to validate new information. They discard information refuting their beliefs as propaganda from the West. This process is progressive. Those who believe that the group has gone too far in their growing radicalization peel off through a process of self-selection. At the end, only the true believers remain.

Once in the group, it is difficult to abandon it because of group loyalties. Comrades become best friends and a substitute for family. The Madrid train bombings capture the intensity of the group ties. The perpetrators were not suicide bombers. They placed thirteen bombs on four trains, killing 191 people and injuring more than one thousand. About three weeks later, the police tracked some of the perpetrators to an apartment. The police tried to discreetly surround the apartment, but one of the bombers detected them and alerted his companions still in the apartment. One of the men inside probably suggested to the others that if the police came in, they should not be captured alive and should take as many policemen as possible in their deaths.

The police evacuated the neighborhood and attempted to negotiate with the perpetrators. The terrorists shouted back in Arabic, sang jihadi songs, and swore that they would die in a blaze of glory. They made phone calls to family, friends, and supporting imams to say goodbye. The police blew up the lock on the door and fired a teargas container in the living room. Almost immediately, an explosion blew up the apartment, killing all seven terrorists and the chief police negotiator.

The point here is that, even if one of the terrorists did not want to die, in that situation he was stuck. Around him were six of his best friends. He could not abandon them even if he disagreed with them. What could he say? "Brothers, you go ahead, I'll join you later"? This group loyalty kept them in the operation even if they were hesitant. They just could not let their best friends down. This also played the other way. If individually they did not have the courage to do something, together they did as their mutual encouragement egged them on to greater heights. This natural and intense loyalty to the group, inspired by a violent Salafi script, transformed alienated young Muslims into fanatic terrorists.

FIVE

The Atlantic Divide

One of the most puzzling issues confronting America since 2001 is the lack of any terrorist follow-up to the 9/11 events. Rather, it is Europe that has suffered from subsequent al Qaeda attacks. Europe was also important to 9/11, as the field leaders came from Hamburg while the "muscle" came from Saudi Arabia. Six years later, unlike in Europe, there is a relatively small and contained threat from "homegrown" Islamist terrorism in the United States, and the various plots discovered in the United States do not seem as serious as those in Europe.

Different agencies in the U.S. government are quick to take credit for this greater security in the United States. They argue that it is due to the success of the Global War on Terror, including the elimination of al Qaeda camps in Afghanistan, the capture or killing of key al Qaeda leaders, the disruption of terrorist plots worldwide, the hardening of U.S. borders and the reliance on foreign liaison military or intelligence services to prevent the renewal of terrorist sanctuaries. Law enforcement agencies would argue that they have aggressively pursued terrorist cells in this country and nipped any domestic terrorist plots in the bud. This is all true, and credit must be granted to those responsible for the increased commitment to security in America and abroad since 9/11. These efforts have denied easy funding for terrorist groups and prevent terrorists from traveling and communicating at will.

However, I would like to suggest another explanation. There have been far fewer homegrown global Islamist terrorists in the United States than in

Europe because of differences in the rate of radicalization of their respective Muslim communities. Numbers support this impression. Since 9/11, there have been over 2,300 arrests connected to Islamist terrorism in Europe[1] in contrast to about 60 in the United States.[2] Some might object that these numbers are not comparable because of different criteria used in the arrests, but European law enforcement officials would reply that the laws in their countries do not allow the arrest and detention of suspects under the harsher provisions of the USA Patriot Act. If anything, these numbers overestimate the threat in the United States. Europe and the United States have comparable general populations: 340 million in Europe and 300 million in the United States. It is far more difficult to estimate their respective Muslim populations because in many Western countries the law prohibits the government from asking religion in its periodic official census. This is the case in France and the United States, for instance. As a result, estimates range wildly on both continents. For Europe, the range is between 12 to 20 million Muslims, while in the United States, the most methodologically sound estimate is 2.35 million Muslims.[3] Putting these numbers all together, the rate of arrests on terrorism charges per capita among Muslims is six times higher in Europe than in the United States.

What accounts for this difference? It is certainly not the lack of efficacy of U.S. law enforcement agencies, which dwarf their European counterparts in resources, numbers, and technical proficiency. Nor is it the lack of aggressiveness in the United States. Terrorist suspects in the States are arrested at a much earlier stage of the evolution of their plots than in Europe. Indeed, plots in America are detected at such an early stage that law enforcement agencies have the luxury of infiltrating these networks with undercover informants. This contrasts sharply with Europe. The early disruption of plots in America presents difficulties later on in the prosecution of these cases, as clear indication of plotters' intent is sometimes lacking at trial. No, the simple fact is that there are far fewer domestic homegrown Islamist terrorists in the United States than in Europe, and this is the main reason why we have not seen another 9/11 in the past six years in the United States. This does not mean that there is no chance of a large-scale Islamist terrorist operation on the continental United States. The May 2007 arrests of young Muslim second-generation immigrants for trying to blow up part of Fort Dix, New Jersey, shows that this threat does exist. But it is not present to the extent that it is in Europe. The reason lies in the differences in the extent to which these respective Muslim communities are radicalized.

Moral Outrage

In my analysis, I will follow the outline for radicalization presented in the previous chapter, which organizes our thinking about this process. First, let us look at the Muslim sense of moral outrage. Since 2003, the war in Iraq has without question fueled the process of radicalization worldwide, including the United States. The data are crystal clear. Opinion polls throughout the Muslim world show outrage at the U.S. invasion of Iraq. Even among Muslim Americans, who are mostly mainstream, a solid three-fourths reject U.S. policy toward Iraq.[4] Muslim reaction to the U.S. invasion of Iraq of course did not create the first two waves of global Islamist terrorism—after all, 9/11 occurred before the invasion of Iraq. But it has since provided a focus for the sense of moral outrage in Muslims all over the world. In all my talks with Muslims at home and abroad, Iraq monopolizes the theme of any conversation about Islam and the West. The humiliations of Abu Ghraib and Guantánamo Bay, media events such as the controversy over the Danish cartoons of Muhammad, and multiple statements from Western leaders implicitly denigrating Islam surface as well in these exchanges.

The White House has justified its Iraq invasion in terms of the "Global War on Terror": "We are fighting them there so we don't have to fight them here." This is a spurious argument and is generally seen as ridiculous by the majority of Muslims I have encountered. U.S. forces went into Afghanistan because there were terrorists there. Terrorists came into Iraq because U.S. forces were there. The consensus in the intelligence community is that there was no operational al Qaeda presence in Iraq before the invasion. They came there after the invasion. But Iraq has galvanized the worldwide Muslim community and become the most compelling argument that the West is engaged in a general war against Islam. Iraq is now the rallying point, radicalizing and inspiring young Muslims to join the third wave of global Islamist terrorism. The U.S. intelligence community agrees: "The Iraq conflict has become the cause célèbre for jihadists, breeding deep resentment of U.S. involvement in the Muslim world and cultivating supporters for the global jihadist movement."[5] Iraq has increased the pool of potential terrorists so that we are fighting them here as well as there—if by "here" we mean the West, including our European allies. The outrage caused by the foreign Western presence in Iraq is creating far more terrorists worldwide than Western governments are arresting. The invasion of Iraq has bred the third wave of global Islamist terrorism.

91

With the ubiquity of the Internet and the media, all Muslims around the world are subjected to similar images of global moral violations against Muslims. I qualify this statement because U.S. television is far more squeamish about showing the real blood and gore that accompanies any war, so that images usually seen on American television are much milder than those on Al Jazeerah and other international networks. However, the Internet equalizes this field, and global issues like Iraq do not explain the differences in outrage between Muslim Americans and Europeans. Rather, a higher level of local moral violations is to blame.

Communities in general are extremely sensitive to local police action. Police in modern societies have the monopoly on legitimate state violence, and society is careful to scrutinize potential abuse of this privilege. Since 9/11, there have been abuses by U.S. law enforcement agencies against Muslims, and this is deeply resented by Muslim Americans. About 9 percent complain that they have been singled out by police, and about 30 percent who flew complain that they were singled out at airports for special scrutiny.[6] A majority of Muslim Americans say that it has become more difficult to be a Muslim in the United States after 9/11,[7] 19 percent complain about discrimination, racism, and prejudice and about 15 percent complain about being viewed as a terrorist.[8] On the other hand, acts of support from the rest of the society mitigate this anger against local police scrutiny and societal prejudice.[9]

Similar questions were not asked of Muslim Europeans. Yet there is evidence to indicate that the situation might be worse in Europe. Police forces in Europe are predominantly Caucasian, with the result that white police officers are patrolling local immigrant enclaves, which are predominantly North African or South Asian Muslim. There is a palpable hostility between the police departments and the newcomers' neighborhoods, for the officers assigned there are not from those communities. This situation is ripe for incidents that might spark riots. Indeed, the French immigrant riots of October–November 2005 were triggered when some local immigrant youths fled from some white police officers in a northern suburb of Paris and accidentally electrocuted themselves. Similar hostility is seen all over Europe. The police force is not viewed as part of the local Muslim immigrant community.

This contrasts with community policing efforts in the United States, where the aim is to develop a police force that is not only a reflection of the community but also an integral part of it. For instance, the population of New

York City is about a third foreign-born, and so is the New York Police Department (NYPD). If local law enforcement officers are seen as part of the community, they are not viewed as enemies, but as trusted intermediaries between the community and its police department. Europeans are conscious of their shortcomings in this area, but they tell me that Muslims do not join either the police or the army despite great efforts to recruit them. Perhaps the NYPD is benefiting from the reputation it acquired when its officers did not hesitate to risk their lives during the 9/11 tragedy. The point is that local police forces in the United States are working toward becoming more deeply integrated within the community, and so they are not invariably seen as hostile outside forces. Officers are embedded in the community, and as a result they receive many tips from the Muslim community about potential threats. This is not the case in Europe, where police are generally limited to weekly meetings with local community leaders, who are not respected and are even rejected by young Muslim militants.

In Britain, authorities face an additional set of problems with the Muslim community. Since the 7/7 London bombings, local police forces have become more aggressive about arresting suspected terrorists. They have made some mistakes, such as the killing of a Brazilian expatriate on suspicion of terrorism and the shooting of two Bangladeshi Muslims who had no link to terrorism. There have been many instances of arrests, followed by later releases without any explanation. These local moral violations have alienated the British Muslim community, which feels singled out. It no longer gives the police the benefit of the doubt. This is compounded by a common-law tradition that gags the authorities from elaborating on the reasons for police action for fear of later negatively influencing a jury and not allowing for a fair trial. British police are losing the hearts-and-minds battle with their Muslim community. In essence, they make arrests and expect the Muslim community to suspend judgment about these arrests until the full evidence is presented in a court of law three or four years later. This is unrealistic. People will fill the information vacuum with explanations of their own, and at this point, those explanations do not support the government's claims. Indeed, the level of trust for government claims generally has sunk so low that most Muslims around the world do not believe that Muslims carried out the 9/11 operations.[10] The gag order designed to guarantee a fair trial is contributing to the growing hostility of the Muslim British population toward the rest of society.

In the United States, the opposite problem exists. Politicians do not hesitate to call a press conference when a potential Islamist terrorist is arrested. These arrests are trumpeted as major victories in the "Global War on Terror." In the process, they elevate incompetent terrorist wannabes to the status of potential heroes and inspire copycats to emulate the plotters. When the smoke clears a few days later and the true facts of the alleged plot emerge, there is much less than originally advertised. These spectacles could alienate Muslim Americans, who might begin to believe that the federal government is wrongfully targeting the Muslim community with trumped-up charges.

The war against the al Qaeda social movement is basically a battle for the hearts and minds of the Muslim community. To win that battle, Western governments need to avoid committing mistakes that risk the loss of good will in the Muslim community.

The War Against Islam and American Cultural Exceptionalism

Anyone who has lived for long periods of time on both sides of the Atlantic is stuck by how differently Americans and Europeans think about themselves and their countries. These differing cultural perspectives may either enhance or undermine people's receptivity to certain ideas, depending on how consistent those ideas are with their underlying beliefs. This has important ramifications for the rates of acceptance of the conviction that the West is engaged in a war against Islam within the different Muslim communities.

When thinking about themselves, Americans often use the metaphor of a melting pot, while Europeans talk of a defining essence, around which their respective nations have been created. Such essence-based nationalism is promoted through the creation of a grand historical narrative, which celebrates national heroes—Joan of Arc and Napoleon for France; Nelson and Wellington for Britain; Bismarck for Germany; Garibaldi for Italy. These myths were so powerful that young men were willing to die for them. This sense of belonging to these imagined communities[11] in Europe reached its peak between 1870 and 1945, when Europe was torn by a succession of nationalistic wars.

In reality, all European nations are the results of mass migrations and mixed ethnic groups.[12] What is a Frenchman? Is he a Gaul; a Frank, the name of the Germanic tribe that gave its name to the country; a Briton; a Basque; a

Roman; an Ostrogoth; a Visigoth, a Vandal, a Viking, or Norman? France is the result of mixed migrant ethnic groups bounded by easily protected physical boundaries. Likewise, what is an Englishman? Is he an Angle, the name of the tribe that gave its name to the country; a Saxon; a Celt; Welsh; a Scot; a Norman or Viking? Europeans seem reluctant to admit their ethnic diversity and cling to the myth of this national essence. About thirty-five years ago, during a trip to Denmark, I was struck by my host's description of the inhabitants of a village as the "Poles" because they were refugees who had fled the Teutonic Knights in the fourteenth century. Later, he expressed pride that he was of pure Danish stock, not like those German usurpers who had drifted to Denmark in the tenth century!

Such a conversation seems bizarre to most Americans, where the burden of history begins about four centuries ago. Selective history, as promoted through national pride, is a true burden for Europe for it excludes outsiders that apparently do not fit into this mythical essence, like people from Asia or Africa. Such exclusion can be couched in an affirmation of national values, as in "We have to maintain our Dutch (French, German, British . . .) values." But all too often, this just means, "We have to keep our Muslim immigrants from becoming part of us." Muslims are treated differently in Europe. This attitude can be seen in the vote against admitting Turkey into the European Union. Romania was allowed into the union, but not Turkey. The Romanians, of course, happen to be predominantly Catholic, even if they are not as economically advanced as the Turks, who happen to be predominantly Muslim.

The national myth of the United States is that it is a melting pot. This myth promotes the acceptance of foreigners and their eventual integration in society. Of course, the reality is different from the myth, but enough people believe it for it to work. When I speak publicly, I regularly ask my audiences to raise a hand if they have an immigrant grandparent. Invariably at least half raise their hand, yet most also think of themselves as fully assimilated Americans. Less than half (47 percent) of Muslim Americans think of themselves as Muslim first and American second, while for Britain, Spain, and Germany the rates are 81, 69, and 66 percent, respectively. Only Muslims in France have a comparable rate to America (46 percent).

Of course, there were times when foreigners, especially from certain countries like Italy, Ireland, or China, were not welcome. Discrimination against some newly arrived ethnic groups has a long history; the incarceration of Japanese Americans during World War II is a blatant example of prejudice. Quotas have been imposed, preventing even humanitarian acceptance of political refugees. But the United States is without question a country built on immigration and generally proud of its diversity. After three generations, these diverse ethnic groups are assimilated into a huge melting pot.

At this point, European audiences point out U.S. rejection of migrants from south of the border. This is not discrimination against Latin Americans because of ethnicity or country of origin. Debates in Congress in 2007 were specifically about amnesty and granting them legal status, given the fact that they had entered the country illegally. Of course, such debates can mask some latent prejudice. But once their legal status is resolved, they can integrate into the fabric of the nation.

Legal immigration is not a major social problem in America, but it is in Europe. Although each continent has become a beacon for immigrants, their welcome varies greatly according to where they land. In America, the melting pot myth facilitates the assimilation of outsiders, while in Europe the emphasis on a national essence prevents the integration of immigrants that "look different." Assimilation makes it less likely for Muslim Americans to believe that they are part of a war against Islam, while exclusion on a basis of a national essence makes it more likely for Muslim Europeans to believe this notion.

A second cultural difference between Europe and the United States is the belief in the "American Dream"—the land of opportunity (not the land of freedom or democracy, as some politicians mistakenly believe). Some scholars dispute the existence of the reality behind the dream, arguing that there is much less equal opportunity and fluidity between social classes in America. They also point to the much greater disparity between rich and poor in the United States than in Europe. This is true, but what matters is that people think they stand a good chance of succeeding in America and immigrants believe that their children will completely integrate into society. Pick up a newspaper in America, and often you will find an immigrant "rags to riches" story. On July 4, 2007, the American national holiday, *The New York Times* published a full-page ad celebrating immigrants as the essence of the country. One does not find such stories or advertisements in European newspapers. There is no European Dream. The reality is that social mobility is probably not as great as advertised in the United States and is greater than advertised in Europe. But when dealing with perceptions, the promise of the American Dream still shines bright for most immigrants.

Polling data clearly show that Muslim Americans are stronger believers in the American Dream (71 percent) than the American general public (64 percent).[13] The variation in this belief within the Muslim American community points to the major American societal problem, the continuing legacy of slavery. Only 56 percent of Muslim African Americans believe in the American Dream in contrast to 75 percent of the rest of the Muslim American community. This lower rate is on par with the rest of African Americans. While integration of immigrants has been a success story, integration of descendants of slaves has been far more challenging. Interestingly enough, black immigrants to the United States seem to follow an immigrant pattern, with some success stories for their children, as illustrated by Colin Powell—the son of a Caribbean immigrant. On the other hand, native African American converts to Islam maintain the social status and beliefs of the general African American population.[14]

This is not the case in Europe. While the Pew Research Center surveys did not ask questions about the pay-off of hard work, Muslim Europeans complain far more about economic discrimination and exclusion than Muslim Americans. Differences in income levels support their complaints.[15] When compared to their European counterparts, American Muslims' strong belief in equal opportunity provides relative protection against the belief that there is widespread discrimination against Muslims as part of a war against Islam.

The American Dream is a mixture of belief in equal opportunity and individualism. Americans are the most individualist people in the world.[16] European countries fall behind, but still in the upper half of the scale along this dimension while Muslim majority countries fall at the bottom of the scale, solidly in the collectivistic spectrum of the scale.[17] As noted in Chapter 1, the differences in answers about economic adversity between Muslim Americans ("I didn't try hard enough") and Muslim Europeans ("I never got a chance because I'm Muslim") can be viewed along an individualistic-collectivistic spectrum. The relevant factor here is that individualism makes it harder for people to see their collective fate and develop a collective identity hostile to the host society. American individualism makes it harder for Muslim Americans to interpret their world in collective terms, as part of a war against Islam.

Finally, American society is generally viewed as more open, and the economy as more dynamic than its European counterparts. The emphasis on individual responsibility and the openness of society encourages grass-roots voluntarism like parent-teacher associations. Such activity further anchors citizens into society and provides a sense of having a stake, a role to play. In Europe, perceived social rigidity discourages voluntarism. This leads to apathy and an expectation that the state should step in and provide social services. Grass-roots voluntarism and its effectiveness in influencing one's proximate environment might divert the energy of disgruntled young Muslims toward positive local changes. These local successes may mitigate the belief that they are involved in a war against Islam. A sense of local empowerment might be protective against a larger strike against society.

The nation as a melting pot, the American Dream, individualism, and grass-roots voluntarism—these cultural values make American Muslims less likely than their European counterparts to accept the interpretation that there is a war against Islam. Muslim immigrants, who come from beyond the oceans, go to great efforts to come to America because they believe in its values.[18] This is a process of self-selection, where overseas people attracted to the promise of the "American Creed"[19] immigrate to the United States whereas economic migrants, like Latin American immigrants to the United States, drift to Europe for simple economic survival and not belief. This creed is not compatible with the belief that America is at war with Islam. Surprisingly, France, the only European nation that advertises itself as being based on a creed—liberty, equality, and fraternity—shares some of the same universal beliefs as America (as we saw earlier in this section), which makes it hard for the global Islamist terrorism ideology to implant itself there.[20]

The "war against Islam" interpretation has become intertwined with anti-Americanism among Muslims, mixing the U.S. government, population, and culture. This rejection of America as a whole has less traction in the United States, where Muslim Americans do not share this oversimplified view and distinguish the U.S. government from its population.[21] Even the Muslim American segment that complained most about bigotry and intolerance reported about equal expression of support from the general population.[22] It seems easier to be anti-American from afar than from within. The absence of anti-Americanism among Muslim Americans undermines the appeal of the global Islamist message.

Resonance with Personal Experiences

Beyond this conflict between immigrant community and host national values, there is another reason the message that the West is engaged in a war against Islam is more credible for European Muslims than for American Muslims. In Europe, this perspective resonates more with their personal experiences, which in turn gives strength to the ideology from indisputable biographical evidence.

Historically, the immigrant experience is very different in each continent. The United States is protected by two oceans, which make it difficult for foreign Muslims who live overseas to enter the country illegally. They must apply for a visa for entry. This allows the United States to cherry-pick professionals—engineers, physicians, businessmen, scholars. The result is that many Muslim Americans are solidly upper middle class.

The history of Muslim European communities is quite different.[23] Europe managed to inflict great damage on itself and eradicate large parts of its labor force during World War II. The devastated countries had to look elsewhere for manpower to aid in their reconstruction after the war. They turned to former colonies and allies for help. The French imported labor from Algeria, the British from South Asian countries, and the Germans from Turkey. Most of these countries were predominantly Muslim or had a large Muslim population, making the labor supply to postwar Europe mostly Muslim. Throughout suburban Europe, male immigrant workers lived in inexpensive, crowded lodgings, and sent money back home to support their families. They frequently traveled between host and home countries, marrying and having children at home but returning to Europe to work.

After a quarter of a century, the Muslim immigrants who had helped to rebuild the countries of Europe were encouraged to return to their homelands. The European economies, suffering the effects of the oil price shocks of the 1970s, contracted, drying up employment opportunities. Governments did not want a large pool of unemployed immigrant workers, so they increased the pressure on foreign workers to go home, even instituting financial rewards for doing so and tightening immigration policies. These new restrictions, however, had a reverse effect. Foreign workers did not want to return home because economic conditions were even worse there than in Europe. At the same time, fearful that they would not be allowed to return to Europe if they visited their home nations, they decided to bring their families to their host country (a process facilitated by new European rules on family reunification).

The measures taken to tighten immigration to Europe thus led to an immigration explosion in the 1970s and 1980s. Unlike the postwar reconstruction wave, made up mainly of working-age men, this new influx included mostly women and children, who demanded schools and mosques.

This historical outline shows that on each side of the Atlantic divide we are dealing with a very different Muslim community. Muslim Americans belong predominantly to a professional middle class while Muslim Europeans are predominantly unskilled laborers and belong to a lower socioeconomic class. Since many Western governments explicitly refrain from asking a person's religion on their regular census because of the separation of church and state, official statistics on Muslims in Western countries do not exist. However, survey data support this analysis that Muslim Americans are solidly middle class, with incomes comparable to the general population.[24] The data probably even underestimates the income of Muslim American families because it was gathered on individuals and the Muslim population is younger than the general population. On the other hand, the average income of Muslim Europeans is below that of the general population of their respective countries.[25]

Labor markets across these two regions are also quite different. In the United States, most workers are hired and fired at will. In Europe, long traditions of social protection are incorporated into statute making it almost impossible to fire an employee without undergoing a lengthy and costly legal process. Since no employer wishes to be dragged into this legal quagmire, businesses want to be sure that their new hires will be good employees. This means hiring on the basis of existing connections, implying prior loyalty, or solid credentials. This also means that because most employers are not immigrants, networks of potential hires will not include immigrants either. This process results in a soft discrimination against immigrants and their children. The outcome is that unemployment among young male Muslims in Europe, who constitute the majority of the second- and third-generation immigrants, is about two to three times higher than the comparable unemployment rate in the "native" population.

I put quotation marks around "native" because the second and third generations were also born in the host country, but as explained earlier, they are not considered native since they lack the mythical "essence" of the various nations. The host population does not consider them to be truly European or treat them like other European citizens. In a sense, the riots that broke out in France in the fall of 2005 had their roots in the desire of the young immigrant rioters to be considered French. Yet they *were* French, since the vast majority was born in France. Most had French parents, who were also born in France. It was their grandparents who had emigrated from Africa. But they were not treated as true French citizens by the rest of the country, especially in terms of equal opportunity.

European governments are starting to understand this problem. The French government passed legislation loosening the labor market. The new laws allowed an employer a two-year window to fire a new employee under the age of twenty-six. The hope was that this might provide the sons of immigrants a better opportunity. From an American perspective, this project seems too timid. But from a French perspective, it was already too much. The vast majority of the student population at the high school and university levels—mostly from nonimmigrant origin, because those from immigrant origin generally drop out of school as teenagers—took to the streets of France in protest. They were later supported by the trade unions, who threatened to paralyze France by calling general strikes. The government backed down and shelved the project indefinitely. This sent a clear message to young immigrants, who are de facto excluded from the rest of economy. I suspect that this problem will continue to fester and explode with any new perceived provocations.

Of course, there is also a soft discrimination against immigrant and minority children in the United States. This is natural because people like to hire people like themselves. But because new hires can in general be fired or laid off, there is fluidity in the labor market and the problem does not reach the level in Europe. There is no evidence that the rate of unemployment in the Muslim second generation is higher than that of the comparable general population. So, while young American Muslims may live in Muslim neighborhoods in New York, Chicago, Los Angeles, or Dearborn, Michigan, these are not ghettos like those that exist in the suburbs of large European metropolitan areas, which breed high unemployment, crime, and potential sympathy for global Islamist terrorism.

Differences in welfare policy between the United States and Europe also have implications for the process of radicalization. The lack of decent employment in Europe is mitigated by generous welfare policies. This creates a problem of its own. Unemployed families, whether from immigrant background or not, receive welfare payments. In many European countries, the larger the family, the larger the welfare checks—often as a result of old policies trying to encourage population growth. Counterterrorist officials worry about terrorist financing and are quick to ban any nonprofit organization that has made contributions to terrorist groups in the past, no matter how small the contribution. The truth is that recent terrorist operations do not cost very much and most of their funding comes from welfare payments to unemployed terrorists. This is especially true in Europe, Canada, and Australia.

For many young people, welfare payments remove the urgency to find regular work and allow some the leisure time to become full-time Islamist terrorist "wannabes," who hang out with their friends at street corners, praising Islamist terrorists, or surf the Internet, dreaming of becoming a jihadi warrior themselves. The harmful effect of idleness and boredom cannot be overestimated. With few other meaningful activities, young Muslims seek out the thrill of participating in a clandestine network, living out the fantasy of being a jihadi warrior and being revered by their peers. The United States, in contrast, has stricter work requirements for those receiving welfare, and it can be difficult for those facing even temporary adversity to receive support. People need to work, or they will starve. This necessity to find full-time employment prevents potential young "wannabes" in America from spending all their time in common jihadi apartments, local halal ethnic fast-food restaurants or barber shops talking about the glory of jihad, like the second wave of terrorists in Europe. The third wave now seems to have migrated to spending a lot of time on Internet jihadi chat rooms like Yunis Tsouli and his two friends, whom I will discuss in the next chapter, or the three young Muslims from the Al-Ansar forum, convicted in Britain in July 2007 for conspiring to use the Internet to incite others to violence. Most of the terrorist wannabes in Europe arrested in the past two years spend a large amount of time on the Internet. Idleness from relative underemployment seems to have been a factor in the growth of global Islamist terrorism in Europe.[26] By the time American young Muslims sympathetic to the jihad get home from work, they are too exhausted to do much.

The multiple terrorist attempts throughout Europe that have marked the first few years of the twenty-first century have heightened the concern of Europeans about the threat of militant Islamic fundamentalism. The new vigor in Islamist militancy and the jealousy about welfare payments to Muslim immigrants and their children have generated a backlash in Europe. This xenophobic right-wing reaction to Muslim immigrant population can be found among about 15 to 20 percent of the electorate throughout Europe. They reject their governments' accommodative policies as a virtual invitation for a Muslim "invasion" of Europe. The hysteria goes so far as to warn about a Muslim Europe in the next half century based on the accession of Turkey to the European Union and the high Muslim birth rate in Europe. But the numbers just do not add up. Europe would have only about 100 million Muslims out of a population of 440 million people with the accession of Turkey. Even counting the differential rate of birth, the numbers are farfetched. This hysteria of course provokes a reaction in the Muslim population and accelerates the radicalization in certain Muslim militant networks. The process generates a vicious cycle of hostility.

Differences in approaches to integration in America and Europe can also contribute to radicalization. The buzzwords in Europe are "radicalization" and "integration." All European countries have an integration policy.[2] Together, they form a natural type of social experiment to see which one might be more effective. In France, the policy is based on the idea of secular republicanism: Muslim women are not permitted to wear veils. The failure of this integration policy is found in the many immigrant neighborhoods surrounding major cities that are declared "no-go" zones by the local police. In England, the policy is based on communitarianism, and yet in poor suburbs there are pockets of immigrants who are deeply hostile to the state. In Germany, young people born in Germany, to parents who themselves were born in Germany of parents who originally came as "guest workers" from Turkey, are converting to Salafi Islam, which is actually foreign to the Turkish culture. All these attempts at integration have failed.

America does not have an integration policy, and this paradoxically may be why it appears not to need one. In Europe, people wait for their governments to develop programs to integrate immigrants into society. These central policies are mostly irrelevant because the experience of newcomers is shaped by their local welcome. It does not matter how generous the government is if your neighbors reject you. The experience of Ahmed Omar Sheikh described in the Introduction is just one example. The success of integration

103

depends on whether your host neighbor will greet you in the morning, invite you over for a cookout, or offer your child a job. Integration is a "bottom-up" process and American grass-roots voluntarism, equal opportunity, and melting pot succeed when "top-down" policies fail. One-third of Muslim Americans reported non-Muslims expressing support for them when they feared intolerance.[28]

The turn to Islam as a frame for political protest in Europe reflects the lack of alternative outlets for social protest. Between the 1960s and the 1980s, social protests in Europe followed a leftist script, corresponding to the third wave of modern terrorism (see Chapter 2). Discrimination against immigrants was interpreted through a Marxist lens and resulted in large protest demonstrations like the 1983 Marche des Beurs in France (*beurs* is a French slang term for Arab). The collapse of the Soviet Union in the early 1990s discredited the leftist dream and dealt the European left a blow from which it has not recovered. Protesters who would have been socialists or communists in earlier times turned to Islam to convey their grievances. Radical Islam has become the hope of the second generation of Muslim immigrants to Europe.[29] It has become the focus of individuals dreaming of glory in defending the downtrodden and the excluded. Even non-Muslims have converted to Islam to take part in this new "crusade," now more properly labeled "jihad." Ilich Ramirez Sanchez, better known as "Carlos," the legendary terrorist of the 1970s, abandoned communism and converted to Islam. Other militants in Europe followed suit.[30]

Differences in attitudes toward religion in Europe and America also influence the way life as a Muslim is experienced and affects the radicalization of the Muslim populations on the two continents. America was founded on explicit religious tolerance. Far from making religion disappear, it allowed waves of all kinds of religious fundamentalism to flourish and gain acceptance in the general population. America not only tolerates but respects fundamentalists, whether Christians, Jews, or Muslims. Indeed, Christian fundamentalist preachers are regularly invited to the White House and are among the strongest supporters of President Bush. Fundamentalist Muslims are treated like any other fundamentalists in the United States.

In Europe, the wave of immigration in the late 1970s and 1980s generated a demand for Muslim cultural institutions for children and women. Coinciding with this demand was a concerted effort on the part of the Saudi government to propagate its own version of Islam. Beginning in the late 1970s, the government of Saudi Arabia, flush with petrodollars, invested heavily in the building of mosques throughout the world to spread the conservative form of Islam practiced in Saudi Arabia. The Saudi offensive was in response to a perceived threat from Iran, where the 1979 Iranian revolution overthrowing the shah in favor of a theocratic regime led by Ayatollah Ruhollah Khomeini reverberated throughout the Muslim world. The Shi'a version of Islam that Khomeini championed had gained a major victory, and the government of Saudi Arabia took notice. The legitimacy of the Saudi family's rule over the "Land of the two Holy Mosques" lay in their claim that they represent a purer form of Islam, derived from the teachings of the eighteenth-century preacher Mohammed ibn Abdal Wahhab. This brand of Islam rejects Shi'ism as an illegitimate version of Islam and condemns Shi'as as apostates. To counter the popularity of the Iranian revolution, the Saudi government embarked on an ambitious program of spreading its fundamentalist version throughout the Muslim world. The Saudis built mosques, funded schools, and sent teachers to Muslim communities throughout the world. They were the main source of Islamic infrastructure in non-Muslim countries, where Muslim immigrant populations were rapidly growing. The teaching at most of the large mosques in the West was fundamentalist, funded through this Saudi initiative. When the young Muslims in Western countries, who until then had generally been raised in a completely secular environment, turned to Islam in the 1990s, the most available form of Islam was the fundamentalist type practiced in Saudi Arabia. The growth of the demand for Islam coincided with a supply limited to the Wahhabi version funded by the Saudis. This version of Islam was consistent with the global jihadi ideology, celebrating heroes who had sacrificed their lives in their attempt to build a Salafi utopia.

While America is fairly religious (about 45 percent of Christian Americans and about 40 percent of Muslim Americans attend religious services on any weekend),[31] Europe is much less so. Churches are for the most part empty and religion is regarded as a curiosity. Fundamentalists are seen as outside the limits of normality. In Europe, disdain for fundamentalists, especially Muslim fundamentalists, and mutual antagonism between the largely secular general population and the Muslim fundamentalists quickly escalate into outright hostility. This hostility toward observant Muslims is exacerbated by the social and political conditions in Europe.

Differences in life experiences distinguish American from European Muslims. Historical differences generated very different classes of population in the two continents. Differences in labor markets show that the American Dream is alive and well in America but constrained in Europe. European welfare policy mitigates against high unemployment rates but leaves restless young Muslims with nothing to do. The allure and thrill of participating in fashionable and clandestine work seems too much to resist. In Europe, top-down integration policies have failed, while, in the United States, the lack of a federal policy in a culture welcoming foreigners allowed society to integrate the grandchildren of newcomers from the bottom up. Finally, religious tolerance in the United States defuses potential escalation of religious disputes. All these factors promote a higher rate of radicalization in Europe as compared to the United States.

Why America Is Not Breeding bin Laden Networks

The differences in the intensity of Muslim outrage and the way they interpret and experience life in Europe and America help explain the disparity between the number of global Islamist terrorist attacks in Europe and the United States. Far fewer global Islamist terrorists are in the United States than in Europe because of the "root causes" conditions that we have just discussed. Some still exist, as seen in the Fort Dix case, but their numbers pale in comparison to Europe. In the United States, the 9/11 attackers came from outside its borders—three pilots came from Hamburg and the other sixteen terrorists from the Arabian Peninsula.

Contrary to the fears of many Americans, there are no sleeper cells in the United States (the possible exception was Ali al-Marri, who was arrested in December 2001).[32] What have been referred to as "sleepers" in the media have not been that at all. Just because someone has not been detected does not make that person a sleeper. A sleeper is a trained terrorist who has been infiltrated to the United States and gone into hibernation to be activated and become totally operational at a later date. The 9/11 terrorists were not sleepers; they would have been detected had the U.S. government been on the lookout—ten of the nineteen terrorists had irregularities with their passports when they entered the country. During their time here, they trained for their mission. They did not try to integrate into the society as sleepers would. U.S. government agencies simply failed to detect them because they were not looking or were obstructed in their efforts.

Since the threat to the United States came from outside its borders, why are not more terrorists like the 9/11 perpetrators coming to America? The U.S. government has done a good job of deterring terrorists from even attempting to come to the United States through the many visible layers of security that have been deployed at airports. Canada is also attempting to harden its borders and has become more aggressive at tracking suspicious individuals as shown by the arrests of over a dozen young Muslims in Toronto in 2006. Very few Islamist terrorists try to cross into the United States from Mexico. This is a major fear for some Americans, but it is groundless since Muslim terrorists would stand out. The "coyotes" who guide Latin American people attempting to illegally enter the United States would be the ones to alert the border patrol in order to safeguard their "business."

Americans in general have also been much more alert about any suspicious behavior since 9/11. People are far more likely to call law enforcement agencies with their suspicions. This creates a hostile habitat for potential terrorists in general. Law enforcement agencies have also been extremely aggressive and efficient in investigating any potential threat in the country. This has made it a difficult environment in which to operate for potential terrorists. There have been few homegrown terrorist networks in America to mobilize angry young Muslims who might have been tempted to join the fight.

Europe does not share many of the geographical and policing advantages that the United States enjoys. Its internal borders are open—there is no need to show a passport once an individual has landed in a European Union country. Its law enforcement agencies do not coordinate well. There have been attempts, but there is no overarching European organization like the FBI that can investigate any member of the EU. And then there is the problem of a restive Muslim population.

This difference in threat levels between Europe and America shows the importance of cultural differences and "root causes" of terrorism, as experienced by Muslims who live in these countries. American Muslims have adopted the American Creed, which makes them less susceptible to the terrorist message. They can watch and read about atrocities against fellow Muslims around the world just as their European coreligionists do and, like them, also feel a sense of moral outrage at those acts. They read and chat about the global jihadi terrorist ideology on the Internet, just like their European counterparts. Yet, for most American Muslims, the terrorist message does not become a catalyst to action as it does for their European counterparts, since it does not resonate with their beliefs or personal experience. For the United States, pursuing policies of political, social, and economic inclusion rather than exclusion has paid an enormous dividend.

SIX

Terrorism in the Age of the Internet

At the end of Chapter 4, I described how radicalized young men were mobilized into terrorism by face-to-face interactions within a given network. The growth of the Internet has dramatically transformed the structure and dynamic of the evolving threat of global Islamist terrorism by changing the nature of terrorists' interactions. The nature of this influence is still misunderstood both by the terrorists themselves and by the people who are fighting them.

The Transformation of the Jihad

When we look over time at the networks comprising global Islamist terrorism, a clear shift in the modes of interaction emerges. Until 2004, most of the networks were a consequence of face-to-face interactions among friends (the 1993 World Trade Center bombings; the 1998 U.S. embassy bombings in East Africa; the 2000 Los Angeles airport millennium plot; the 9/11 attacks; the 2001 Singapore plot; the 2003 Casablanca bombings; the 2004 Madrid train bombings) or family (the 1994 Bojinka plot organized by Ramzi Yousef and Khalid Sheikh Mohammed; the 2003 Istanbul bombings). Starting around 2004, communications and inspiration shifted from face-to-face interaction at local halal ethnic restaurants or barber shops in the vicinity of radical Islamist mosques to interaction on the Internet. People involved in the Crevice case spanned two continents and kept in touch via the Internet. The Madrid bombers were inspired by a document posted on the Global Islamic Media Front website in December 2003. The Hofstad Group in the Netherlands interacted through dedicated forums and chat rooms and inspired other young Muslims to join them physically after making contact with them on the forums. The April 2005 Cairo Khan al-Khalili bombing was aided by the Internet, with the perpetrators downloading bomb-making instructions from jihadi websites. One of the largest international terrorist cases of its kind—the arrest of the Toronto group in Operation Osage in June 2006—had its roots in the group's linkage through an online forum to a group in Copenhagen that sent some of its members to Bosnia to bomb the U.S. embassy there, to a group in London that acted as general coordinators, and to two people in the state of Georgia in the United States. The people who tried to plant bombs on trains in Germany in the summer of 2006 met in an Internet forum. This clearly shows the change from offline to online interaction in the evolution of the threat.

The Internet is ubiquitous in Europe, where about 90 percent of young people have access to it. Although only about 6 percent of the population in the Middle East has access to a computer, young people gather in Internet cafés to surf the Internet and link up with each other. The various Middle Eastern governments are aware of the threat that this new form of communication poses for them and are actively monitoring the activities of young people at these cafés. Nevertheless, the young are able to circumvent this scrutiny and communicate with each other. Even in Indonesia, where Internet usage is very low, all of the young people who belong to terrorist networks connect to each other through the Internet, using laptops that they share or computers at cafés.

This role of the Internet is a spontaneous evolution. It was not planned by any central organization; it simply coincided with the growth of the Internet and the close monitoring of physical meeting spaces, such as mosques, by local police. The hostile environment prevented likeminded young people from physically meeting, so they started exchanging information, views, and visions of the future in Internet forums. This is a recent phenomenon, dating from about 2004.

Another aspect of the Internet is its profound effect on the traditional media. Instead of printed media like newspapers and magazines, the young generally obtain news and information from friends (instant messaging and cell phone conversations) and from the Internet, in blogs and forums. This has very important implications for the efforts to counter this terrorist threat.

Computer-mediated communication directly influences those who participate in it. The people who participate in this form of communication are young, often teenagers who grew up with the Internet. Computer-mediated communication is therefore transforming the threat in terms of the age and gender of the terrorists.

The average age of terrorists arrested in Europe and Canada from 2005 onward has dramatically decreased. My original sample of global Islamist terrorists before December 2003 was about twenty-six years of age. The average for those detained since 2006 is about twenty years of age. This is a significant decrease. Most of the new arrests have a strong linkage to the Internet. Teenagers are the greatest users of the Internet and are therefore most likely to be influenced by it. By the time they evolve into terrorists, they are in their late teens or early twenties.

At the same time, gender separation among terrorists is starting to disappear because of the Internet. Women have been largely absent from the ranks of global Islamist terrorists. The few references to the role of women in this social movement advocated a strictly supportive role. In August 2004, *al-Khansa*, a magazine published by "Al Qaeda's Arabian Peninsula Women's Information Bureau," appeared on the Internet. Although it celebrated the martyrdom of two Palestinian women, it advocated a strict supporting role for women engaged in the jihad: help finance the jihad; care for her jihadi husband and learn first aid; educate her children for jihad; and be fit and learn to use weapons to defend her family and honor. This conventional and secondary role is all the more surprising because historically this limited role for women in terrorism is not the norm. Women have been an integral part of most terrorist movements, comprising about a third of committed terrorists throughout history. In some instances they formed the majority of a terrorist group. Like men, women have political opinions and are as willing as men to sacrifice for them. So, what might account for this small and subordinate role?

The global Islamist terrorists previously practiced strict segregation between women and men. Women were excluded by men from a more active operational role, not because of religious proscription (some women were active in war during the time of the Prophet and are celebrated as female heroes) but because of the masculine conception of heroism among these terrorists. Since many terrorists are attracted to this movement by dreams of fame and glory, the fear was that a more active role for women might lessen the repute of

111

the men's actions. Women were relegated to supporting their husbands, who were allowed to sacrifice themselves for the cause. Palestinian terrorist leaders were also hesitant about using women more operationally. They changed their minds after they noticed the positive response of the Muslim world to women sacrificing themselves for the Palestinian cause. In global Islamist terrorism, this has not yet happened and women are still mostly held back by men from a more operational role.

Now two major developments are taking place simultaneously, which are expanding the role of women in this movement. First, as mentioned above, they are more active in chat rooms. Although many forums are segregated and have chat rooms for women only, some women can still participate in some of the most popular terrorist forums whereas they had been previously largely excluded from such discussions. With the semi-anonymity of the Internet, there is no way of keeping them out. The discussions on certain forums inspire some to want to become more operationally active. However, this more operational role is obscuring the true importance of women in this movement, as a motivational inspiration for men. This role is well documented for the women of the Hofstad Group, the Dutch group that killed Theo van Gogh. Women tried to lure potential recruits to their informal network and motivated their men to become more active. As they had more time on their hands, they learned Arabic and translated some classical jihadi texts into Dutch, thereby becoming the true ideologues of their group.[1] The wives of the alleged terrorists arrested in Toronto in June 2006 in Operation Osage belonged to a chat room where they openly preached violent jihad. Malika el-Aroud, the widow of the suicide bomber who killed Ahmad Shah Massoud on September 9, 2001, was convicted in 2007 in Switzerland of encouraging on the Internet young Muslims to join the ranks of al Qaeda.

Second, as the women's desire to become more operational is increasing, the obstacles in their way are disappearing as their brothers or husbands are either killed or arrested. The remaining women believe they must do something and become operationally active. The wives of the arrested Belgian terrorists, known as the Asparagus 18 case (because they came from the Belgian town of Maaseik, which is known for its cultivation of asparagus) wanted to become more active when their husbands and brothers were arrested and convicted. They asked an unrelated acquaintance in the al Qaeda social movement for dynamite. The male terrorist refused after checking with his superiors. In another case, in April 2005 the wife and the sister of a recently killed terrorist in Cairo shot at a bus, which they believed was filled with Israelis, and then killed themselves. The Belgian convert Muriel Dugaugue became the first European female suicide bomber to die in Iraq on November 9, 2005. On the same day Sajida al-Rishawi, an Iraqi woman, tried but failed to blow herself up at a wedding celebration in Amman, Jordan.

The Importance of Interactivity

Most analysts of the influence of the Internet on Salafi terrorist movement focus on the wrong part of the Internet.[2] The Internet is really two major systems, which need to be distinguished. The first part is the worldwide Web, which is the collection of all websites and provides information to its users. It has grown to enormous proportions, but is still essentially passive. It has the same role as books, newspapers, radio, or television. People access those sites but passively absorb the information provided. These websites do play an important educational role in terms of providing information relevant for the jihadis and especially operational knowledge in the absence of training camps. Such bomb-making knowledge is now available on jihadi websites in the form of very detailed step-by-step video instructions showing how to build improvised explosive devices. There is strong evidence that such online instructions played a critical role in the March 2004 Madrid bombings, the April 2005 Khan al-Khalili bombings in Cairo, the July 2006 failed attempt to bomb trains in Germany, and the June 2007 plot to bomb London's West End and Glasgow.

Some experts are skeptical about the importance of these online instructions in terrorist operations. They claim that there is no substitute for personal instruction in a terrorist camp. It is true that people who have learned to make bombs only from the Internet are not as proficient in their skills as trained bombers. The Khan al-Khalili bombings had fewer than a handful of victims, and the German bombs and London 2007 bombs failed to detonate. The Madrid bombers succeeded in getting dynamite and did not have to manufacture the explosive material. Manufacturing bombs from scratch with just the Internet as guidance presents a real challenge. It requires faith in the instructions and courage to follow them. But it is not impossible and does not require special expertise. Of course, when such expertise acquired in a terrorist training camp is combined with an informal Internet network, the results can be literally devastating.

No matter how important for propaganda purposes these passive websites are, they are not the engine of radicalization. People in general do not change their minds or harden their views by reading newspaper articles or books. They usually read what conforms to their original bias, and thereby only confirms their views, which were created elsewhere. Yet, the images and general direction found on the websites fascinate communication analysts, who assume that these are the active elements in fostering a terrorist worldview. Most of the work on the importance of the Internet to this terrorist movement has focused on these passive websites and assume that the images found therein have intrinsic power to influence people into taking arms against the West.[3] I disagree. These sites merely reinforce already made-up minds.

The Internet is also a vast active system of communication between individuals and between individuals and groups. The best known Internet communication systems are e-mail, listservs, and, especially, forums or chat rooms. In this way, they are similar to other forms of communication, namely letters, telegrams, and the telephone. It is their interactivity that is revolutionary and rapidly changing human relationships in ways of which we are not yet fully aware.

People's relationships are being completely transformed through computer-mediated communication. Because of its apparent anonymity, people are more likely to self-disclose via computer-mediated technology, which contributes to feelings of greater intimacy. This may lead them to fall in love; computer-mediated dating has become as common as meeting at a bar. The curious thing is that when people meet after exchanging communications through computers, they feel that they know the "core" of the other person, which quickly leads to strong bonds. Many people who have met on the Internet have gone on to marry, including some of the terrorists.

The intensity of feelings developed online rival those developed offline. Some terrorist experts are skeptical that online relationships can generate the intensity of trust and emotions required to sacrifice oneself for cause or comrades. However, many psychological studies have compared the strength of positive feelings that people develop toward each other online and offline. It seems that online feelings are stronger in almost every measurement than offline feelings. This is a robust finding that has been duplicated many times.[4] Even for suicide, the Internet has already demonstrated its fatal contribution. Suicidal Japanese teenagers meet in special forums online and get together the next day to collectively commit suicide. If individually they lacked the courage to commit suicide, collectively they gained strength from their mutual support. These collective suicides have already claimed more than several hundred lives as of mid-2007. This fashion has spread to South Korea, where dozens have already killed themselves this way.

Conversely, there is very little "cost" associated with transaction on the Internet. People can just cut off their interaction without any explanation. Because there is no consequence, people can act on the Internet in ways that they would not dare offline—such as insulting someone. Offline, they would risk a variety of unpleasant responses, but online, they are shielded by the Internet's anonymity. The resulting lack of civility online, such as the intensity of hate speech that is not conceivable offline, is the flip side of the greater intimacy that people feel online. These two forces—greater intimacy and lack of civility—are competing with each other, and online society has not come to the kind of communicative compromise that took centuries to develop in face-to-face communications.

This new medium of communication is changing people's relationships as well. The previous major revolution in communication—the invention of movable type printing by Johannes Gutenberg around 1450—resulted in the Reformation, the Counter-Reformation, the various religious wars that plagued Europe, the universal spread of education (once books were available, there was a reason to learn to read), the dramatic rise of mail (now that people knew how to read and write, they could write letters to each other), the Enlightenment (including the rise of science, which was mediated through books), and many far more subtle changes. Interpersonal relationships that were developed and sustained by written means of communication differed from those dependent on oral means of communication, making people more introspective and giving rise to the novel and the scientific study of introspection (psychology, for example). Computer-mediated communication, which seems to collapse time and eliminate space, has the potential to transform human relationships faster and to an even greater degree.

Our interest at the moment is in the effect of this communicative revolution on terrorism. We already see that some networks were created wholesale from forums, which radicalized their members. The interactivity is what

115

is important. In my previous book, I described how the interactivity among a "bunch of guys" acted as an echo chamber, which progressively radicalized them collectively to the point where they were ready to collectively join a terrorist organization. Now the same process is taking place online. Since physical militant sites, like radical mosques, are closely monitored by law enforcement authorities, militants have moved online. The new forums have the same influence that these radical mosques played in the previous generation of terrorists. It is the forums, not the images of the passive websites, which are crucial in the process of radicalization. People change their minds through discussion with friends, not by simply reading impersonal stories. People discuss these stories online and draw their own conclusions. Sometimes the discussion refers them to stories and images on these passive sites, but it is in support of an active argument from a friend or relative. The images and text of the horrors of Chechnya and Iraq found on websites play a supportive role in the transformation of the individuals, but the forums are the engine of this transformation. Just as people are rarely convinced or radicalized by simply reading a newspaper story, so no one is converted by a website alone. It is the discussion of the newspaper article with one's friends and family and the interactive exchanges in the chat rooms that inspire and radicalize.

The Terrorist Chat Room

Young Muslim men and women share their hopes and dreams with their virtual friends on these radical forums. Some might have joined a given forum out of a sense of alienation, of feeling alone. The forums, where people seem to care for each other, provide them with ready friends. In the forums they feel at home and safe enough to explore their fantasies and aspirations with their friends. This mutual sharing makes them feel ever closer to each other, in a virtual process similar to the one previously described as in-group love with face-to-face interactions. This provides them with a sense of belonging to a greater community on the basis of what they have in common, Islam. The forums demonstrate for them that the ummah, or imagined Muslim nation, truly exists, and is represented on the Internet.

The Internet was self-consciously built to be egalitarian, a place where anyone can have a voice and directly reach anyone else. This contrasts with more traditional hierarchical form of organization, where information from the base must pass upward through a host of intermediaries before reaching a leader and vice versa, where it flows downward from a leader through these intermediaries to followers. On the Internet, information can reach anyone directly, so everyone has a voice, without regard to his or her position in the organization. Through email and forums, it is now possible to reach very important people without passing through their subordinates, which was not true several years ago.

Internet egalitarianism provides a concrete example of what the utopian ummah can look like: a community of friends, where everyone is equal and cares for everyone else. This utopia becomes something worth fighting for. The mutual validation of ideas among the participants may not only lead them to develop ideas at odds with the rest of society, but also harden their beliefs through a process called the illusion of numbers. Let's assume that a very few people in the world share the same strange belief, say that the moon is made of green cheese. Through a process of self-selection, they find each other on the same forum. Since the forum provides a friendly and safe environment to share this strange belief, some participants will become very vocal in promoting it to a receptive audience. Lurkers in the forum, who were not sure about their beliefs, will stay silent rather than voice their doubts. Soon, they will assume that everyone shares this conviction because only the true believers air their views and the rest stay silent. The skeptics will become more convinced that perhaps the belief is true since their whole social universe accepts it. This hardening of strange beliefs via partisan chat rooms feeds the ubiquitous conspiracy theories found on the Internet.

Participation is an active process; individuals seek and select the rooms most compatible with their views and abandon the ones they disagree with. In a sense, the followers vote with their mice and select the views they like. This is already one of the major differences between forum-mediated communication and communication in more traditional terrorist organizations. On the Internet, various ideologues compete with each other on different websites. Participants in the forums can discuss the merits of each and voluntarily access them. These competing leaders can coexist peacefully on the Internet side by side without the need to eliminate each other, as is often the case in offline terrorist organizations, where an ideological deviation is viewed as a challenge to the authority of the leader, who then feels compelled to eliminate his rival. The

117

always delicate problem of leadership succession in traditional terrorist organizations thus becomes irrelevant. The followers choose whom to follow, and the other leaders fade away. This is similar to a shopping mall, where customers flock to the store carrying the most popular merchandise, and the other stores see sales plummet. As in the market, the customer, or in this case, the follower is king.

This Internet egalitarianism is also undermining the hierarchy of traditional terrorist organizations. Even if the undisputed leader of the al Qaeda social movement, Osama bin Laden, were to participate in a forum, he could not exert complete authority and control over the rest of the participants. Of course, his voice would be much "louder" than any individual participant, but it would not be the unchallenged voice of a traditional terrorist leader. Cloaked by the semi-anonymity of the Internet, followers would interpret his words according to their wishes, and together would contribute more to the creation of the collective discourse of the forum than any individual leader. The true leader of global Islamist terrorism is the collective discourse of the half-dozen influential jihadi forums. It provides general guidance to the participants in the absence of physical command and control found in traditional terrorist organizations.

It is important to understand that the forums may foster a true conversation. And any conversation has a built-in sense of indeterminacy. Even if we know those speaking, it is difficult to anticipate where the conversation will go. Six frequent guests at dinner will have different conversations on separate occasions. The conversation is likely to depend on the context of the day's events, but it is almost impossible to know exactly where the conversation will lead. The same is true in the forums. There is a sense of open-endedness, and it is difficult to anticipate with precision the future of global Islamist terrorism. The U.S. government is investing heavily in computer models trying to predict terrorist attacks or tactics. They are doomed to failure because of this built-in indeterminacy. It is impossible to predict the turn of the virtual conversation, and whether people will stay together or split in smaller groups or forums that cater to their shared opinions.

In a sense, leadership of the virtual jihad may be up for grabs, a function of the energy of the participants. It seems that regardless of their position when they begin to participate, a person chatting in a forum has influence proportional to the number of postings he or she contributes, if the content of his posting is consistent with the general discourse of the forum and his contributions provide an added value for the rest of the forum. Participation in these influential password-gated entrance forums is by invitation only. Online jihadis are promiscuous, belonging to several closed and open forums at the same time. When they notice a like-minded ongoing participant on an open forum, they invite him to their closed one. From the discussions in the closed forum, the gist filters through dual participants to the open forums, attempting to set the tone for the much greater number of open jihadi forums. Closed forums also receive material from al Qaeda Central for distribution to the greater audience. Dual participants accomplish this with ease, as illustrated by the constant videos from al Qaeda Central and local leaders.

The promiscuity of online jihadis belonging to multiple forums and the decentralized structure of the Internet, which had been originally designed to survive nuclear strikes, give online jihadi networks great resilience. One website taken down can be easily recreated elsewhere. The structure of the Internet with its egalitarianism and built-in redundancy strongly influences the evolution of the shape of global Islamist terrorism, as will be shown in the next chapter.

The case of Younis Tsouli, the famous Irhabi007 (Terrorist 007 in Arabic), is an example of an online jihadi. Tsouli was a twenty-year-old student in London and the son of a Moroccan diplomat there when he was invited to join two password-protected forums in early 2004. He had no history of terrorist activity. He immediately became a prolific participant in both forums and people started deferring to him, out of familiarity and his rapidly growing proficiency with the Internet. When a spokesperson for al Qaeda in Iraq leader Zarqawi started using the Internet to post videos and communiqués, he chose Muntada al-Ansar al-Islami, one of these two forums. At first, participants did not know what to make of the newcomer, but Tsouli welcomed him, setting the tone for the rest of the forum. The forum started distributing Zarqawi's material and became his public relations mouthpiece. This earned Tsouli specific praise from Zarqawi later on. Tsouli took his role seriously, became more skilled in the use of the Internet, such as how to hack into dozens of websites to host huge computer files, mostly videos of beheadings and suicide bombings filed in Iraq. He spend a great deal of time creating and disseminating tutorials on hacking and hiding one's identity online for the rest of the forum participants. With the help of two accomplices, he began using stolen credit card numbers to buy web hosting services in the United States and Europe. He also incited others to commit terrorist acts and guided them to reliable websites where they could learn how to build bombs. He was a critical link between local terrorist networks, such as the Toronto network eventually arrested in Operation Osage in June 2006 and the network arrested in Copenhagen and in Bosnia in October 2005. Tsouli was arrested in London in October 2005 on charges of incitement of terrorist murder using the Internet. He pled guilty in July 2007 and received a ten-year prison sentence.

The career of Younis Tsouli illustrates the inversion of power in the age of the Internet. Traditional leaders can post suggestions in chat rooms, but it is up to the followers to pick and choose among them and follow whatever they like. In this sense, it is similar to a marketplace of ideas. The leaders have no way of enforcing their commands on the Internet, as would have been the case in offline organizations, through incentives like funding or intimidation. They may banish people from certain forums, but the exiles can seek refuge in competing ones. Thus, the followers are in command, anonymously and freely choosing among the competing suggestions in the forums. Instead of traditional leaders being in control of the global Islamist terrorist social movement, it is the unnamed followers who decide to act. The leaders can then retrospectively award legitimacy to some of these operations.

It is likewise in the physical world, where al Qaeda Central leaders by and large do not know who their followers are, have little or no physical contact with them, and do not know what plots they may be hatching. After the fact, the leaders can pick and choose what activities or groups they want to sanction as a legitimate part of their movement. Operations that are outside what might be acceptable to their potential constituency—such as the killing of children in Baghdad in the summer of 2005 or at a school in Beslan, Russia, in the fall of 2005—are ignored or even blamed on the enemy, while more traditional operations like the bombings in Bali, Casablanca, Istanbul, Madrid, and London are celebrated, especially if they involve martyrdom.

The forums are virtual places where active participants post and consume ideas about their goals, perspectives, and hopes. It is where terrorism "cool" is discussed. Debates over the relative merits of various strategies and tactics are held. The resulting collective discourse becomes the ideology, the vision, and the guidance of the participants. They inspire young members to become more active, promote images of inspirational heroes for the participants, and result in overall radicalization. The forums are the true marketplace of ideas guiding this form of terrorism. To use Adam Smith's analogy, the Islamist Internet has become the virtual invisible hand organizing global Salafi terrorism worldwide. Computer-mediated communication is what makes this decentralized leaderless organization of global Islamist terrorism possible and the forums have become its center of gravity.

The forums have become the virtual equivalent of the militant mosques that radicalized about half of the subjects of my original sample. Terrorist wannabes congregate in the forums and gradually form virtual cliques, randomly distributed over large geographical areas. (The group in the Operation Osage case in Toronto was connected to groups in Copenhagen, Bosnia, London, and the United States.) They can plot online and decide to carry out an operation together. When they meet physically, the time before they carry out an actual operation is dramatically shortened, and may be only a couple of days.

Implications of the Internet

The structure of the Internet has become the structure of global Islamist terrorism. It has evolved organically through the search and exploration of new safe methods of interaction by thousands of terrorist sympathizers given the fact that their physical habitat had become very hostile post–9/11 and especially post–Iraq invasion, when the al Qaeda social movement started attacking countries that had previously tolerated them. There was no central intent of moving the terrorist social movement online; it just happened by itself, like a Darwinian evolution by natural selection. They simply adapted to their hostile physical environment by accidentally finding the relative safety of chat rooms and thriving there.

Although I have focused on online forums, I do not mean to neglect offline networks. Most online participants also have friends who share their views and desires but do not spend so much time on the Internet. Terror networks consist of a mixture of online and offline elements, and their respective in-person and virtual discussions mutually influence each other. The Toronto-based Osage case was a mixture of online and offline elements. The overall situation is therefore more complicated than just pure online or offline networks. They are networks within networks, offline and online links, which cross geography and time. The Internet connects them to a truly global network.

The Internet can encourage another special case, namely loners. These loners appear as "lone wolves" only offline. Most are part of a forum, where they share their plans and are encouraged by chat room participants to carry them out. In this sense, they are like the loner high school shooters, such as the two teens who were responsible for the Columbine killings in 1999 or the shootings at Red River in Bemidji, Minnesota, in 2005. In the latter case, a Native American boy stole his grandfather's rifle, killed him, and then took it to school where he killed eight of his classmates before killing himself. He appeared to be a loner but was an active member of a neo-Nazi forum, where he told his online buddies what he was going to do and was in turn encouraged by them. More generally, several apparent loners have been active participants in radical chat rooms, where they were encouraged to carry out terrorist activities. These lone wolves are usually teenagers, who build bombs in their bedrooms in their parents' homes, like Yehya Kadouri, a seventeen-year-old boy, who was arrested and convicted in the Netherlands in 2005. He used the online name AIVDkiller but had never physically met any other wannabe, let alone a true terrorist. He had built a homemade bomb, which failed to detonate in two attempts.

This Internet-mediated form of terrorism survives through media and Internet dissemination. The news media (especially television) becomes its propaganda machine and broadcasts its ideas and actions. Sometimes government officials are complicit by boasting about their arrests, usually elevating unknowns to the status of heroes. Successful actions are copied by sympathizers, and spectacular action inspires young people to join the movement. Unsuccessful actions are generally neglected, giving the impression that the movement is more effective than it really is. The Internet now allows for the distribution of propaganda of successful action through dissemination over the Internet. This allows the groups involved to brag about their victories and inspire young people to join. Failures are ignored.

The Internet and the traditional news media can keep a martyr's action alive forever as an inspiration to potential new members. Even if a perpetrator survives and later regrets his action, his deeds become separated from him and carry their own weight. Terrorist websites do not have to reveal the later career of the perpetrators. Computer-mediated communication makes it possible for the movement to survive mostly in the virtual world. There are no membership lists, no financial records, and no direct communication between the independent groups. On the down side for those combating terrorism, there is no way to negotiate with such a virtual social movement.

Unlike traditional terrorist organizations that have physical sites and more territorial ambitions, there is no incentive for a leaderless virtual social movement to moderate or evolve beyond terrorism. Because there is no formal organization, with assets, sunk costs, physical commitments, or other stabilizing elements, participants who become more moderate in their views simply leave the forum and move on, or are banished from the forum by the webmaster. But their legacy lives on; their previous commitments and activities (writings, videos, and terrorist operations) are still archived in the forums and could continue to inspire new generations of dreamers to capture the glory that had inspired the old stalwarts in the first place. Indeed, if the forums and websites grow dormant because of a large-scale elimination of their participants, they are still present in a latent phase on the Internet, waiting to be rediscovered perhaps by accident by a future generation that might then become inspired by the dreams of glory contained on these sites. Thanks to the Internet, global Islamist terrorism may fade away, but will never completely die.

SEVEN

The Rise of Leaderless Jihad

The global Islamist terrorist threat continues to evolve. Before 9/11, most countries did not take the threat seriously enough to mobilize against it. The United States did create a special unit within the CIA, Alec Station, which tracked and tried to eliminate al Qaeda,[1] but this was a low-grade international law enforcement strategy. Responses to actual terrorist operations were anemic. After the 1998 East African embassy bombings Washington launched a limited cruise missile attack against an al Qaeda training camp in Afghanistan and an alleged al Qaeda "chemical factory" in Sudan. That weak response was followed by no response at all after al Qaeda's bombing of the USS *Cole* off Yemen in 2000. This lack of serious response in the years before 9/11 might have emboldened al Qaeda Central to escalate until its enemy took the threat seriously.[2] September 11, 2001, changed all of that.

Within weeks of the airplane attacks, U.S. forces invaded Afghanistan to destroy al Qaeda sanctuaries. This seemed to have surprised its leaders, who expected a more moderate response, such as another cruise missile attack. With the Afghan population rapidly turning against the al Qaeda foreigners, U.S. forces and their Afghan allies quickly toppled the Taliban regime and destroyed al Qaeda's sanctuary—and training camps—in Afghanistan. Pressure on the Saudi regime and the help of the international financial community allowed the tracking and drastic reduction of funding for al Qaeda activities. Communications among al Qaeda members came under increased monitoring and key leaders were either arrested or killed. The international community supported the U.S. government in this large-scale action and the global Muslim community offered only minimal protest. The link between al Qaeda and the Taliban had been clear for all to see, and the U.S.-led action was generally accepted as appropriate retaliation for the atrocities of 9/11.

The United States also mobilized its allies, after an initially lackluster response, to fight this threat globally. It took several bombings or killings in Tunisia, Indonesia, Saudi Arabia, Morocco, Turkey, Spain, the Netherlands, and Britain to bring most countries in the world into the same fight against al Qaeda Central and to make them realize that this was not just an American problem, but a global concern with domestic consequences for them as well. As a result, the international community has been far more cooperative and vigilant against the terrorist threat, making it more difficult for the old al Qaeda to operate as it did before 9/11.

Al Qaeda Central in particular was neutralized operationally. But as long as some of its leaders were still at large, it was not eliminated. Osama bin Laden and Ayman al-Zawahiri still deliver speeches via video and through the Internet, exhorting their followers to continue the fight. There is also evidence that the two had limited communication with some of their followers, as shown by the case of Naeem Khan, arrested in Lahore in the summer of 2004. Khan, an al Qaeda operative, sent messages to al Qaeda affiliates that he had received from the leadership. In general, however, communications had degraded to the point that there was no meaningful command and control between the al Qaeda leadership and its followers.

On the March—or On the Run?

The West's muscular response to 9/11 and other terrorist attempts in Europe created a hostile environment for al Qaeda Central and its affiliated social movement. The severe blows to al Qaeda Central in Afghanistan in the proximate post–9/11 period degraded the central organization's capability. In mid-2007, several commentators on global Islamist terrorism argue that we are seeing a resurgence of al Qaeda Central.[3] One went so far as to claim that "Al Qaeda is a more dangerous enemy today than it was ever before."[4] They point to the training camps that have sprung up in Waziristan in the Federally Administered Tribal Areas (FATA) of Pakistan; the fact that some of those arrested for their association with a number of planned and executed terrorist attacks in London were connected to al Qaeda Central; the merger of al Qaeda and the Taliban in Afghanistan; attempted strikes at financial institutions in the United States in 2004; the merger of the Algerian GSPC with al Qaeda to form al Qaeda in the Islamic Maghreb; a growing propaganda operation, especially the material of As Sahab Production; and of course a dramatic growth of al Qaeda activities in Iraq.[5] The July 2007 *National Intelligence Estimate: The Terrorist Threat to the U.S. Homeland* also shares this alarmist tone,[6] which the media immediately amplified.

I am skeptical of the claim of a resurgent al Qaeda Central. The evidence mustered in support is anecdotal and without any explanation of the dynamics underlying the fluctuations in al Qaeda operations. To respond to the arguments, yes, al Qaeda Central is better off in the summer 2007 than it was a year prior for the reason hinted in the first argument. Between 2004 and 2006, Pakistani President Pervez Musharraf signed a series of truces with tribal leaders in the FATA, which specified that tribal leaders would police their neighborhoods and prevent fighters from launching cross-border raids into Afghanistan in return for Pakistani military withdrawal from the region. The Pakistani army kept its end of the bargain and stayed clear of the FATA. At first, the tribal leaders tried to oust Uzbeks and Chechens from their territory, but seemed to have left more traditional al Qaeda Central leaders alone. The result is that al Qaeda leaders seem to be coming out of their hiding places and meeting each other more openly. While I would reject the notion that al Qaeda is resurgent (there is no surge here, and there has not been an al Qaeda Central fatality since July 7, 2005), I would agree that at this juncture al Qaeda leadership is regrouping and consolidating in Waziristan. The report of new "training camps" there is consistent with this analysis.

I put quotation marks around the words "training camps" because what exist are not camps at all. There is no sign that Pakistan contains "training camps" similar in size and importance to those that existed in Afghanistan in the 1990s. But the training facilities seen in Waziristan since the September 2006 truce seem more open than the facilities that were available in the previous five years. From the testimony at the Crevice trial in London, it seems that jihadi wannabes went to Pakistan to search for a trainer, who was generally sympathetic to al Qaeda's ideology but might not have been in al Qaeda himself. The deals were concluded between the students and the trainer, on a case-by-case basis. The class consisted of up to ten students, who spent at most four weeks with the trainer and an assistant in a house surrounded by a wall, like most of the houses in northern Pakistan. There, the students studied with the trainer and learned to make bombs. It is unclear whether they had the opportunity to test the bombs during the course. The trainer was often a "fellow traveler," belonging to a Kashmiri group that has a similar outlook to that of al Qaeda—Laskar e-Toyba or Jaish e-Mohammed, for example—but which is focused on liberating Kashmir from India. It appears that these one-month sessions were conducted sporadically, whenever some students could find an appropriate instructor.

The new facilities in Waziristan seem to be slightly bigger, more visible, and the number of students may even reach twenty.[7] So the new training camps in Waziristan are indeed worrisome (who is training there, and are they going to come back to Europe or the United States?), but they are indications of a consolidation rather than a surge. The people attending these camps are also cause for concern. Up to the 2006 truce, the only Western wannabes who succeeded in making contact with terrorist trainers were British second-generation immigrants, whose parents came from the Mirpur District of Azad Kashmir. They still had relatives in Pakistan who could vouch for them and make the introduction. An enthusiastic wannabe from elsewhere would not be trusted and would have difficulty finding a trainer. With the now more receptive North Waziristan habitat, the new leaders of al Qaeda Central are becoming more visible, and foreigners can more easily make contact with them. This is changing the composition of those Westerners able to receive training. The arrests of four German Muslims in the first half of 2007 in Pakistan triggered alarm bells in Germany. The greater ability of Western wannabes to get training and advice from seasoned terrorists is reason for concern, and a threat to the West. Again, this is a sign of al Qaeda Central's consolidation and regrouping, but not yet of its resurgence. All indications are that the number of these wannabes is still quite small, several dozens at most, as compared to the hundreds or thousands that traveled to Afghanistan in the second wave of global Islamist terrorism. So far, this consolidation within al Qaeda Central has not effectively spilled beyond the borders of Waziristan. In that sense, there is no surge.

The specific British cases mentioned in the alarmist argument date from about 2002 to 2005 at the latest. Scattered reports of training have been trickling in at a constant pace since 9/11. Many references to al Qaeda Central are now surfacing because some past cases with links to al Qaeda Central or its fellow travelers are now going to court several years after the relevant terrorist activities. These old stories are not evidence of a recent resurgence of al Qaeda Central. Likewise, the plot to bomb U.S. financial facilities that surfaced in August 2004 with the arrest of Naeem Khan in Lahore, Pakistan, was also an outdated story. The casings took place in 2000, with no new developments since. The plot was discovered four years later, and it was an old story even then. These plots came from the remnant of the second wave or the transitional period to the third wave. Because they had some connection to people with links to some middle managers of al Qaeda Central, they could make the connection through these intermediaries. They did not involve the third wave.

One commentator added the 2004 Madrid bombing to the evidence of al Qaeda "on the March."[8] He based his claim on allegedly secret information about Amer al-Azizi, whom he identified as the link to al Qaeda Central. He also credited Azizi as being the host of the meeting between Mohammed Atta and Ramzi bin al-Shibh in Spain at the last tune-up for the 9/11 operation. Azizi disappeared from Spain in October 2001 ahead of a warrant for his arrest. Since then, Azizi sightings in Europe have rivaled those of Elvis in the United States. The 9/11 Commission report completely rejected any alleged Spanish involvement in the meeting.[9] During the five-month trial for the perpetrators of the Madrid bombings concluded in July 2007, considerable evidence has become publicly available about the evolution of the plot, including the testimony of several human penetrations of the responsible network. There is no hint of any direct al Qaeda Central connection. Hiding behind so-called secret information is no substitute for careful investigation of the facts and sober analysis. On this, the Spanish prosecutors have it right. The plot was not by al Qaeda, but was definitely inspired by al Qaeda Central. Again, Madrid does not provide any evidence of a resurgence of al Qaeda Central.

In terms of the new al Qaeda in Islamic Maghreb, little "al Qaedas" have sprung up everywhere in the world. They are just al Qaeda in name, trying to acquire the reputation of al Qaeda by using its name. There is strong evidence that the acquisition of the name by some leaders of the old Algerian GSPC (Groupe Salafiste pour la Prédication et le Combat) has generated a lot of debate in jihadi chat rooms, with many of the traditional leaders rejecting this move. In any case, Algerian terrorist groups have always been fiercely independent and have more often fought with each other than joined for combined operations. It is unlikely that al Qaeda Central will be able to dictate anything to these groups. The modus operandi of the April 11, 2007, bombing in Algiers differed from other Algerian operations and was more similar to the typical al Qaeda operation. It remains to be seen if this will become a trend or simply experimentation with new terrorist techniques. Many Algerian terrorists have complained that this type of bombing was alienating their constituency, and the April 11 bombing may herald yet another split among the Algerian terrorist groups.

Jumping to another part of the world, media commentators were pointing to al Qaeda success in Iraq in the spring of 2007. As of the summer of 2007, Iraqi Sunni tribes have combined with U.S. forces to administer severe blows to al Qaeda in Anbar Province. In any case, al Qaeda's affiliate in Iraq has been independent from al Qaeda Central, although since the death of Zarqawi, there has been an attempt to combine the two organizations. The verdict is still out on this. However, the 2007 NIE is right to note that al Qaeda in Iraq is probably the most competent, active, and resourceful constituent of global Islamist terrorism. It remains to be seen whether the combined U.S. and local Sunni tribal forces will succeed in eradicating this most dangerous organization.

The growth of al Qaeda propaganda operations is real enough. If there is one major improvement for al Qaeda since 2004, it is its use of the Internet. Its production arm As Sahab is of very high quality. The evidence that came out of the Tsouli trial also showed the sophistication of the communication between al Qaeda and some of its trusted followers online. Communication between al Qaeda Central and some of its peripheral members has improved since 2005. This is potentially dangerous, especially in the context of regrouping of al Qaeda leadership.

The new fears about a resurgent al Qaeda Central are not commensurate with the apparent danger. In the first three years after 9/11, al Qaeda was fairly active in Pakistan, especially in the many assassination attempts against Pakistani officials from 2002 to 2004. Amjad Farooqi, who orchestrated many of the attacks against Pakistani President Musharraf, evidently acted as an intermediary between people he recruited in Pakistan and Abu Faraj al Libi, the al Qaeda military leader after the capture of Khalid Sheikh Mohammed. But again, these are now old stories, and not indicative of a resurgence of al Qaeda Central. Since 2004, al Qaeda seems to have been less active in Pakistan outside of Waziristan. After the outrage caused by the storming of the Red Mosque in Islamabad in July 2007, there has been a spike of suicide bombings in northern Pakistan. These indiscriminate bombings differ from the past targeted violence sponsored by al Qaeda Central against high Pakistani government officials. These types of bombings seem to reflect a lack of discipline, which might well turn the Pakistani population against the Islamist terrorists, as it did in so many other countries.[10]

The general trends about al Qaeda Central simply do not support the resurgence theory. The rapid succession of al Qaeda military commanders since 9/11—Abu Hafs al Masri, Khalid Sheikh Mohammed, Abu Faraj al Libi, Hamza Rabia, Abdur Rahman al Muhajir, Abdel Hadi al Iraqi—indicates that the operational leaders of al Qaeda Central are still members of the first wave. Their number is rapidly dwindling because of capture or death. There is no indication that members of the second wave are stepping up to leadership positions. Given the fact that the number of members keeps diminishing, with no real replacement from the third wave, which has trouble making contact with al Qaeda Central, I would venture that the trend is quite the opposite of that argued by the alarmists. Far from having depth at many positions, al Qaeda's bench is shrinking. Yes, there are still trained and quite competent terrorist trainers around, and they are more visible in Waziristan, but the long-term prospect of al Qaeda Central in the Afghan-Pakistani theater is diminishing. Given the fact that three al Qaeda operational chiefs have been captured, I suspect that they did not know where bin Laden was hiding, for they might have betrayed him. This probably means that, after the disappearance of the previous military chief, a new aggressive one simply steps up and becomes de facto leader himself. This may account for the fact that some of the 2007 al Qaeda Central leaders were at most middle-level leaders just a few years earlier. Bin Laden's approval of the new promotions might come later, after the fact, sent through trusted messengers.

Nevertheless, al Qaeda seems to be spearheading a campaign of terror in Afghanistan. In the first two waves, there were no Afghans in al Qaeda despite the latter's twenty-year presence in Afghanistan. There was no love lost between Afghans and al Qaeda foreigners. Now, al Qaeda and the Taliban find themselves in the same situation, as fugitives in the Afghan-Pakistani border. Since 2005, there has been a strong collaboration between the two networks. Taliban leaders have started using al Qaeda themes and terminology in their public statements. They publicly admit that they are collaborating with operations and al Qaeda has named a specific commander for Afghanistan. Taliban insurgents have adopted al Qaeda tactics and techniques.[11] This seems strong evidence that Taliban fighters have been trained by al Qaeda veterans. So, it seems that the growing gap left by the departure of the first- and second-wave global Islamist terrorists is being filled with local Afghans.

This virtual merger between al Qaeda and the Taliban has unleashed a local resurgence (yes, the term is correct in this context) of the Taliban in Afghanistan with increasing bombings and damages. However, Afghan peasants do not travel well to the West. They are a local threat because they mix well with their Afghan habitat, but they would be immediately detected in the West. I suspect the great increase in al Qaeda membership now comes from these local Afghanis. But theirs is a limited marriage of convenience. The mutual dislike and distrust between Pushtuns and foreigners prevents the Taliban from truly merging with al Qaeda. The Pushtun al Qaeda members have a dual loyalty, and if push comes to shove, they will again betray the foreigners, as they did in the fall of 2001. For now, this marriage has resulted in a Taliban resurgence in Afghanistan and greater protection for Arab al Qaeda members in the tribal areas on both sides of the border.

Al Qaeda Central is of course not dead, but it is still contained operationally. It puts out inspirational guidance on the Internet, but does not have the means to exert command and control over the al Qaeda social movement. The surviving leaders of al Qaeda are undoubtedly still plotting to do harm to various countries in the world and have the expertise to do so, but they are hampered by the global security measures that have been put in place. They remain in hiding, but seem to have consolidated in Waziristan since the Pakistani military relaxed its efforts against them. So far al Qaeda Central has been confined to that area, but the increase in wannabes coming for training and its renewed ability to communicate with followers are disturbing developments. However, the long-term trend does not favor al Qaeda. The number of the trained global Islamist terrorists continues to dwindle along the Afghan-Pakistani border, and there is no sign that they are being replenished with competent new recruits. The recent consolidation and training efforts from al Qaeda Central terrorists demonstrate the dynamic and delicate balance between networks and their habitat. The relaxation of hostility in their immediate environment due to the evacuation of Pakistani forces from Waziristan allowed the al Qaeda network to reemerge from hiding and become more active. This might be a short-term event, which can be easily reversed by Pakistani authorities. On the other hand, the long-term trend of diminishing numbers of experienced terrorists cannot be so easily reversed. Over time, this trend will prevail.

The handfuls of wannabes that succeed in making contact with al Qaeda terrorists do get trained and dispatched back to wreak havoc in the West. These newly trained terrorists must escape detection on the way back and then proceed with their plot without being discovered by vigilant law enforcement agencies. We cannot relax our worldwide vigilance against global Islamist terrorism, because it may indeed become resurgent. While al Qaeda Central is still very much in hiding, the al Qaeda social movement has flourished, fueled by worldwide Muslim resentment against the Western invasion and occupation of Iraq.

Homegrown Terrorism

The worldwide governmental hostility to al Qaeda Central and its affiliated terrorist social movement has broken up the physical links between them, intercepted or monitored their communications and generally disrupted their financial links. The informal groups forming the post-9/11 and post-Iraq third wave of global Islamist terrorism are still being self generated as described above, but with few exceptions can no longer establish any physical link to al Qaeda Central. Disconnected from one another, each of these existing or newly formed networks is basically on its own. Because of the greater scrutiny at borders, members of these networks hesitate to travel to another country and have begun to conduct operations within their own borders. This "new" phenomenon was labeled the homegrown terrorist. The attacks in Casablanca, Spain, London, and Amsterdam are successful examples, but the arrests of thousands of terrorist plotters in Britain, America, Spain, France, Morocco, Algeria, Tunisia, the Netherlands, Germany, Denmark, Sweden, Norway, Italy, Bosnia, Egypt, Jordan, Syria, Saudi Arabia, Kuwait, Yemen, Pakistan, Malaysia, Indonesia, Canada, and Australia show that this phenomenon is far more widespread than indicated by the small number of countries in which terrorists have succeeded in killing people.

This homegrown phenomenon is not new. The dynamic of self-organized networks and their radicalization in the host country in the third wave is the same as it was in the second wave before 9/11. The second wave had both homegrown and expatriate groups, which could link up with al Qaeda Central by going to Afghanistan. Now the third wave groups generally no longer can do so, and so they are left to their own devices. What distinguishes the groups in the respective waves is not the process of radicalization, but their ability to connect with al Qaeda Central and their different homegrown/expatriate mixtures.

The concept of homegrown indicates that the members of these mainly Muslim diaspora groups in the West were born and radicalized in the host country. In the second wave, host Western governments did not appreciate that these groups radicalized locally because their ideology was foreign, imported from the Middle East. It was assumed that the second generation of Muslim immigrants would not pose a problem to their host countries, but would direct their ire against the Middle East (Egypt, Jordan, Yemen, and Algeria), Europe (Bosnia), Central Asia (Chechnya), or South Asia (Kashmir).

The exception to this reaction to the second wave was France, which had suffered from several rounds of Islamist bombings dating back to the mid-1980s. In the mid-1990s, France clamped down on its Islamist radicals, who took refuge in the neighboring European countries and especially London, which earned the French label "Londonistan." But even the French authorities blamed the radicalization of these homegrown second-wave groups on the developments in Algeria and did not appreciate the domestic dynamics of the radicalization. Meanwhile, with the influx of French Muslim radical expatriates in London, British authorities attributed their radicalization to events in France and not to domestic factors. So, they missed the radicalization of people like Habib Zacarias Moussaoui, the alleged twentieth 9/11 bomber, who was convicted of belonging to al Qaeda in 2006; Richard Reid, the "shoe bomber," who pled guilty to the December 2001 attempt to blow up an airplane en route to Miami; and the Courtailler brothers, David and Jerome, who were later convicted of terrorist activities in France and the Netherlands. The list is long, but the British assumed that this was a foreign problem and did not appreciate that the radicalization of these people took place in England, not in France. They dismissed the radicalization of Richard Reid, who had grown up in Britain, because he seemed to socialize with these French expatriate networks.

It is true that expatriates were a very prominent element of the second wave, and many of these had come to the West as students, where they became radicalized. Since many of these well-educated expatriates travelled to Afghanistan in hopes of being selected for al Qaeda Central, it was easy for European governments to miss the process of radicalization that took place on their soil and simply blame it on indoctrination in al Qaeda camps in Afghanistan. Yet there were already hints that radicalization was a homegrown phenomenon. During the second wave, several second-generation sons of Pakistani immigrants like Ahmed Omar Sheikh were radicalized in England and went to fight in South Asia for the Islamist cause. Other British-born and raised Islamist militants went to Yemen to participate in the bizarre kidnapping and killing of Western expatriates in December 1998.[12] What European governments missed was that homegrown radicals actively sought out al Qaeda and not the other way around. They were already radicalized by the time they went to Afghanistan.

To be fair, the pre-9/11 second-wave threat appeared to be an external one, as most of the attempts were carried out by expatriates. The leadership of the wave of bombings in Paris in the summer of 1995 came from Algeria and the financing might have come from bin Laden, even though the foot soldiers were homegrown. The 1998 bombings of the U.S. embassies in Nairobi and Dar es Salaam were organized and directed from Khartoum and Afghanistan. Algerians who lived in Canada were responsible for the millennium plot to bomb the Los Angeles airport. The USS *Cole* attack was orchestrated from Afghanistan. The Strasbourg Christmas Market bombing plot of December 2000 was orchestrated by Algerians living in London and funded from Afghanistan. Of course, the coordination, leadership, financing, and perpetrators of the 9/11 operation came from outside the United States. All these plots seemed to come from outside the target country, obscuring the domestic radicalization process. This meant that the strategy to counter this threat was to deny expatriate entrance into the host country and fortify the host country's borders against those outsiders who tried to sneak in illegally.

The comfortable belief that there was no internal problem in Western countries was shattered when third-wave terrorists no longer had any significant physical link to al Qaeda Central. In the third wave, the threat was recognized for what it is, namely endogenous to host countries, coming from within. Crossing international borders is now more difficult for terrorists, both because of the much stricter security measures and the greater coordination among nations attempting to combat terrorism. Most of the third wave plots involved local homegrown terrorists. This shift from an exogenous to an endogenous

threat makes it appear that the dynamics of mobilization into the terrorist social movement has changed. This is not so. The dynamics of becoming part of
the social movement are the same as before, but now that young people consider themselves part of it, they have greater difficulty getting in touch with al
Qaeda Central and therefore stay at home. Al Qaeda Central does not know
who its followers are, and is reduced to accepting them after the adherents declare themselves in an act of terrorism. Their official acceptance into al Qaeda
comes after the fact, as in Madrid. In effect, the bombing itself is the offering to
al Qaeda Central leaders for official recognition and admission into the ranks
of global Islamist terrorism. The bombing is the de facto official initiation ceremony into the al Qaeda social movement. Since the third-wave threat comes
within each host country, the host government countermeasures evolved to
counter the second-wave outside threat (denial of entry) no longer work.

Incidentally, the 2007 plot to blow up a nightclub in West London and
the Glasgow airport reminds us that the third wave can also include expatriates, who might look very similar to the second-wave expatriates. The dynamics of homegrown and expatriate radicalizations proceed in parallel during
each wave, with different relative magnitudes, and should not be neglected.
Expatriate terrorists dominated the second wave, now homegrown terrorists
dominate the third.

Between Waves

The attacks of 9/11 galvanized the U.S. government to enter into a full-scale
war against al Qaeda Central. The invasion of Iraq galvanized young Muslims
worldwide to join the fight against the West and become the third wave. Span-
ning these two events was a transition between the two waves.

The invasion of Afghanistan by coalition forces did not generate widespread negative reaction from Muslims worldwide. The Taliban had never been
popular with the Muslim world, except for a very small minority who refused to
see its drawbacks and limitation (only three countries recognized the Taliban as
Afghanistan's legitimate government: Pakistan, the United Arab Emirates, and
Saudi Arabia). In the 1990s, when Afghanistan experienced its worst drought in
years and the population suffered mass starvation, the governing Taliban regime
was unable to aid the population because there was no functional central gov-

ernment. Moreover, the Taliban's main concern was not the physical welfare of the population, but its spiritual salvation—that the Afghan people abide by the tenets of the Taliban's interpretation of Islamic law. The most visible part of the government was the Committee to Command Virtue and Forbid Vice. Members of this committee enforced Taliban dictates among the population: that women were covered and did not work or go to school; that men had a beard of the required length; and that no one watched television, listened to music, or flew a kite. The only positive element that they had brought to Afghanistan was security. This was a major achievement after two decades of internal fighting among local warlords. Whether the population lived or died was left up to God. Most Muslims around the world found such a disregard for human life repulsive, and hence, were not sorry to see the Taliban go.

In the months following the toppling of the Taliban, there was a worldwide surge in terrorist attacks from the second wave. Richard Reid's plot in December 2001; the Singapore plot to blow up the U.S., British, French, and Israeli embassies in December 2001; the Djerba bombing in Tunisia in April 2002; the Gibraltar plot to blow up military vessels in the Strait of Gibraltar in May 2002; the *Limburg* bombing in October 2002 in the Persian Gulf; the Bali bombing of October 2002, which killed more than two hundred people, many of them Australian tourists; the Mombassa Hotel Paradise bombing in November 2002; the French Ricin plot of December 2002; and Iyman Faris's plot to topple the Brooklyn Bridge in March 2003. All of these attempts or plots were carried out by the second generation of al Qaeda and directly linked to al Qaeda Central. All the perpetrators or plotters had received directives from al Qaeda Central to scatter around the world and continue the campaign of terror worldwide. They had all received training in al Qaeda camps in Afghanistan and were directed from Pakistan or Afghanistan, and most had received financial support from the central organization. However, by March 2003, a large number of major al Qaeda Central terrorists had been captured or killed, including some of the top military commanders: Subhi Mohammed abu Sittah (aka Abu Hafs al-Masri or Mohammed Atef, really part of the first wave); Abdal Rahim al-Nashiri (abu Bilal al-Makki); Waleed Mohammed Tawfiq bin Attash (Khallad); and Khalid Sheikh Mohammed (Mokhtar). There was some evidence that the second-wave campaign was fading away.

In March 2003 the United States invaded Iraq, supported by a small coalition of countries. There was considerable international resistance to this

military action and intense protest from the Muslim world. The main ratio-
nales for the invasion—namely that Iraq was a threat because of its weapons
of mass destruction and that it was linked to al Qaeda and the 9/11 atrocities—were later exposed as false. No weapons of mass destructions were discovered, and the 9/11 Commission report clearly refuted the alleged link between Saddam Hussein and the 9/11 plot.[13] While the White House initially
blamed the U.S. intelligence community for an "intelligence failure," reports
later emerged that the administration had intimidated the intelligence community to issue a NIE that was consistent with the administration's ambition
in Iraq.

The Muslim world's outraged response to Iraq stood in stark contrast to
its nearly mute response to Afghanistan. The U.S. government appeared as a
hypocritical bully, throwing its weight around and embarking on a war against
Islam. Compounding the outrage were the secret detentions at the U.S. prison
camp at Guantánamo, the scenes of humiliation and torture at Abu Ghraib,
and the reports of the kidnapping of prominent Muslims in Europe and their
rendition to countries where they could be tortured. Especially frustrating to
Muslims was America's apparent double standard of turning a blind eye to Israeli occupation in the West Bank. All this hardened the belief that the United
States was indeed at war with Islam.

U.S. policy, especially in Iraq, has poured oil on a fire that was in the process of being extinguished. The second wave was disappearing as the appeal
of global Salafi terrorism was waning among Muslim youths before the Iraqi
invasion. Of course, there were remnants of this wave, consisting of peripheral
members of these networks. These "members" were uninvolved friends and
relatives of full-fledged Islamist terrorists. The worldwide crackdown on the
terrorists radicalized some of these previously hesitant friends and relatives,
who through their social bonds belonged to the larger networks that included
the second-wave terrorist groups. These peripheral members would become
the vanguard of the third wave. Products of this transition were the members
of the Crevice case, Mohamed Sidique Khan of 7/7 London bombing fame
(but not the rest of the group, which was definitely third wave), and Serhane
bin Abdelmajid Fakhet and Jamal Zougam, two of the 2004 Madrid bombers,
who were linked with the second-wave group around Barakat Yarkas in Madrid. The transition perpetrators, who seem to surf both waves, are probably
confusing the "al Qaeda Central on the march" advocates.

After the invasion of Iraq, the types of terrorist attacks that the third wave perpetrated had no or very faint connection to al Qaeda Central. Beginning in 2004, the clear operational links (command, control, training, personnel, or financing) of the second-wave operations gradually disappeared. The Madrid bombings of March 2004; the Asparagus 18 case in Belgium of March 2004; the Yanbu raid in Saudi Arabia in May 2004; the Taba, Egypt, bombings in October 2004; the Nova plot to blow up the Madrid courthouse in October 2004; the Hofstad Group's assassination of Theo van Gogh and its attempt to bomb Schipol airport in Amsterdam in 2004; the Khan al-Khalili bombing in Cairo in April 2005; the Sharm el-Sheikh bombings in Sinai in July 2005; the Sarajevo bombing plot in October 2005; the Melbourne and Sydney bombing plots (Operation Pendennis) in November 2005; the Toronto plot in June 2006; the plot to bomb the Sears Tower in Chicago in June 2006; the Koblenz train bombing plot in Germany in July 2006; the Odense plot to bomb facilities in Denmark in September 2006; the plot to bomb London and Glasgow in June 2007—not one of these had any significant al Qaeda Central link. Moreover, when the perpetrators were arrested or had left videos behind, they all mentioned Iraq as their prime motivation.

This list of terrorist attacks *outside* Iraq convincingly refutes the post hoc U.S. administration justification for the invasion of Iraq: "we are fighting them there so we don't have to fight them here." In Chapter 5, I argued that global Islamist terrorist attacks in the United States are unlikely because the al Qaeda ideologies do not resonate with the personal experience of American Muslims. Unless the government allowed outsiders to come to the United States to carry out terrorist operations on U.S. soil, it would be unlikely for the U.S. government to have to "fight them here," meaning the continental United States.

The Iraqi invasion and occupation has certainly increased the pool of terrorists worldwide. Some from the neighboring countries of Saudi Arabia, Syria, and Jordan come to fight American forces in Iraq. So, we are definitely fighting them there. However, only a few from the West have gone to Iraq. Most have stayed home and, inspired by Iraq, they are conducting operations in places that they seldom targeted before in Europe, Canada, and Australia. So if we expand the meaning of "here" to include these new places, we are also "fighting them here." From a few hundred terrorists in the second wave, there are now thousands in the third wave.

The Third Wave

Groups forming in the third wave become radicalized on their own initiative—even the "preachers of hate" can no longer espouse violence openly without being arrested or deported. These groups are autonomous and unknown to al Qaeda Central. These new groups must finance their own operations. However, from the evidence in Europe, terrorist operations are not expensive, and they do not need to raise much money. Since many of the new terrorist aspirants receive public assistance because of unemployment or refugee status, their operations are often financed by the host state via these payments.[14] The rest is either from their jobs or from petty crime or drug traffic. Prevention of terrorist operations through the interdiction of financial resources may work for large, expensive, coordinated attacks, but not for these self-financed actions. The major obstacle to a terrorist operation is not finance but expertise.

The major impact of not being able to link up with al Qaeda Central is lack of access to technical expertise. By default, most of the third-wave terrorist groups are self-trained. This explains the deterioration in the quality of operations and tradecraft in the past few years, which allows many potential terrorists to be detected and arrested before they come close to carrying out an operation. Many of the new terrorist groups perform paramilitary exercises together. Some like to play paintball and pretend that they are mujahedin fighting in Afghanistan or Iraq. Others engage in paramilitary camping on weekends, strapping on a thirty-pound backpack and running up and down some hills, again pretending to be glorious mujahedin. At the very least, these exercises solidify their esprit de corps and determination to carry out operations.

For the third wave, the instructions for building bombs are on the Internet. However, it takes a courageous person to mix the chemicals to make bombs, because any small mistake can result in death. Even experienced bomb makers have mishaps and many are missing a finger or two. Most of the bombs manufactured from Internet tutorials, like the May 2003 Casablanca bombings and the April 2005 Cairo Khan al-Khalili bombing, have not been very powerful, or they have simply failed, like the attempted bombings in Koblenz in the summer of 2006, the failed attempts of Yehya Kadouri, the Dutch teenage lone wolf, or the plots in Britain in June 2007. These new groups do, however, become dangerous when they hook up with a trained bomb maker, as the

London 7/7 bombers group did. But even training does not guarantee success, as the London 7/21 group demonstrated.

These third-wave groups form in the same way the second-wave groups formed, so they are already friends and family. Most have known each other all their lives. Locally, their communications are informal and they do not need sophisticated and expensive equipment to stay in touch. They are therefore typically difficult to detect and monitor. If they try to make contact with al Qaeda Central, they can be detected and arrested as was Ryan Anderson, a National Guardsman arrested in February 2004 for spying for al Qaeda.

There has been a dramatic expansion of new groups in the third wave. Unlike the second wave, when al Qaeda Central picked the best, brightest, and most committed of the volunteers who came to the training camps, now anyone can call himself an al Qaeda warrior; no one will stop him from doing so. There is no initiation ceremony or any entry barrier for anyone who declares himself part of the al Qaeda social movement. This means that the average third-wave global Islamist terrorist is far less skilled and adept than the terrorists prior to 9/11. This lack of good tradecraft accounts for the continued increase in their arrests worldwide. But law enforcement authorities should not become complacent, the number of wannabe terrorists remains large, and by the law of averages some are bound to be smart and bold enough to pull off an attack.

The informality of these local networks makes it difficult to identify who is a terrorist and who is simply a sympathizer—or a potential terrorist who did not yet have the opportunity to carry out an operation. There is no clear boundary to the networks, which often include loose acquaintances, distant relatives, as well as much closer friends and family who actively encourage violence. There is a spectrum of activities, from moral support to actual operations. Within a network, not everyone is as enthusiastic as the zealots who try to entice their friends into perpetrating a terrorist act. Some who are a bit reluctant to join in are nonetheless fully aware of their friends' activities, and will not betray them out of loyalty. This variation in the intensity of commitment and involvement in global Islamist terrorism complicates the picture. The loose networks of varying involvement present difficulties for prosecutors. Juries have become skeptical of district attorneys' inflated claims against Muslim defendants on terrorism charges when the evidence at court looks skimpy. Likewise, the Muslim community is carefully following these trials for evidence of prejudice or persecution. Apparently unwarranted harsh punishment of those who had a minimal role in terrorist attempts generates a feeling of moral outrage among their friends, who may then become inspired to overcome their reluctance in order to avenge their friends. Quite a few family members or friends at first rejected terrorism, but became so angry after the arrest and harsh punishment of their loved ones that they later became terrorists.

Some third-wave terrorists attempt to get in touch with al Qaeda Central in order to receive the blessing of its leaders, obtain training from the group, become involved in fighting American forces in Iraq or Afghanistan, or solicit funding for terrorist operations. They travel to Pakistan, Turkey, Iran, Yemen, Egypt, Syria, and Saudi Arabia in order to link up with al Qaeda. Most are unsuccessful and return disappointed, or are arrested by local law enforcement authorities and repatriated to their home countries. A few succeed in reaching Afghanistan, Iraq, or Chechnya, where they dream about becoming martyrs for the cause and killing Americans or Russians in uniform. In general, young Muslims are most attracted to the appeal of a glorious death on behalf of their imagined ummah (the worldwide Muslim community). Their preference is to die fighting the hated American military. But except for the countries bordering Iraq, it is now difficult for young Muslims to go to Iraq and fulfill their desire. As a result, many choose to act locally, and become heroes to their local friends and relatives that comprise the informal network of potential terrorists around them.

This desire to become a martyr marks a major difference between this wave and the preceding one. Members of the second wave went to Afghanistan for training and to join the Al Qaeda social movement. They stayed in Afghanistan, then returned to their country or went elsewhere to carry out terrorist operations worldwide. The return to the West of trained terrorists, who know how to make bombs and carry out other terrorist operations, was an especially dangerous situation. In contrast, the new wave goes to Afghanistan, Iraq, Chechnya, or Kashmir to die. Until now, very few have returned. Most have taken themselves out of the fight through death.

Starting in 2003, some new terrorists have been turned around by their trainers in Pakistan. These young men hoped to cover themselves with glory by sacrificing themselves. Their trainers in Pakistan convinced them that they might be more useful for the social movement if they took the war to the West by carrying out their sacrifice in their host countries. The return of these now trained third-wave terrorists, who can reconnect with their former friends and relatives who did not have the opportunity to experience the new "training camps," is a new threat for Western countries. The returnees are often treated as local heroes and use their enhanced reputations to help radicalize family members and former friends. This link between the few trained terrorists and the latent networks of sympathizers can have devastating effects for the West. There is evidence that this was part of the history of the networks that carried out the 7/7 London bombings, the attempted 7/21 London plot, the Melbourne and Sydney bombing plots of November 2005, the Toronto plot of June 2006 (Operation Osage), and the August 2006 British plot to blow up several airplanes over the Atlantic.

Leaderless Jihad

In this chapter, I examined several factors in the evolution of the structure of global Islamist terrorist network. the breakup of the global network; the hostile local environment; the hardening of national borders; and the availability of the Internet. The process of radicalization that generates small, local, self-organized groups in a hostile habitat but linked through the Internet also leads to a disconnected global network, the leaderless jihad. This is the natural outcome of a bottom-up mechanism of group formation in a specific environment shaped by top-down counterterrorist strategy. If the habitat changes, the network will adapt to its new niche. In Waziristan, its environment suddenly became less hostile after the tribal leaders' agreement with the Pakistani army. The central network regrouped, consolidated, and became bold enough to test the limits of its local opportunities by setting up mini-camps for terrorist wannabes. If the whole of Pakistan or Afghanistan becomes more receptive to al Qaeda, there will definitely be a resurgence, for the network will flourish in its friendlier niche.

Before the advent of the Internet, the evolution of a leaderless form of terrorism was an admission of failure of traditional terrorism. It was a last attempt to keep the struggle alive in the face of overwhelming opposition. The theory of leaderless resistance was developed by Louis Beam to continue the right-wing militias' fight against the U.S. government despite overwhelming FBI opposition.[15] In the global Islamist terrorism context, Hakim (better known as

143

Abu Musab al-Suri or Mustapha Setmariam Nasr) developed a similar analysis in his book, *The Call to Global Islamic Resistance*.[16] It is a strategy of fighting an overwhelming enemy using self-organizing clandestine networks. Hierarchical organizations are easy prey to efficient state law enforcement agencies. The solution is to convince like-minded people to form independent groups that will continue the fight without any linkage to leaders or other groups, for these linkages are the vulnerability of the network. These networks operate independently and are protected from detection if members of another group are questioned. Its leaderless and disconnected structure constitutes at the same time its strength (in terms of survivability and adaptability) and its weakness (lack of clear direction and political goals).

The third wave of global Islamist terrorism has degraded into a leaderless jihad.[17] Each local network carries out its attacks without coordination from above. But while this campaign of terror lacks a firm overarching strategy, it still has an agenda set by general guidelines found on the Internet, which is the virtual glue maintaining a weak appearance of unity. Without the Internet, a leaderless terrorist social movement would scatter all over the political space without any direction. The Internet makes the existence of a leaderless jihad possible. However, without direction, it cannot coalesce into a political organization able to govern a country. The leaderless jihad can be a terrorist network and nothing more. Its strength is that it is all things to all people, who can project their favorite fantasies onto the movement.

The common agenda of the third wave found on the Internet is basically anti-Western political violence, which is the lowest common denominator of the various ideologies of global Islamist terrorism. These ideologies are woven together in a general narrative of a world polarized between good (Salafi Islam) and evil (the West). But they do not add up to a coherent political strategy and there is little evidence of a grand coordinated international plan. Of course, a continuing pattern of political violence exists throughout the world, with each perpetrator claiming to be part of the overall strategy of global Islamist terrorists, but these attempts, successful or not, are neither coordinated nor focused in a way that reflects long-term goals or strategic aims. Each local group lives in its own world, connected to the overall social movement through the Internet. Their attempts are all ad hoc, each with its local internal logic and directed against its own local targets. Commentators and journalists are quick to imagine an overall coordination and conspiracy to these events,[18] but no central coordinator, whether part of al Qaeda Central or not, has been found or even suggested in the vast majority of terrorist operations.

The little coherence that the al Qaeda social movement displays is mediated through a virtual market. In effect, through its spokesmen Osama bin Laden or Ayman al-Zawahiri, al Qaeda Central advertises demands for terrorist operations on the Internet and local networks provide terrorist activities, just as the marketplace coordinates the distribution of goods and services in a country. No one is in charge of the market. Each buyer or provider pursues his or her own interest, but the overall pattern is that everyone is fed, housed, and clothed. Such coordination does not require a feeding, housing, or clothing czar. The coordination is generated spontaneously from the bottom up, through the "invisible hand" of the market. This is identical to Adam Smith's argument about the emerging overall pattern of coordination of goods and services by market forces from below. "As every individual . . . intends only his own gain, and he is in this, as in many other cases, led by an invisible hand to promote an end which was no part of his intention. By pursuing his own interest he frequently promotes that of the society more effectually than when he really intends to promote it."[19] Each small terrorist network pursues its own activity for its own local reasons, and in doing so promotes far more effectively the overall goals and strategy of the al Qaeda terrorist social movement than al Qaeda Central could. The overall pattern of international violence is an emergent trend far more effectively carried out by "market forces" than by a single intentional entity. Markets are probably far more efficient at organizing large-scale activities than bureaucracies. This difficulty of national bureaucracies trying to combat terrorist market forces will be revisited in the next chapter.

The leaderless social movement has other limitations. To survive, it requires a constant stream of new violent actions to hold the interest of potential newcomers to the movement, create the impression of visible progress toward a goal, and give potential recruits a vicarious experience before they take the initiative to engage in their own terrorist activities. The Internet permits the terror movement to survive any loss, no matter how important. Jihadi websites survive as well because of the built-in redundancy of the Internet and the promiscuity of forum members. I am often asked whether global Islamist terrorism could survive the death of bin Laden or Zawahiri. The answer is, of course, yes. The real direction today comes from the continued discourse on the Internet. Sayyed Qutb and Sheikh Abdullah Azzam continue to be a source of inspiration for young radical Muslims long after their deaths. Their memory is kept alive through the discussions in the forums, reinforcing the resolve of the newcomers to continue their work.

Although a virtual leaderless social movement may survive even the most repressive state strategy, it is also self-limiting. It dares not move beyond this stage for fear of creating a leadership that might finally provide a target for effective law enforcement agencies. It cannot negotiate this shift from violence to political compromise for it does not have any method to terminate violence, except by general consensus on the Internet, which is probably impossible. Some more militant individuals trying to establish their reputation as tough-minded will always take the challenge and push the envelope of violence.

A leaderless jihad also suffers from other weaknesses. It is vulnerable to whatever may diminish its appeal among the young. By definition a leaderless social movement has no way to impose discipline on its participants. It is permanently at their mercy. If its leaders become discredited by being exposed for making false claims, followers may simply desert them. If its ultimate goals become discredited over time, as the collapse of the Soviet Union put to rest the dream of a Communist utopia, followers may again desert the movement. But I suspect its greatest vulnerability might be that new dreams of glory will displace old Islamist dreams and make them irrelevant. With any of these scenarios, global Islamist terrorism will fade away, no longer able to attract new adherents.

The leaderless jihad will probably fade away for such internal reasons. The danger is that too vigorous an eradication campaign might be counterproductive and actually prolong the life of the social movement. The eradication efforts may be seen as unjust and therefore attract new recruits to the movement, just when it was dying out on its own. A measure of restraint is necessary to prevent new members from joining. The leaderless jihad should be allowed to expire on its own. What can be done to accelerate this demise is the subject of the final chapter.

EIGHT

Combating Global Islamist Terrorism

How can we defeat the threat of global Islamist terrorism? First, it is critical to be explicit about our goals, and then fashion a strategy according to those goals and our understanding of the enemy. Most of the officially proposed solutions to counter this threat suffer from too strong a reliance on ideology. The July 2006 *National Strategy for Combating Terrorism* (NSCT) continues to advocate the advancement of democracy to combat terrorism.[1] This approach is misguided and continues to show its deficiencies six years after it was first articulated. The U.S. strategy of promoting democracy and freedom in the Middle East as the antidote to terrorism has not borne any fruit in the region.[2] This strategy is calculated to win the "war of ideas" among the converted, namely conservative Americans who deeply believe in the values of freedom and democracy. Although the U.S. government needs the support of voters at home, to counter the terrorist threat it is essential to focus on the terrorists. Let us examine what a truly effective program to combat this form of terrorism would entail.

Establishing Homeland Security

The ultimate goal of any campaign to fight terrorism is homeland security: the protection of the population. The fight against global Islamist terrorism is no exception. We must not let ourselves be carried away by our own rhetoric, uttered for domestic political gains at election time. It does not help further this goal to accuse one's political opponents of "being soft on terrorism," "playing into the terrorists' hands," or "capitulating to terrorists." These slogans are designed to score political points with the electorate. Repeating them does nothing to develop an effective strategy against the threat; it encourages each party to prove that it is "tougher" on terrorism and forces it to take aggressive actions against Muslim fence sitters, which backfires, as we shall see. Politicians should immediately stop playing on the fears of the American public and end the posturing to show who is toughest on terrorism. What should matter is finding the most effective means to counter the threat. Security should be the metric—a term the government is so fond of using—against which all strategy and tactics must be measured.

What would ensure homeland security against the specific threat that we confront? About sixty years ago, when the United States faced a menacing Soviet Union, George Kennan analyzed that threat in his long telegram that became the basis of his classic article "The Sources of Soviet Conduct" in *Foreign Affairs* under the pseudonym "X."[3] As the title suggests, the article discussed the essence of Soviet behavior and concluded that the threat was self-contained, and that the United States should enter "with reasonable confidence upon a policy of firm containment." The notion of containment for Kennan was geographic, based on frustrating the expansionist aims of an enemy. Given this book's analysis of the violent Islamist threat, what kind of strategy would best promote homeland security?

The threat confronting the United States consists of both al Qaeda Central, the remnant of the organization that committed the 9/11 atrocities, and the leaderless al Qaeda social movement. Members of al Qaeda Central must be eliminated or brought to justice. However, the al Qaeda social movement constitutes the real threat, because its attempts to inflict violence upon the United States could garner the support of potentially millions of Muslims (only a handful of whom would carry out the attacks). To counter this greater threat is the real challenge for the United States (the NSCT, to its credit, also makes this point).

In devising a strategy, it is important to understand whether the danger the United States faces is in fact a threat to the existence of the nation. The Soviet Union had thousands of nuclear missiles poised at the United States, ready to destroy the entire country within a few hours. This is definitely not the case with global Islamist terrorism. September 11, despite being an atrocity and the largest single terrorist event in world history, did not come close to wiping out the United States. Even the worst imaginable event, a biological or a nuclear strike by terrorists, will not destroy the nation. In fact, at this point in history, only the United States could obliterate the United States. If the United States transforms its fight against global Islamist terrorism into a war against Islam, which might mobilize all Muslims against the United States, then this expanded enemy could become an existential threat. However, only America has the power to transform this small threat into a much larger one. The key is to keep the threat contained in its present limit.

Containment for the Twenty-First Century

Will the threat grow or will it fade by itself? George Kennan argued that the Soviet threat had inherent limits, and the United States should simply ride out the threat. The previous chapter argued that global Islamist terrorism is also a self-limiting threat. For all its emphasis on building a just world, based on the community of the Prophet, the projected utopia is not an appealing one. The few manifestations of this utopia, the Taliban regime in Afghanistan and some parts of Algeria or the Philippines during the 1990s, were not inspiring for most young Muslim people. Indeed, a good countermeasure against this threat is to advertise what life was like under the Taliban, which was never popular with Muslims and did not motivate them to take up arms against the West.

Moreover, al Qaeda Central has been unable to forge any strategic alliances. It is hunted everywhere and has managed to make only enemies. Indeed, this failure to attain protected sanctuary is the very reason that the third wave evolved, out of necessity, into a "leaderless jihad." This is the only form in which it can still survive.

The key to the social movement's continued existence will be its ability to attract young Muslims to its ranks. The sources of its appeal to young people are not universal, but are sustained by U.S. actions that are perceived to be a war on Islam. Without this fuel, young Muslims will no longer find the hopes and aspiration of their elders to be "cool" and will move on to new ones. The fact that rioting young French immigrants in the fall 2005 self-consciously re-

149

jected militant Islam as a frame for their action might be indicative that the message no longer appeals to French Muslim fifteen- or sixteen-year-olds, as it did with their older brothers. Elsewhere right now there is a "jihadi cool" talk on the Internet, but generations have a way of defining themselves anew, mainly in contrast to the older generation, which by nature is no longer considered "cool." Young Muslims are attracted to the goals of al Qaeda by dreams of glory and the thrill of clandestine activities. As al Qaeda and those acting on its behalf continue to commit ever greater atrocities, this appeal will fade and be replaced with new ways of covering oneself with glory and new forms of "cool" thrills.

All of this leads me to conclude that just as the threat from al Qaeda is self-limiting, so is its appeal, and global Islamist terrorism will probably disappear for internal reasons—if the United States has the sense to allow it to continue on its course and fade away. This need not be a long war, unless American policy makes it so. Thus far, in the fight against global Islamist terrorism, the United States has committed grave strategic mistakes that fuel the ire of angry young Muslims. The correct strategy should be one of restraint with respect to the greater challenge: preventing young Muslims from joining the terrorist social movement (or what the NSCT calls the long-term approach).

At present the U.S. government has focused on a strategy of pursuing high-value targets in the hope of decapitating al Qaeda and allowing the movement to implode. As the NSCT states, "the loss of a leader can degrade a group's cohesiveness and in some cases may trigger its collapse."[4] This may be true in some cases, but in this instance, it is wishful thinking. The loss of Osama bin Laden or Ayman al Zawahiri will not have this predicted effect. The leaderless jihad will survive, for it is not especially cohesive and lacks central operational command and control. It is important to bring the principal leaders to justice for past atrocities, but their loss in terms of the future of the movement will be easily overcome.

Because the potential long-term threat—hostility against the United States growing beyond the few thousands in the al Qaeda social movement to encompass tens of millions of Muslims—is far more serious than any present threat, the approach to fighting global Islamist terrorism beyond the present situation is the real challenge. It is definitely a battle for the hearts and minds of Muslims, who might be tempted to join the ranks of the al Qaeda social movement. Like the strategy proposed by Kennan sixty years ago, the U.S. program to fight this danger should be based on an accurate understanding of the internal dynamics and behavior of the enemy.

If national security is the true aim of the fight against this type of terrorism, and the threat is self-limiting, then the logical strategy is one of containment while waiting for the threat to disintegrate for internal reasons—just as it was our strategy in dealing with the much greater and truly existential threat from the Soviet Union. The key is to accelerate and not slow down or stop this process of internal decay. Nothing should be done that will make the threat grow to include almost all Muslims; such an escalation may become an existential threat to the United States.

With the first two waves of global Islamist terrorism, the threat came from outside the West, from the radicalized expatriates, who trained in the camps of Afghanistan. It could have simply been countered by denying trained terrorists access to the West. This was not done before 9/11. Aggressive border protection, especially at airports worldwide, has effectively countered this threat. It should be continued, lest terrorists be tempted again to come and wreak havoc in the West.

With the third wave, the threat is now internal to the West, and border security is no longer relevant. A successful strategy will disrupt the process of radicalization before it reaches its violent end.

Take the Glory out of Terrorism

Over the past century and a half, young people have joined terrorist movements for individual and collective glory, to build a better world on behalf of an imagined constituency.[5] Our strategy should be to take the glory and thrill out of terrorism. It should be based on how potential terrorists view themselves and the world.

Terrorists want to be elevated to the status of a person on an FBI wanted poster. In this sense, distributing the pictures of terrorists in areas such as Pakistan in a misguided attempt to get the population to denounce them has exactly the opposite effect: the Rewards for Justice Program, which posts and ranks terrorists according to the price that the U.S. government is willing to pay for information leading to their capture, has been a general failure and instead turns nobodies into heroes.[6] Very few have turned in their now famous friends and acquaintances. This program is based on an American ethnocentric economic model, while terrorists and their friends reject materialism for status and respect.

Terrorists see themselves as selfless heroes devoted to their less fortunate brethren. They are sacrificing their lives for a greater good, and therefore feel morally different from criminals who are out for material gain. Their fight is for justice and fairness, manifested in a desire to punish the perceived oppressors—usually the United States. Anything that elevates them to the status of heroes in their friends' eyes encourages them. Their constituency consists of other like-minded groups that might join the al Qaeda social movement and now populate the Internet. They are heroes to this audience. Martyrdom lifts them from insignificance and paradoxically ensures their immortality. The prospect of such exaltation is intoxicating. A heroic literature with songs and poems glorifies their martyrdom on the Internet.

The terrorists ask for nothing more than to fight American soldiers. The courage to fight this apparently invincible enemy covers them with glory in the eyes of their sympathizers. The United States has thus committed a strategic mistake by relying on its unmatched military might to stop the threat by capturing and killing Islamist militants. It has militarized the fight against these terrorists, as enshrined in the 2006 *Quadrennial Defense Review Report.*[7] The sight of U.S. soldiers fighting Muslims around the world triggers moral outrage and inspires sympathizers to join the movement. The sight of Muslims fighting back provides a heroic model to emulate. The result is that military action creates more terrorists than it eliminates. To young Muslims, the conflict is a modern version of Robin Hood fighting the evil sheriff's henchmen.

The pursuit of a military strategy was initially popular in the United States, but it is completely counterproductive and self-defeating because it undermines the ultimate goal of protecting the U.S. homeland. This is emphatically the case with the invasion and occupation of Iraq, which has radicalized a new wave of young jihadists who have been led to believe that America is establishing a base in the Middle East in order to exploit oil resources and dominate the region.

Use of the military should be a last resort. Indeed, the only military role in the overall strategy to fight global Islamist terrorism should be to deny terrorists sanctuary. Al Qaeda's creation of a sanctuary in Afghanistan contributed to 9/11 by giving al Qaeda the ability to coordinate the operation internationally. The presence of a sanctuary allows terrorists the leisure to transform a local operation into an international one. Sanctuary denial, especially in ungoverned regions like Afghanistan or the FATA, is an appropriate military strategy. However, American troops cannot linger on the ground after the operation is over, for their continued presence—labeled as occupation—will become a rallying cry for the enemy. Military operations must be conducted swiftly, precisely, with as much restraint as possible to minimize collateral civilian deaths and with as low a profile as possible in order to deny terrorists the argument that this campaign is a war against Islam. The American public must be educated about the need to resist the temptation to militarize the conflict.

The most effective way to remove the glory from terrorism is to reduce the terrorists to common criminals. There is no glory in being taken to prison in handcuffs. No jihadi website carries such pictures, as opposed to the thousands of video clips of American military vehicles blowing up, as well as martyrs blowing themselves up in the vicinity of uniformed American personnel. Arrested terrorists will fade into oblivion and no longer inspire young people to join the fight against the West.

This strategy of taking the glory out of terrorism also means putting a stop to press conferences at which representatives from the Department of Justice, the Federal Bureau of Investigation, and the Department of Homeland Security hold self-congratulatory celebrations of their newest victories in the "war on terror." The press conferences are good for electioneering, but they are counterproductive. Homeland security will be better served through quiet arrests and prosecutions of potential terrorists. This apparent neglect of terrorists and their reduction to common criminals robs them of the stage they crave and undermines the effective promotion of their cause through propaganda by the deed. Reducing the terrorists' profiles deprives their potential followers of seeing them as feared major players.

If in a civilian jurisdiction, the ensuing trials should be low-key demonstrations of the poverty of their ideas and the vicious nature of their acts, with prominent testimony from victims and their families presented at the penalty phase of their trials. These trials must be above reproach, which means that the government must present a strong case before a jury, something it has so far failed to do in several instances, where overzealous federal attorneys overreached their limits.[8] Such apparent lack of fairness may antagonize the domestic Muslim community and trigger a sense of moral outrage. The U.S. government needs to keep its attention focused on protecting the public. It cannot allow individual civil servants to exploit the issue of terrorism for personal political gain. This is counterproductive against this form of terrorism.

Diminish the Sense of Moral Outrage

Young Muslims the world over are enraged at the United States, and the situation in Iraq is the main fuel for this anger.[9] The NSCT is correct to argue that terrorism is "not simply the result of hostility to U.S. policy in Iraq,"[10] but to leave it at that is disingenuous. The first two waves of global Islamist terrorism preceded the U.S. invasion of Iraq, and 9/11 was planned during a period in which the Israeli-Palestinian conflict was being actively addressed. Old hardcore al Qaeda members were simply anti-American and wanted nothing more than to engage the United States in a war. However, the invasion of Iraq galvanized Muslims into forming the third wave. These new self-appointed members of the al Qaeda social movement explicitly refer to Iraq and the Palestinians in communiqués or videos released after their deaths. Pictures of dying Iraqi civilians inflame Muslim youths worldwide. It is irrelevant whether the killing is by American soldiers, although if it is, the outrage is multiplied, since the blame is placed on the U.S. presence in Iraq. It provides the terrorists with a ready excuse, partially exculpating them of the atrocities they are committing.

The presence of the U.S. military on the streets of Baghdad and in the other cities and towns of Iraq enables al Qaeda and its fellow travelers to portray the situation as one of American imperialism and provides a ready target for novice terrorists. The deployment of U.S. soldiers in civilian areas and the heavy-handed tactics that necessarily go along with that deployment garner popular support for al Qaeda in its role as the self-designated defender of Islam and adversary of the United States. Muslims find ridiculous the claims that the United States is occupying Iraq to defend New York and export democracy. Instead, they believe al Qaeda claims that the U.S. military is an army of occupation interested only in dominating the region, which is almost entirely inhabited by Muslims, and exploiting its oil wealth. The U.S. invasion has proved to be a rallying cry for a new generation of young Muslims, who are willing to sacrifice themselves on behalf of their Iraqi brothers (regardless whether these brothers welcome or reject such sacrifice). The presence of even one American soldier in uniform in Iraq will trump any goodwill policy the United States attempts to carry out in the Middle East. Withdrawal from Iraq is a necessary condition for diminishing the sense of moral outrage that Muslims feel.

Removal of American forces from Iraq and a good faith attempt to broker a solution to the Israeli-Palestinian conflict are absolutely essential if the United States wants to counter al Qaeda propaganda. Only deeds, not words, will count in this arena. Muslims realize that the Israeli-Palestinian conflict is complicated. They also realize that a solution will be difficult. But the appearance of an honest broker is all that is required of the United States. Since the start of the second intifada, the U.S. government is seen as siding too closely with Israel, and as complicit in Israeli operations against the Palestinians. It is a sore that continues to fester and requires urgent and even-handed attention.

A sense of moral outrage is not the exclusive province of global politics. Local events also fuel it. There is strong evidence that the Madrid bombers were upset at the arrest of close friends and relatives by both Moroccan and Spanish authorities for their alleged involvement in the 2003 Casablanca bombings. They believed that their friends were innocent, and so far the evidence supports this. The arrests were a major step in their radicalization, which eventually contributed to the horrors of the March 11, 2004, train bombings in Madrid. This illustrates the importance of appearing to apply the law fairly to all of society. No element can be singled out for special treatment.

Again, the NSCT is correct to point out that "terrorism is not simply a response to our efforts to prevent terror attacks."[11] Counterterrorism measures need to be seen as fair. People who have committed criminal acts should of course be arrested and prosecuted. The population understands that, and puts the blame on the criminals. It is when Muslims are indiscriminately singled out that they become angry. Any campaign against terrorism must be focused specifically on the perpetrators, and not on a more general segment of the population. This was the lesson learned, after many years of failure, by the British in their attempt to contain Irish terrorism, and by the Egyptian authorities in the late 1990s against the Egyptian Islamic Group terrorist organizations. In the Egyptian case, some of the more militant elements of the Islamic Group tried to derail their leaders' peace initiative by killing sixty-two people in Luxor in the fall of 1997. The Egyptian government refrained from carrying out waves of mass arrests as it had previously done; it had learned that its previous strategy of sweeps had inspired many young people to join the terrorists out of anger. Since Luxor, there has not been any Egyptian Islamic Group attempt against the population.

If homeland security is the goal, this type of restraint is the only policy democracies can follow. They must ensure that legitimate police actions against the suspected perpetrators of violence do not harm or alienate the broader population from which the suspects come. A slip can negate years of careful development of the relationship with the community. This is partially what happened in Britain after the 7/7 bombings, with unwise police actions such as killing a Brazilian expatriate on suspicion he was a Muslim terrorist or the shooting of two innocent pious Muslim Bangladeshi expatriates. Potential short-term gains cannot be allowed to interfere with this ultimate goal of homeland security. This means that in the pursuit of suspected terrorist-criminals, law enforcement agencies must follow the rules so as not to be perceived as prejudiced and singling out Muslims. If the threat can be contained without arrests of presumed perpetrators, it is best to keep them free until enough evidence is accumulated to convince the public of their guilt. This calls for restraint in our law enforcement activities, because local action vividly brings home the idea that there is discrimination against Muslims, and polarizes the community to an unhealthy level.

Counter the Enemy's Appeal

Muslims join the al Qaeda social movement because they respond to its appeal. Al Qaeda Central has several ideologies,[12] but its essence is that the West is waging a war against Islam and all good Muslims must join the fight, lest they be destroyed. This is definitely a war for "hearts and minds." The United States has interpreted it as a "War of Ideas" and its strategy is, according to the NSCT, "to counter the lies behind the terrorists' ideology and deny them future recruits."[13] The NSCT promotes "effective democracy" as the way to counter terrorist ideology: "terrorism ultimately depends upon the appeal of an ideology that excuses or even glorifies the deliberate killing of innocents. Islam has been twisted and made to serve an evil end, as in other times and places other religions have been similarly abused."[14]

I am not sure that this strong emphasis on ideology, religion, and fighting "extremist Islam" is fruitful. I have traveled to several trials of terrorists in Western Europe, spoken to people who knew them as children and as young men, and read the open-source literature about them, including shreds of conversations attributed to them when they surfaced in the press or in trials. I have come to the conclusion that the terrorists in Western Europe and North America were not intellectuals or ideologues, much less religious scholars. It is not about how they think, but how they feel. Let us not make the mistake of over-intellectualizing this fight. It is indeed a contest for the hearts and minds of potential terrorists, not an intellectual debate about the legitimacy of an extreme interpretation of a religious message.

The terrorists' lack of religious education is most striking for the third wave of global Islamist terrorists. Members of this wave are poorly educated (unlike those in the preceding waves) and do not even know the Quran. Their relative ignorance of their religion contributes to their vulnerability to extreme interpretations of the Quran. Religious education might have inoculated them against such interpretations since it would have given them a context with which to assess the legitimacy of terrorist messages. The entire effort to dissuade wannabes from joining the ranks of the al Qaeda social movement by debating them with religious arguments and selective quotes from the Quran and hadiths is misguided. The defendants in terrorism trials around the world would not have been swayed by an exegesis of the Quran. They would simply have been bored and would not have listened. Those potential terrorists visiting sites on the Internet would avoid those with overt religious content because they are not interested in religious disquisition. Radical Islamic theology is not the main source of appeal for the vast majority of arrested global Islamist terrorists. Theological debates may appeal to a few autodidactic scholars that populate some of the radical Internet sites, but they seem to only talk to each other and hold little appeal for the real terrorist rank and file, who join for other reasons.

A counterterrorist focus on Islamic ideology is dangerous. We cannot afford to allow the terrorists to control the debate by framing the context of this war to their advantage. It is not the role of the West to tell Muslims what is Islam and what is not Islam. Let them define it however they want, and focus our efforts on undermining the appeal that global Islamist terrorism has for young Muslims.

At the same time, "effective democracy" as advocated in the NSCT is not going to appeal to potential terrorists either. The recent NSCT document provides a number of reasons as to why promotion of "effective democracy" is a strong counterstrategy to the terrorist ideology. Advancement of "effective

157

democracy" is a worthwhile goal by itself, which I strongly endorse, but it will not affect terrorism. In fact, the unrest that might accompany the transition to "effective democracy" might promote terrorism, as it did in Indonesia in its transition to democracy. There, the unrest was so widespread that a wave of bombings that damaged about forty churches on Christmas Eve 2000 went unnoticed at the time. The NSCT even admits that its strategy might not work. "Democracies are not immune to terrorism. In some democracies, some ethnic or religious groups are unable or unwilling to grasp the benefits of freedom otherwise available in the society. Such a group can evidence the same alienation and despair that the transnational terrorists exploit in undemocratic states. This accounts for the emergence in democratic societies of homegrown terrorists—even among second- and third-generation citizens. Even in these cases, the long-term solution remains deepening the reach of democracy so that all citizens enjoy its benefits."[15] In other words, young Muslims in the democratic West who chose to join global Islamist terrorism were "unable or unwilling to grasp" the gift of democracy. This is not a convincing explanation of the "homegrown terrorist" phenomenon, which I analyzed in a previous chapter. I am afraid that promoting "effective democracy" as a strategy in the war for "hearts and minds" falls flat. Muslims know all about democracy: they have it in Egypt, in Morocco, in Algeria, and now in Iraq. They do not want this type of democracy. Muslims around the world also do not believe that the United States is trying to promote "effective democracy" when they see that it seems to backtrack on its commitment to democracy each time parties hostile to the United States win elections in the Middle East (the case of Hamas in the Palestinian Authority being the most recent example). And in Europe, Muslims realize that although they do have a voice in the government, the numbers are against them and they do not have any effective influence over their government. They then reject democracy as an effective tool and turn to violence instead to influence their government. Indeed, they celebrate their alleged victory in Spain in the election of March 14, 2004, where Prime Minister Aznar's government, which sent troops to Iraq, was defeated by Prime Minister Zapatero's government, which promptly brought the troops home. Although this is not my reading of why this sequence of events took place, this use of violence three days before elections has been celebrated in jihadi chat rooms (and ironically also denounced in right-wing U.S. chat rooms) as a major victory for al Qaeda.

A focus on "effective democracy" in the context of an occupation of Iraq and support for some of the greatest violators of democratic principles strains the credibility of the United States. Credibility is a key issue in a battle for hearts and minds. At present, the U.S. government has no credibility in most of the world, and this has been a self-inflicted wound. On the other hand, the willingness of an extremely wealthy civil engineer and a promising physician to sacrifice all for the sake of their beliefs makes it credible that they preach what they actually believe. So far, we are badly losing the battle of credibility and we must work hard to reverse that. We will do so only by matching words and deeds and regain the moral high ground by eliminating the contradictions between our high ideals and our actual policies. Only after we regain our credibility will a campaign for "effective democracy" start to gather support among Muslims.

Earlier, I argued that Muslims join this terrorist social movement because they want to be viewed as heroes. The desire to escape insignificance and become famous seems to be a powerful motivator for joining the terrorist social movement. Young Muslims need alternative local heroes with whom they can identify and who can be role models for them. During a 2007 trip to Tetouan, a city in northern Morocco, my colleague, Scott Atran, and I spoke with Moroccan children in front of the mosque that five of the Madrid suicide bombers had attended. When we asked them their names, they responded with the names of soccer superstars. After an exchange of pleasantries, we asked them who they would be if they could not become soccer stars. They responded almost without thinking, "Osama bin Laden." A soccer star or "Osama bin Laden": this is the dilemma the West is facing. There is a dearth of local role models in Muslim countries and the slums surrounding major Western cities. In the Middle East, the region of hereditary democracies, leaders do not allow anyone to become so famous as to potentially challenge their legitimacy. After a certain threshold of fame, they are systemically cut down. Instead, Osama bin Laden is a hero to many Muslims for his willingness to sacrifice his riches for the cause of the Muslims. This does not mean that they like his policies or his goals, but they admire him and many want to become like him.

In the United States there are Muslim local heroes who have become successful in the community. They can be a source of inspiration for local ambitious young Muslims. In Europe, local heroes to the younger generation are rare, and in the Middle East, they are even rarer. Now, the local heroes to imitate are terrorists. There is a "jihadi cool" and "jihadi talk" in Europe, where it is fashionable to emulate terrorists. This makes jihad fun and interesting to young Muslims, who join global Islamist terrorism because it's cool and thrilling to be part of a clandestine undertaking. It is imperative that the Muslim community create new models of success for their youth to emulate. These models should be recognized by the rest of the population. At present, non-Muslim populations give an inadvertent advertisement to bin Laden and al Qaeda by their obsession with them. This is the wrong message to send. The key is to diminish the fame and therefore the appeal of these violent models.

Much of the discussion about "jihadi cool" takes place informally in Muslim enclaves in Europe and in Internet chat rooms. As we have seen, the chat rooms have become the arena where the war for the "hearts and minds" takes place. This battle is completely one-sided. The true believers, who populate the radical forums, are working themselves into a frenzy with no moderate voice present to calm them down. This leads to ever greater radicalization on the part of the participants, who slowly take on the views of their friends. The greater Muslim community cannot allow this to happen. This is a fight for the soul of the Muslim community. Muslims who reject violence need to enter this arena and participate in the discussions to influence and stop this slide toward ever greater radicalization. This is an internal Muslim debate about the nature of their community in the West. Non-Muslims have no role to play in this debate, for any intervention on the side of those rejecting violence might simply discredit them and leave them open to accusation of having sold out. The Internet should become the battleground of this war of interpretations, hopes, dreams, and aspirations.

In this online battle for hearts and minds, it is important to identify the influential opinion leaders in the various forums frequented by Muslim youths. These leaders should be the focus of a subtle campaign to influence them to embrace nonviolence as a way to fulfill Muslim aspirations. This campaign should be conducted by other Muslims, who can benefit from advice on the process of political and cultural influence.[16] Of course, conflicts between Muslims and non-Muslims are bound to arise in any complex society. The point is to informally persuade influential Muslims—those whom young Muslims look up to—to advocate the resolution of such conflicts in a law-abiding and peaceful manner.

Terrorist groups often do make mistakes and go too far—even for their own supporters. Most commonly, this happens when they start killing women and children. The bombing of a wedding in Amman, Jordan, in November 2005 dramatically turned the Jordanian population from one that generally supported terrorism (especially directed against Israel) to one that rejected it. Such mistakes offer a hugely important opportunity for those who want to mobilize public opinion against the terrorists. If we keep our eyes on the objective of isolating the terrorists and prevent the spread of their appeal, we should try to capitalize on their atrocities and use them to further that objective rather than acceding to the provocation of the terrorists. This calls for restraint and nimble exploitation of the opportunity offered by the overreach of the terrorists.

I have heard many Muslims reject violence and terrorists as beyond the pale of Islam, calling them "just killers." However, the mass media and most Internet sites do not cover this majority voice[17] for they do not deem it as newsworthy when imam after imam rejects violence. As a result, many non-Muslims believe that they do not condemn violence. Indeed, many fairly sophisticated students of terrorism have often asked me why no one from the Muslim community condemns global Islamist terrorism. They mistake the lack of coverage for lack of activity. When I tell them that the majority condemns such action, they seem surprised and say they have never heard a major imam condemn it. However, have just one imam express sympathy for terrorist aims and it hits the front page of the Islamophobic press and is displayed prominently on Islamophobic websites. Ironically, the same bias operates the other way, when the most outrageous statements from Sunday morning evangelists in the United States are posted on Saudi websites within a day or so, and people in Saudi Arabia believe that these statements represent majority belief in the United States. Sensationalism sells. Editors and producers need to provide more balanced reporting on this issue.

Perhaps a more active engagement between non-Muslims and Muslims in the West would give more visibility to mainstream Muslims through this relationship. Both sides can issue joint statements condemning moral violations against Muslims and non-Muslims alike, advocate universal civil rights for all and condemn discrimination against Muslims in the West, and promote the idea of a partnership for justice and fairness for everyone around the world, including Muslims. This will require the West, and especially the United States, to distance themselves from local violations of civil rights, often perpetrated by putative allies in the name of the "war against terror"—the Russian intervention in Chechnya, the Uzbek crackdown against dissidents, the Egyptian government's campaigns against dissidents, for example. These violations must be condemned no matter what their origin. There can be little doubt that many U.S. allies in the Middle East and the Muslim world do not share a Western commitment to civil rights, let alone "effective democracy." If we want the world's Muslims to believe that we are committed to our words, our deeds must follow through. We must regain our credibility and the moral high ground internationally, which will refute the notion that we are engaged in a war against Islam. We must advocate political reforms where they are needed. We should demonstrate that we are aware that elections alone do not constitute "effective democracy" and that Iraq has demonstrated that democracy cannot be successfully imposed from outside. Instead, we should support the development of civil society and moderate opposition parties in countries with a democratic deficit. The election of parties hostile to the United States will test American resolve, but should be viewed as evidence of success. We must also do a better job of explaining our policies and the reasoning behind them. This requires a significant commitment to public diplomacy, which must take our case to Muslim communities worldwide. Our media and technological skills may give us an advantage here. But, as I noted earlier, deeds speak louder than words. Public diplomacy must be matched by global action, and that means withdrawing American troops from Iraq and making a good faith effort to resolve the Palestinian-Israeli conflict.

National security is not just a matter for government officials. In the battle for hearts and minds, the American public must also be educated about the real nature of the threat facing the United States. The fear of terrorism has reached the bogeyman threshold. Terrorists are not as well organized as the Communist Party that the United States faced just two decades ago. The real threat to the United States comes from two sources: spontaneously self-organized groups of homegrown wannabes, who are still undetected by local law enforcement authorities and who join the terrorist social movement in the act of committing their first (and last if it is a suicide mission) terrorist attack; and outside terrorists, especially from Europe, who succeed in sneaking into the country to carry out their attacks. With the possible exception of Ali al-Marri, there has not been any infiltrated trained long-term sleeper cell in this country. Al Qaeda is not an insidious, silent presence. Since 9/11, most successful terrorist networks actually had been detected by local law enforcements agencies, but the seriousness of the threats was not recognized.

It is time that we begin an honest conversation about our core values and see where security fits in our priorities, particularly when it may involve compromises in privacy or personal rights. This debate should also encompass new technologies, such as computer-mediated communications, that are transforming how people relate to one another. This nationwide conversation must take place in public, in the various media, including the Internet; it is a conversation that will touch on the essence of what we want our nation to be. This conversation may allow radicals of all kinds to join in a peaceful debate about our respective visions of what we would like our society to be, and perhaps help defuse some of the violent "propaganda by the deed."

Although the United States, Asia, and the Middle East have been the focus of the "war on terror," the real battleground for "hearts and minds" is Europe. European governments should begin a campaign to educate their population about the benefits of new immigrants. Once immigrants are accepted as full citizens of their countries, the friction between Muslims and non-Muslims will begin to fade away.

The duration of the threat is determined by the influx of newcomers into the global Islamist terrorist social movement. As long as young Muslims sign up, the threat will persist. As the flow into the movement dries up, so will the danger. In essence, any threat requires some form of periodic successes to inspire new young people to join the movement. As the successes vanish, so will the movement's appeal to the young, who will look elsewhere for inspiration.

Eliminate Discrimination Against Muslims

The global Islamist terrorist interpretation appeals to Muslims because it resonates with their personal experiences of discrimination and economic exclusion. This is mostly a West European problem, for the "melting pot" mentality and American dream (whether myth or reality) partially protects the United States. European countries must provide their Muslim immigrant populations with equal opportunity in the labor market that refutes the claim that the West is at war with Islam. They must strive to eliminate any bias against Muslims and treat them on an equal footing with other members of their societies. Of course, Muslims should have legal remedy against such discrimination and I am sure that each Western society has the equivalent of the equal protection clause of the U.S. Constitution. This ecumenical program would convince the Muslim community that it is an integral part of the nation, isolate the rejectionists from which potential terrorists emerge, check the spread of their appeal and inoculate potential recruits against terrorism.

In order to actively engage the Muslim community to fight violence, the rest of the population must not provide potential terrorists with any support for their claim that there is strong discrimination against Muslims, part of a War against Islam. Any slander or discrimination against Muslims should be vigorously exposed and protested not only by government officials, but also representatives of society and nongovernmental watchdog groups, such as the Anti-Defamation League, the American Civil Liberties Union, or the American Arab Anti-Discrimination Committee. Non-Muslim organizations should have a prominent role in extending protection of civil rights to Muslims, denounce discrimination and defamation against them and put such action on the more universal footing of the protection of civil rights. These organizations should encourage private initiatives by Muslims to denounce the more discriminatory and defamatory practices they see. Of course, such initiatives must be endorsed by the political leadership of each country and the population in general. This general condemnation of civil rights violations will in turn give Muslim leaders legitimacy and a platform to criticize violations within their midst, such as those of terrorists who happen to be Muslim. This will encourage Muslims to feel part of the larger community and distance them from the extreme elements within. This is very much the situation in the United States, where Muslim Americans are largely assimilated, happy with their lives and moderate with respect to many of the issues that have divided Muslims around the world. Muslim Americans are very much like the rest of the country.[18]

The everyday discrimination against Muslims in Europe in the labor market must be fought with the same vigor as the more blatant social discrimination. The French government's attempt to liberalize the labor market in the spring of 2006 was a good first step. However, this law was shelved after huge demonstrations of host students were joined by labor unions. The Council of State later declared the law unconstitutional. This is a bad precedent, which sends a very negative message to the children of immigrants, who are in a majority Muslim. The liberalization of the labor markets in Europe should be on a universal footing, and not appear to include measures specifically aimed at Muslims. This appearance might trigger a major blowback from the host population and needlessly polarize society between mostly Muslim immigrants and the rest of the general population. For instance, liberalization of labor markets should be presented as a necessary measure for competition in a global economy.

To provide Muslims options other than joining terrorism out of boredom and idleness, welfare policy must be modified. It should provide some relief for the unfortunate out of work, but it should not allow them to spend their free time surfing the Internet and becoming full-time terrorist wannabes. State-sponsored work programs should keep them busy on tasks useful for society, a little like the various work programs under the New Deal. Such programs would not have to be so extensive since the national unemployment rate is not as dramatic as the one during the Great Depression. The point is that young people of working age should not be idle and thereby seek to escape boredom in the thrill of joining a forbidden movement.

Any governmental singling out of the Muslim community will be viewed with suspicion in these extremely tense times because of the global Islamist terrorist threat. Muslims resent being viewed as terrorists by the rest of the population and reject this label. Even measures to protect some segments of the Muslim population will be viewed as discriminatory. Because of the German government's desire to prevent forced marriages, common in the Turkish immigrant community, which imports very young brides from Anatolian villages, it enacted a law that grants a residency permit to spouses of immigrants only if they are at least eighteen years of age and have a basic knowledge of German. This law does not pertain to spouses of nonimmigrant Germans and does not apply to Americans, Japanese, or European Union citizens. Groups representing Germany's Turkish population claimed discrimination and refused to participate in the German chancellor's integration summit in mid-July 2007. They claimed that if the law was intended to protect women, it should be adopted to make it easier for women to flee violent husbands. According to current regulations, a spouse who joins a partner in Germany could get his or her independent residence permit only after two years.

Eliminate Terrorist Networks

While the fight against this new infectious form of terrorism is a battle for hearts and minds, there are physical terrorists who are plotting to kill people.

These terrorists must be eliminated before they can indiscriminately harm innocent victims. This is a local law enforcement task, which must be carried out with restraint and in accordance with the law to maintain the trust and confidence of society.

The recommendation for police restraint was already articulated in the section on diminishing moral outrage. The local police force must never be seen as the enemy by the Muslim community. An effort must be made to change that perspective, so that local law enforcement is viewed as part of the community. This means that local law enforcement should be recruited from the neighborhood itself, so that its composition reflects the local population.

The New York City Police Department is an example of successful community policing. New York City's population is about one-third foreign born. The NYPD decided that the city's police force should be a reflection of the city's residents and it actively solicited applications from young immigrants. The result is that now the NYPD is also one-third foreign born. Officers from different backgrounds understand what is going on in their neighborhoods and act as intermediaries between the department and their communities. A level of trust has developed between immigrants and the police.

In contrast, police departments in European cities draw heavily on the host population, which treats the immigrant populations and their progeny with some condescension. There is a palpable hostility between the police departments and the newcomers' neighborhoods when the officers assigned there are not from those communities. This is ripe for incidents that might spark riots, such as those in France in the fall of 2005.

The fight against terrorism is a community affair. The community must become responsible for its protection. Its vigilance against violent threats should alert local law enforcement authorities about them. British authorities complain that they do not get tips about potential terrorist threats from their local Muslim communities, which view the police with suspicion. This contrasts sharply with U.S. law enforcement authorities, who get so many tips that they must deal with the opposite problem: How to recognize real threats from the fears of the citizenry? A local police force that is seen as an integral part of the community will increase trust in local enforcement authorities and encourage Muslims to become the eyes and ears of the police. It is not sufficient for a police department to meet with Muslim leaders on a weekly basis. This might be a good first step, but it is essential that the police force to be viewed as an organic part of the community.

Trust in the local police, a crucial ingredient of the fight against terrorists, is undermined by excessive secrecy imposed by trial judges attempting to shield potential jurors from news reports that might prejudice them at trial. In the United States, law enforcement and prosecutorial authorities are allowed to present the case in an unsealed indictment, laying out the accusation. Likewise, the principle of freedom of the press is interpreted as allowing investigative reporting on government allegations. In many Commonwealth countries, however, such as Britain, Canada, and Australia, this kind of reporting is banned because of its potential prejudicial effects on juries. The gag orders imposed on the media and authorities by the judiciary in these countries prevent the authorities from informing the Muslim community about the scope of the terrorist threat because the evidence against the suspects cannot be disclosed until the trials are over. Nor can newspapers publish what their investigative reporters have found out on their own until the trials are over.

These gag orders have contributed to broad public and especially Muslim skepticism and suspicion about the scale of the Islamist terrorist threat. The breakdown in the public's trust of the police and the public's unwillingness to accept the government's explanations of the threat of terrorism has severely affected the ability to collect important information from the public that could help tip them off to potential plots. The idea that the public can suspend judgment about such dramatic events as arrests and wait for three or four years to discover the evidence runs against human nature. The public will fill in the gaps in its knowledge and this can potentially turn against the authorities. Compelling evidence of crimes or intended crimes must be shared with the public, and especially the Muslim community, lest it become suspicious that such arrests are unwarranted and discriminative, target Muslims and therefore are part of a more general war on Islam. The U.S. legal system demonstrates that one can conduct a fair trial while still allowing the authorities to release enough evidence before the trial to convince the public that a threat exists and permitting the press to conduct and publish its own independent investigation. Defendants are entitled to a fair trial, but this does not require jurors to know nothing about a case. I see no evidence that investigative reporting prejudices juries. Jurors may know something about the events under litigation, but not so much as to prevent them from deciding fairly about the responsibility of the defendants. The law should aim for a fair trial as opposed to an ideal one. British appellate courts must ease up on the gag orders that feed the skepticism of its Muslim community.

With the help of the community, local police forces would be the first ones to detect any potential terrorist threats. However, they must understand the nature of threat reported to them. Given the differences between local criminals and terrorists, the local police might not appreciate the warning signs. Federal authorities, because they have become the repository of information about other terrorist groups, are more likely to understand the process of radicalization and acts in furtherance of homegrown terrorist wannabes. Therefore, greater collaboration and even integration between local and federal law enforcement agencies must be set up in Western countries to detect and perhaps dissuade these groups from the path of violence. The creation of regional fusion centers under the Department of Homeland Security providing this link between local police departments and federal agencies is a step in this direction.

It is possible that the appeal of global Islamist terrorism might be a temporary romantic rebellious urge in Muslims transitioning to adulthood. They might not be hardened terrorists, and may grow out of it and settle into a more peaceful and responsible life. The law should also allow for leniency for minor infractions in exchange for important information and cooperation with authorities. Grants of leniency have proved successful against terrorist organizations, especially those past their peak appeal for potential new members. Such partial leniency, which may give the appearance of not fully punishing criminals, does carry political costs, especially from families of victims. These two imperatives, elimination of a threat and fair punishment, must be weighed by prosecutorial authorities on a case-by-case basis. However, if the ultimate goal is to reduce the actual threat to homeland security, and the arrested perpetrator has valuable information to bargain, the resulting apprehension of further perpetrators will diminish the likelihood that the public would view such bargaining as rewarding terrorism.

If the law does not allow for the fair prosecution of some suspects, then the law must be changed to reflect current realities. This is especially true when dealing with potential plots involving weapons of mass destruction. For Western jurisprudence, the problem of terrorism offers a major challenge. Because of the extent of potential atrocities committed in the name of terrorism, no government can afford to sit back and wait for these events to occur. The goal for governments is to prevent them and disrupt or arrest terrorists before they have the opportunity to act.

This poses a problem. Western criminal jurisprudence has evolved to give a fair trial to a suspect who is alleged to have already committed a criminal act. Criminal thoughts or words without criminal behavior cannot be prosecuted. So, what can we do about people who talk about doing things, but have not yet committed any acts? This is exactly the situation of potential terrorists, who are arrested before they get a chance to carry out their intent. It is hard for the prosecutor to prove that such a person really intended to do a criminal act beyond a reasonable doubt. Defendants always have an easy defense: "We were just talking, this was not serious." Juries tend to be skeptical when finding guilt means serious prison time.

Many jurisdictions are thus trying to criminalize the status of being a terrorist. The problem, as I have shown before, is that there is no commonly agreed upon definition of terrorism or formal status of being a terrorist. The law can provide a definition, but the defense attorney can undermine it with the common argument that a terrorist for some is a freedom fighter for others. The official definition of a terrorist also glosses over the difficulty that juries face when confronted with real cases of prosecution, namely to what extent is the indicted person guilty. Not all terrorists make and explode bombs that kill innocent bystanders. In fact, most are supporters who make terrorism possible through the dissemination of literature or Internet postings, raising money for activities that include terrorism. Or they may be people who might know about future operations but choose not to become involved and instead tell authorities about them. So, the law tries to provide more concrete criteria by making criminal the simple act of belonging to a terrorist organization. The French have had some measure of success with this approach, which assumes that formal terrorist organizations exist. This misunderstands the true nature of modern terrorism, which is carried out by informal groups of people who do not call themselves anything but "brothers." These groups are given names in the media and sometimes within law enforcement authorities as a form of shorthand. These labels over time acquire a reality of their own, leading people to make the mistaken assumption that these groups formally exist, when in fact they are usually informal and fluid in composition according to the situation, which depends on many chance events.

This obsession with legal minutiae can result in absurd decisions. On December 2, 2006, a court in Amsterdam found that three defendants were individually engaged in preparing terrorist attacks, but were acquitted of belonging to a terrorist organization. In reading out his judgment, the presiding judge contrasted the group that they belonged to—which the prosecution labeled the Lions of Tawheed (tawheed means monotheism)—with the Hofstad Group (also previously labeled by the prosecution), which had been found in another trial to be a terrorist organization. In the Lions case, the judge argued that the Hofstad Group was a terrorist organization for three reasons: its members met regularly, these meetings were presided over by a spiritual leader, and the members devoted themselves to disseminating their ideology in writing.[19] Although the Lions of Tawheed were much further along than the Hofstad Group in making preparations for one or more attacks, they did not seem to form a terrorist group because the suspects rarely met face to face. When they met each other on the street, no structure was involved. The Lions had never met in plenary session, and some members had never met each other during the period in question.[20] Under this reasoning, if the Madrid or London bombers who carried out the atrocities on March 11, 2004, and July 7, 2005, respectively, had been caught, they would also have been exonerated on charges of being terrorists because they did not belong to a formal terrorist organization. I suspect that no terrorist in the third wave of Islamist terrorism could be proven to belong to a "formal" terrorist organization.

The legal consequences of this fiction of membership in a formal terrorist organization cannot be underestimated. The Foreign Intelligence Surveillance Act of 1978 (FISA) prescribes procedures regarding requests for judicial authorization for electronic surveillance of those engaged in international terrorism against the United States on behalf of a foreign power. FISA includes in its definition of "foreign power" a "group engaged in international terrorism or activities in preparation thereof." This is construed as meaning a formal group.[21] Unfortunately, most suspected terrorists threatening the United States are not part of a formal group, which means that law enforcement officials cannot go to a FISA court to request authorization for electronic surveillance of suspects. Since such surveillance has not been formally authorized, the results cannot be used in court, for it is not admissible evidence. This prevents the prosecution of some suspects for whom the government has amassed considerable evidence. The assumption that terrorists are organized in formal groups is an obstacle to the rightful prosecution of terrorists. This assumption needs to be rethought in light of the present evidence, and the laws altered to reflect the reality on the ground.

The core group of people who comprise al Qaeda Central—those who have blood on their hands or are plotting against the United States—must be eliminated or captured and tried for their crimes. Actions to ensure this result should be carried out according to the rule of law. If not, a double standard will inflame young Muslims and lead them to believe that the United States is conducting war against Islam and undermine the goal of keeping Americans safe. The imprisoning of terror suspects at Guantánamo while declaring them to be outside of the Geneva Conventions may have played well to domestic American audiences, but it has been a complete disaster for the United States in the fight against global Islamist terrorism. It has undoubtedly helped inspire more terrorists while providing minimal benefits from an operational point of view. The base must be closed immediately, and the inmates transferred to the United States, where they can receive due process. At present, their status is a continuing source of moral outrage for Muslims everywhere, even among those who have little sympathy for al Qaeda. In this fight, the United States must try to recapture the moral high ground, and its detention policies—at Guantánamo and at Abu Ghraib—have been strategic mistakes.

For these hardened terrorists captured abroad, Congress needs to establish a new system of preventive detention that is overseen by a specialized federal court to deal with terrorism. This court would be composed of specifically chosen federal judges with special clearance, like the present pool of FISA court judges, and who would serve for life. This court would have a permanent staff of prosecutors and defense lawyers, with the same level of security clearances. Given the privileges bestowed on this group, it is imperative that they be lawyers with impeccable integrity, willing to share contrary evidence with the opposite side. The interest of justice should trump the desire to "win" a case. This court would be able to hear evidence that could not be presented in regular civilian courts to protect intelligence sources and methods and assess evidence collected in places that might not meet the strict standards of American criminal jurisprudence. There would be a right of appeal to a second layer of judges, who would review the proceedings for fairness, as the detainees would probably not have the full range of criminal protection, such as immediate access to a lawyer (especially when captured in a very hostile environment), Miranda rights, and full access to family, public, and the press.

Ideally, networks would not progress to the point that police detection, disruption and defeat of global Islamist terrorist networks and fair prosecution of the defendants are necessary. Probably the best way to prevent such progression to violence is to provide informal networks of Muslims an alternative path to follow. One of the ways is to divert them into joining pro-social groups like the Boy Scouts of America, which was created in 1910 partially because of the fear that young boys migrating from rural to urban environments might no longer be learning core American values. The movement was able to capture a large portion of young people and keep them out of trouble through discipline, outdoor activities, and good deeds. A similar large and formal network of young Muslims, based on peaceful Muslim traditions, might provide a sense of belonging and self-help to deal with some of the problems that children of immigrants invariably face. The desire for thrill and fame could be quenched through a hierarchy of promotion that would recognize the talents and efforts of the members. This would be an alternative to informal gangs that evolve into homegrown terrorists.

Fund Scientific Research on Terrorism

In order to develop an effective strategy based on an accurate understanding of the enemy's behavior, policymakers need access to an empirical research project on global Islamist terrorism and terrorism in general. More than six years after the tragedy of 9/11, such evidence-based terrorism research is generally lacking. Self-appointed terrorism experts still ask the public to accept their declarations on faith.

Just as the federal government initiated nationwide projects on Soviet studies in the 1950s and 1960s to develop expertise to deal with our adversary, it should embark on a similar project in terrorism studies. Some small programs already exist, but they are isolated from the rest of the academy and do not yet attract the best graduate students. Since global and local terrorism is a definite threat to national security, programs to support a variety of projects on terrorism should be funded. The graduates from these programs will constitute an ever-renewing pool of potential experts, which the government could tap in its aim to provide homeland security for the American people.

The government should resist the temptation to develop this expertise by hiring young graduates without any advanced training in social methodology and then provide instruction. This has been tried and does not work. The in-house training programs are simply not good enough and the government does not foster the inquisitive and rebellious spirit that drives scientific advancement. There is just too much pressure to conform in the government, as the disastrous run-up to the Iraqi invasion demonstrates. Some of the best social science is done in protected areas of free inquiry, where mutual challenges and disputes lead to new insights. The atmosphere in government agencies is not conducive to such leaps of creativity because inquiry into areas of disagreement is prematurely cut off, especially when scientists' evaluations, which form the basis for promotion, are written by their superiors. By stimulating the academy to develop evidence-based terrorism research, the government will be able to draw from this pool of talented new Ph.D.s in the field to help promote national security.

Any attempt to foster the scientific study of terrorism requires accurate data. There are two obstacles to acquiring that data presently: the first is prejudice in government funding in favor of modeling over data collection. The second is a mania for secrecy.

The politics of government funding favors contracts for concrete products. In other words, at the end of the contract, there must be an unambiguous tool or "deliverable." Enter the software developers and modelers, who have been tasked to model terrorism in order to anticipate and predict the threat facing the United States. These projects, unfortunately, have no relevance to reality because they draw on inaccurate or poorly developed concepts regarding terrorism and terrorists. Models based on preconceived and false notions of how terrorist networks behave are worthless.

Although a model is a "deliverable," it is just a tool to help manipulate concepts. It is only as useful as the purpose to which it is put. Generating data for these models is a very difficult process. Indeed, in the creation of software programs to analyze real social trends, such as forecasting the stock market, for instance, the generation of data itself that is the most difficult, complicated, and expensive step. And yet, this is exactly what is not funded because the government does not like to support the collection of information from open sources.[22]

Tools can advance the study of terrorism, but they are just tools. The person in charge of these projects should understand terrorism and be able to gauge the usefulness of a tool for the study at hand. Federal contracting officers need to change their policy for funding terrorism research, so that many important basic projects such as "How does one become a terrorist?" or "How is a terrorist different from people who had a chance to become one but did not?" or "How do new technologies of communication transform the terrorist threat?" will be funded. Some visionary federal contracting officers are beginning to understand the problem and provide seed money for such projects. Unless real social scientists with expertise in terrorism are in charge of projects about terrorism and not software modelers who cannot assess their model's relevance for the field, there is little chance of any real progress in the field.

The second obstacle is obtaining accurate data. This is nearly impossible because of the widespread secrecy surrounding government acquisition of information about terrorism. Some of this governmental concern with secrecy is legitimate. However, such tactical information is not eternally sensitive and should not be maintained as secret only because of bureaucratic inertia. Homeland security was not compromised by the declassification of large parts of the interrogations of Khalid Sheikh Mohammed, Ramzi bin al-Shibh, and others for the publication of the 9/11 Commission report. This worthwhile initiative should be followed up for less important terrorist suspects currently in custody. This would make available the data necessary to pursue terrorism research on a sound empirical footing, rather than to generate opinions based on speculation.

Most government data need not be secret. I understand that there is some information that does require classification, but this should not apply to every snippet gathered about terrorists. The situation now is such that scholars dealing with terrorism know less about the new developments in the field than at any previous time. As a result, they continue to base their analysis on outdated concepts rather than evolving facts on the ground. This is especially true with the evolution of global Islamist terrorism, partly driven by the greater use of the Internet. Once, governments implicitly asked the help of the academy in the attempt to understand terrorism, as illustrated by the publications of the German Interior Ministry's findings about the psychology and sociology of the Red Army Faction wave of terrorism in the 1970s.[23] This kind of initiative should be emulated since it provides the raw material that anchors a major program of true evidence-based terrorist research.

Deny the Acquisition of Weapons of Mass Destruction

The NSCT correctly singles out the possibility of weapons of mass destruction (WMD) terrorism for special consideration. The scenarios the NSCT considers, however, are too focused on terrorists gaining WMD from rogue states and too dismissive of the principles of deterrence. The NSCT does not analyze the possibility that terrorists, whether Muslim or not, could acquire WMD without relying on a state sponsor. The recommendations are based on hypothetical worst-case scenarios and surprisingly ignore the empirical data on terrorists using WMD.

The difficulties of generating a nuclear device have so far prevented terrorists from seriously embarking on this path. Several terrorist groups such as al Qaeda have shown great interest in acquiring nuclear weapons, but they have not gone beyond that point. The far more serious threat in terms of both feasibility and destructive potential is from live biological agents (as opposed to biologically derived poisons) used as terrorist tools. In the past century, there have been six such non-state-sponsored serious attempts to use biological weapons: RISE in Chicago in 1972,[24] the Rajneeshees in Oregon in 1984,[25] Aum Shinrikyo in Japan (in 1990, 1993, and 1995),[26] Larry Wayne Harris in Ohio and Las Vegas in 1995 and 1998, respectively,[27] al Qaeda in 2000 and 2001 in Afghanistan, and the still unsolved anthrax cases in the United States in the fall of 2001. Only the last instance resulted in fatalities. With the exception of al Qaeda, none of the groups or individuals started out as terrorist groups. RISE was an ad hoc extreme environmentalist duo, and the Rajneeshees and Aum Shinrikyo were cults. Nor did all of them have an apocalyptic ideology, nor could they be deterred. Indeed, as police were closing in on RISE and Aum Shinrikyo, they accelerated their operations rather than abandoned them.

The odds are that a WMD attack on the United States might come, not from any of the well-known terrorist groups, which are already monitored by law enforcement authorities, but from an informal group that is not yet the focus of such scrutiny. This group might very well fly under the radar of authorities, and the strategy contained in the NSCT may prove ineffective against such an informal group. Detection will instead come from local law enforcement, which might not have the expertise—present in federal agencies—to recognize and correctly interpret what they see on the ground. Local coordination was crucial in Chicago in 1972, Oregon in 1984, and in Japan in the early 1990s; greater resources for foreign intelligence would not have detected any of these cases. To protect against WMD terrorism, we need much closer coordination between federal expertise and local police on this issue.

Even if a terrorist group were able to obtain a nuclear device and explode it, the attack would not threaten the existence of the United States. However, the reaction to such an attack could. This was the purpose of the Aum Shinrikyo attacks in the 1990s: to trigger a global war, which the cult believed it would survive. After a WMD attack, the pressure in a democracy to "do something" immediately would be overwhelming. The outraged public would demand instant retaliation against any enemy, even if it turned out to be the wrong one—as was the case with the false accusation against Iraq of involvement in the 9/11 plot. This reaction, especially if it is a nuclear strike against a traditional enemy of the United States, might escalate into a global nuclear exchange, which would be much worse than the original attack and potentially threaten the existence of the human race.

To avert such a nightmare scenario, new mechanisms must be immediately put in place. The nuclear powers need to revisit the question of nuclear war. The cold war doctrine of mutually assured destruction as the deterrent against retaliatory nuclear attacks may prove obsolete in the event of a terrorist nuclear detonation. A different strategy must be put in place that will satisfy the demands of rightfully outraged crowds in the victim state and bring the perpetrators to justice in a fair and just way. There must be immediate and transparent international cooperation to avert an even greater tragedy.

Although I focus on the WMD threats from terrorists who happen to be Muslim, we need to consider that an even greater threat may be awaiting us. Global Islamist terrorists have argued that their beliefs can legitimate the use of WMD in certain circumstances. So, too, have radical environmentalist extremists, who make the case that humans are destroying the world through pollution, global warming, and overuse of national resources and that the only way to preserve the earth and the human race is to eradicate a large portion of the world population. Such logic practically invites the use of biological agents, for no other weapon has the potential to kill so efficiently. We must not allow our obsessive focus on the horrors caused by a wave of terrorism perpetrated by a small group of radical Muslims to blind us against the potentially far more cataclysmic devastation engineered by a completely different type of terrorism that could threaten the existence of the human race.

Conclusion

The complexity of the recommendations should alert the reader that there is no simple solution to fight global Islamist terrorism. The strategy is composed of multiple steps under an overarching idea of homeland security, defending the population.

It is important to take the glory out of terrorism by demilitarizing the conflict except for sanctuary denial and by reducing terrorists to the status of common criminals. Diminishing Muslim moral outrage can be accomplished globally by withdrawing from Iraq and locally through restraint in the aftermath of terrorism operations. The battle for the hearts and minds of the Muslim community must be based on the promotion of peaceful local heroes who can inspire young Muslims to emulate them. Muslims who reject violence should also join the battle online and confront terrorist sympathizers with the horrors perpetrated in their name. The worldwide media should give far more play to prominent Muslim leaders who censure terrorism. The majority view should be that terrorism is simply beyond the pale and must be rejected.

The West should regain the moral high ground and condemn any atrocity or persecution committed by any government, including some of our staunchest allies in the Middle East, often in the name of the "war on terror." In Europe, the elimination of discrimination and economic exclusion against Muslims would strongly undermine the Islamist terrorist appeal. Current terrorist networks must be eradicated through good community policing. Once arrested, alleged terrorists are entitled to due process and the impartial application of justice in order to win over the worldwide Muslim community and refute claims that Muslims are treated unfairly.

The strategy to counter global Islamist terrorism must be strongly grounded in scientific empirical research. It is important for the Western governments to restructure their funding strategy in order to support relevant research. Finally, denial of weapons of mass destruction must remain a critical priority for every government. But despite all precautions taken, we must still face the possibility of the unthinkable and put into place right now a mechanism that would prevent the even greater disaster of overreaction that could trigger the annihilation of a large part of the human race.

Because the threat of al Qaeda is self-limiting in terms of both structural capability and appeal, homeland security is best accomplished through a strategy of bringing to justice real terrorists, containing potential terrorists, and exercising restraint with respect to the Muslim community. Only then will the leaderless jihad expire, poisoned by its own toxic message.

NOTES

PREFACE

1. Sageman, 2004.

INTRODUCTION

1. Levy, 2003: 128.
2. Stock, 2002.
3. Williams, 2002.
4. O'Neill, 2001.
5. Hannaford, 2005.
6. Lees, Syal, and Pukas, 1994.
7. Williams, 2002.
8. Hannaford, 2005.
9. McGinty, 2002.
10. Ibid.
11. Hannaford, 2005.
12. O'Neill, 2002; Levy, 2003: 123; and Hannaford, 2005.
13. Fielding, 2002.
14. Hannaford, 2005; Fielding, 2002.
15. Unless otherwise noted, all quotations from Peter Gee are from Stock, 2002; see also Levy, 2003: 141.
16. Levy, 2003: 185–188.
17. O'Neill, 2001.
18. Hannaford, 2005.
19. McGinty, 2002.
20. Hannaford, 2005.
21. McGinty, 2002.
22. Fielding, 2002.
23. O'Neill, 2002.
24. Fielding, 2001.

25. Linzer, 2002.
26. O'Neill, 2001.
27. Fielding, 2002.
28. Linzer, 2002.
29. Ibid.
30. O'Neill, 2002.
31. Lees, Syal, and Pukas, 1994.
32. O'Neill, 2001.
33. Linzer, 2002.
34. Fielding, 2002.
35. Fielding, 2002.
36. Fielding, 2001.
37. Fielding, 2002.
38. Fielding, 2001.
39. Fielding, 2002.
40. Gallagher, 1994.
41. Sheikh, 2001.
42. Videnieks and O'Brien, 2000.
43. Levy, 2003: 182.
44. Lees, Syal, and Pukas, 1994.
45. Khan, 2002.

CHAPTER 1. HOW TO STUDY TERRORISM IN THE TWENTY-FIRST CENTURY

1. Godfrey-Smith, 2003.
2. Schmid, 1984.
3. See Baeyer-Katte, 1982; Horgan, 2005; Hudson, 1999; Schmidtchen, 1982; Silke, 2003.
4. Examples of this approach include Akhtar, 1999; Gilmartin, 1996; Pearlstein, 1991; Volkam, 1997.
5. See Post, 1984, 1986, 1990/1998; Robins and Post, 1997.
6. Milgram, 1975.
7. Christakis and Fowler, 2007.
8. This is the approach espoused by Scheuer, 2006.
9. See Gupta, 2001; Gurr, 1970; Hafez, 2003; Kepel, 2002; Moaddel, 2005; Roy, 2004.
10. Emerson, 2002; Habeck, 2006; Lewis, 2003.
11. See especially Habeck, 2006.
12. On this point see Abou el Fadl, 2005; Baker, 2003; Esposito, 2002.
13. As argued by Gerges, 2005; McCants and Brachman, 2006.
14. Benschop, 2005.
15. Sageman, 2004.
16. Chaliand and Blin, 2004.

CHAPTER 2. THE GLOBALIZATION OF JIHADI TERROR

1. See Al-Fadl, 2001.
2. National Commission on Terrorist Attacks upon the United States, 2004: 150.
3. Rapoport, 2003.
4. Engel and Rosenthal, 1992: 19–20.

5. Quoted in Engel and Rosenthal, 1992: 78.

6. Ulam, 1977: 269.

7. Kucherov, 1952.

8. Borowitz, 2005.

9. Democracy (in the Western sense) and freedom (as practiced in the West) are ways to achieve justice and fairness. These more abstract concepts can be realized in a variety of ways, according to local customs. The prevalent social system of wasta (favors on the basis of kinship and friendship) is designed to protect the locals from the authority of their government. Yet these local customs will undermine any attempt to build a Jeffersonian democracy in their midst.

10. The death of the Prophet split the Muslim community in two. The majority of the community accepted the choice of Abu Bakr as its new political leader and became known as Sunnis (followers of the Sunnah, or example of the Prophet). A minority argued that the leader must be a descendant of the Prophet, in this case Ali, and became known as Shi'a (meaning the followers of Ali). The full split between the Sunnis and Shi'a came in 662, ending the reign of the Golden Age of Islam.

11. See Sageman, 2004: 1–24 for an in-depth discussion of this evolution.

12. Qutb, n.d.

13. Faraj, 1986.

14. Gerges, 2005.

15. For histories, see Benjamin and Simon, 2002; Bergen, 2006; Burke, 2003; Coll, 2004; Kepel, 2002; Sageman, 2004: 25–59; Scheuer, 2006; National Commission on Terrorist Attacks upon the United States, 2004; Wright, 2006.

16. See Bergen, 2006: 75–81 for the minutes of the founding meetings of al Qaeda.

17. Roy, 1994.

18. Al-Fadl, 2001.

19. Bin Laden, 1996.

20. National Commission on Terrorist Attacks upon the United States, 2004: 66, 169–172.

21. Bin Laden, 2005: 58–62.

CHAPTER 3. THE JIHADIST'S PROFILE

Note to epigraph: Buruma, 2006: 192–93.

1. See Club de Madrid, 2005.

2. See Bakker, 2007 for a description of this third wave.

3. I will elaborate further on the three waves in Chapter 7.

4. Mansour, 2003.

5. Chadi, 2003.

6. Rerhaye, 2004 (translation mine).

7. "Two Fifteen-year-olds Behind Bars," 2004.

8. Najib and Serraj, 2003a.

9. Najib and Serraj, 2003b, 2003c.

10. Najib and Serraj, 2003d.

11. Najib and Serraj, 2003e.

12. Najib and Serraj, 2003f.

13. Bennani, 2007 (translation mine).

14. Ibid.

15. Ibid.
16. Zawahiri, 2005.
17. See my previous discussion in Sageman, 2004: 80–91.

CHAPTER 4. RADICALIZATION IN THE DIASPORA

1. Stern, 2003: 32–62.
2. Ferrarella, 2004. In October 2007, Spain's National Court acquitted Rabei and two others of organizing the 2004 Madrid train bombings.
3. Caloprico, 2004.
4. Rousseau, 1997.
5. Nilus, 2003.
6. Zawahiri, 2001.
7. Gerges, 2005.
8. Wiktorowicz, 2005.
9. The New York Police Department report *Radicalization in the West* (Silber and Bhatt, 2007) describes this process.

CHAPTER 5. THE ATLANTIC DIVIDE

1. Personal communications, Europol, June 4, 2007, which tabulated about 1,800 arrests, which excluded British numbers; Joint Terrorism Analysis Center in Britain, June 8, 2007, which tabulated about 500 arrests since 9/11.
2. Updating Eggen and Tate, 2005. Lustick, 2006: 151–52 agrees with this estimate.
3. Pew Research Center, 2007.
4. Pew Research Center, 2007: 48.
5. National Intelligence Council, 2006. The NIE summary of July 2007 confirms this key judgment. "Its association with AQI [al-Qa'ida in Iraq] helps al-Qa'ida [Central] to energize the broader Sunni extremist community, raise resources, and to recruit and indoctrinate operatives, including for Homeland attacks" (National Intelligence Council, 2007).
6. Pew Research Center, 2007: 38–39.
7. Pew Research Center, 2007: 35.
8. Pew Research Center, 2007: 36.
9. Pew Research Center, 2007: 38.
10. See Pew Research Center 2006 and 2007.
11. Anderson, 1991.
12. Geary, 2002.
13. Pew Research Center, 2007: 30.
14. Pew Research Center, 2007: 30.
15. See next section on the economic disparity between these two populations.
16. Hofstede, 1980: 222; Hofstede, 1991: 53.
17. Hofstede, 1991: 53.
18. Pew Research Center, 2007: 95, shows that over half of Muslim immigrants come to the United States for educational or economic opportunities.
19. See Lipset, 1997, who defines the American Creed a little differently: liberty, equal opportunity, individualism, populism, and laissez-faire.
20. Allen, 2006. As an example, the second- and third-generation immigrant children, who

rioted in the fall of 2005, did not do so in the name of militant Islam, but in the name of equality, a more universal value. This is clearly the case, even though the majority of rioters were Muslims who resisted the takeover of the protests by Islamist groups.

21. This may imply that U.S. homegrown wannabe terrorists might be more likely to target official U.S. installations, as opposed to U.S. expatriate terrorists, who might be more likely to target the population itself.

22. Pew Research Center, 2007: 38–39.

23. See Arkoun, 2006; Cesari, 2004; Fetzer and Soper, 2005; Khosrokhavar, 1997 and 2002; Roy, 2004.

24. Pew Research Center, 2007: 19, 98.

25. Pew Research Center, 2007: 3.

26. The same element of idleness seems to have contributed to the growth of gangs, both in the 1920s and the 1980s in the United States. See Thrasher, 1927, and Decker and van Winkle, 1996.

27. See Buruma, 2006; Fetzer and Soper, 2005.

28. Pew Research Center, 2007: 38.

29. Khosrokhavar, 1997.

30. Ramirez Sanchez, 2003.

31. Pew Research Center, 2007: 27.

32. Schmidt, 2007.

CHAPTER 6. TERRORISM IN THE AGE OF THE INTERNET

1. See Groen and Kranenberg, 2006.

2. An exception is Cilluffo, Saathoff, et al., 2007.

3. See Weimann, 2006 as one of the most sophisticated examples of this view.

4. See Bargh and McKenna, 2004.

CHAPTER 7. THE RISE OF LEADERLESS JIHAD

1. See Coll, 2004.

2. The only exception was France, which reacted strongly against the Islamist threat after its two waves of bombings in the summer of 1995 and the spring of 1996.

3. See Bergen, 2007; Hoffman, 2007; and Riedel, 2007.

4. Riedel, 2007: 24.

5. This is a summary of Peter Bergen's arguments, by far the most articulate of the three above.

6. National Intelligence Council, 2007.

7. Bergen, 2007: 13.

8. Hoffman, 2007.

9. National Commission on Terrorist Attacks upon the United States, 2004: 530.

10. Pew Research Center, 2006: 4.

11. Bergen, 2007, astutely notes this local virtual merger between the Taliban and al Qaeda.

12. See the account of Quin, 2005.

13. National Commission on Terrorist Attacks upon the United States, 2004: 228–229.

14. Most of the money for the 2005 Pendennis case in Australia—which involved the arrest of twenty-two global jihadi terrorists planning to blow up sites in Melbourne and Sydney— came from the suspects' public assistance checks and the rest from petty crime.

15. Beam, 1992.

16. Hakim, 2004.

17. The first two waves are still more formally and hierarchically organized.

18. See especially the articles by Michael Scheuer in Heffelfinger, ed., 2005, and in Hutzley, ed., 2007.

19. Smith, 1776/1937: 423.

CHAPTER 8. COMBATING GLOBAL ISLAMIST TERRORISM

1. National Strategy for Combating Terrorism, 2006.

2. See Pew Research Center, 2006 for the worldwide rejection of U.S. foreign policy.

3. "X," 1947.

4. National Strategy for Combating Terrorism: 11–12.

5. See recent arguments of Borowitz, 2005, and Richardson, 2006, which parallel mine.

6. See its website at http://www.rewardsforjustice.net/.

7. Department of Defense, 2006.

8. Lustick, 2006.

9. See Pew Research Center, 2006.

10. National Strategy for Combating Terrorism, 2006: 9.

11. National Strategy for Combating Terrorism, 2006: 9.

12. See Gerges, 2005.

13. National Strategy for Combating Terrorism, 2006: 11.

14. National Strategy for Combating Terrorism, 2006: 10.

15. National Strategy for Combating Terrorism, 2006: 10.

16. The two-step process of personal influence is clearly described in the classic study by Katz and Lazarsfeld (1964). This process was popularized in Gladwell's (2002) best-seller *The Tipping Point*.

17. It is a majority voice. See Pew Research Center, 2006 and 2007.

18. Pew Research Center, 2007.

19. Benjamin and Simon, 2005: 88-95; Benschop, 2005; Buruma, 2006; Vidino, 2006, 337–364.

20. Reported in Olgun, 2006.

21. FISA, 1978.

22. A government funder once told me, "If it's free information, why should we pay for it?"

23. See Schmidtchen, 1981; Baeyer-Katte, 1983.

24. Carus, 2000.

25. Carter, 1990.

26. Reader, 2000; Kaplan and Marshall, 1996. The group is better known for carrying out the Sarin gas attacks in the Tokyo subway in March 1995. It killed dozens through chemical weapons, but no one with biological agents.

27. Stern, 2000.

BIBLIOGRAPHY

Abou el Fadl, Khaled. 2005. *The Great Theft: Wrestling Islam from the Extremists*. New York: HarperCollins.

Akhtar, Salman. 1999. "The Psychodynamic Dimension of Terrorism." *Psychiatric Annals*, 29 (6): 350–355.

Allen, Jodie. 2006. *The French-Muslim Connection: Is France Doing a Better Job of Integration than its Critics?* Philadelphia: Pew Research Center Publications, at http://pewresearch. org/pubs/50/the-french-muslim-connection.

Arkoun, Mohammed, ed. 2006. *Histoire de l'islam et des musulmans en France du Moyen Age à nos jours*. Paris: Editions Albin Michel.

Al-Ashhab, Muhammad, and Al-Shammari. 2002. "Rabat Interrogating Five Saudis Who Planned to Attack U.S. and British Ships." *Al-Hayah*, June 12, 2002, Open Source Center GMP20020612.0000055.

Baeyer-Katte, Wanda von, et al. 1983. *Analysen sum Terrorismus--3, Gruppeprozesse*. Darmstadt: Deutscher Verlag.

Baker, Raymond William. 2003. *Islam Without Fear: Egypt and the New Islamists*. Cambridge, Mass.: Harvard University Press.

Bakker, Edwin. 2007. *Jihadi Terrorists in Europe*. The Hague: Netherlands Institute of International Relations, Clingendael.

Bamber, David, and Francis Elliott. 2002. "Blair's Iraq Dossier Will Show How Saddam Trained Al-Qa'ida Fighters." *Sunday Telegraph*, September 15, 2002.

Bargh, John, and Katelyn McKenna. 2004. "The Internet and Social Life." *Annual Review of Psychology*, 55: 573–590.

Beam, Louis. 1992. "Leaderless Resistance." *The Seditionist*, 12 (February 1992) at www.louisbeam.com/leaderless.htm.

Benjamin, Daniel, and Steven Simon. 2002. *The Age of Sacred Terror*. New York: Random House.

———. 2005. *The Next Attack: The Failure of the War on Terror and a Strategy for Getting It Right*. New York: Times Books.

Bennani, Driss, with Ahmed Najim. 2007. "Portrait Enquête: L'incroyable histoire des soeurs Laghriss." *Telquel*, No. 260, February 16, 2007.

Benschop, Albert. 2005. *Chronicle of a Political Murder Foretold: Jihad in the Netherlands.* www.sociosite.org/jihad_nl_en.php.

Bergen, Peter. 2006. *The Osama bin Laden I Know.* New York: The Free Press.

———. 2007. "Where You Bin? The Return of al Qaeda." *New Republic,* 236, no. 5 (January 29): 16–19.

Bin Laden, Osama. 1996. "Declaration of War Against the Americans Occupying the Land of the Two Holy Places." *Al-Quds al-Arabi* (London), August 23, 1996, available at www.pbs.org/newshour/terrorism/international/fatwa_1996.html.

———. 2005. *Messages to the World: The Statements of Osama bin Laden.* London: Verso.

Borowitz, Albert. 2005. *Terrorism for Self-Glorification: The Herostratos Syndrome.* Kent, Ohio: Kent State University Press.

Burke, Jason. 2003. *Al-Qaeda: Casting a Shadow of Terror.* London: I. B. Tauris.

Buruma, Ian. 2006. *Murder in Amsterdam: The Death of Theo van Gogh and the Limits of Tolerance.* New York: Penguin Press.

Caloprico, Piero. 2004. "Mohammed the Egyptian: 'I Am the Madrid Strand.'" *La Repubblica* (Rome), June 9, 2004, Open Source Center EUP20040610000060.

Carus, W. Seth. 2000. R.I.S.E., in Jonathan, Tucker, ed., *Toxic Terror: Assessing Terrorist Use of Chemical and Biological Weapons,* 55–70. Cambridge, Mass.: MIT Press.

Cater, Lewis. 1990. *Charisma and Control in Rajneeshpuram: The Role of Shared Values in the Creation of a Community.* Cambridge: Cambridge University Press.

Cesari, Jocelyne. 2004. *L'Islam à l'épreuve de l'Occident.* Paris: La Découverte.

Chadi, Taieb. 2003. "Tous coupables." *Maroc Hebdo International,* 574, October 3, 2003: 5.

Chaliand, Gerard, and Arnaud Blin. 2004. *Histoire du Terrorisme: De l'Antiquité à Al Qaida.* Paris: Bayard.

Christakis, Nicholas, and James Fowler. 2007. "The Spread of Obesity in a Large Social Network over 32 Years." *New England Journal of Medicine,* 357 (4): 370–379.

Cilluffo, Frank, Gregory Saathoff, Jan Lane, Andrew Whitehead, and Sharon Cardash. 2007. NETworked Radicalization: A Counter-Strategy. George Washington University Homeland Security Policy Institute and University of Virginia Critical Incident Analysis Group, found at www.healthsystem.virginia.edu/internet/ciag/publications/NETworked-Radicalization_A-Counter-Strategy.pdf.

Club de Madrid. 2005. *Addressing the Causes of Terrorism, The Club de Madrid Series on Democracy and Terrorism, Volume I,* found at www.safe-democracy.org/docs/CdM-Series-on-Terrorism-Vol-1.pdf.

Coll, Steve. 2004. *Ghost Wars: The Secret History of the CIA, Afghanistan, and bin Laden, from the Soviet Invasion to September 10, 2001.* New York: Penguin Press.

Decker, Scott, and Barrik van Winkle. 1996. *Life in the Gang: Family, Friends, and Violence.* Cambridge: Cambridge University Press.

Department of Defense, United States of America. 2006. *Quadrennial Defense Review Report,* found at www.defenselink.mil/pubs/pdfs/QDR20060203.pdf.

Eggen, Dan, and Julie Tate. 2005. "U.S. Campaign Produces Few Convictions on Terrorism Charges: Statistics Often Count Lesser Crimes." *Washington Post,* June 12, 2005.

Emerson, Steven. 2002. *American Jihad: The Terrorists Living Among Us.* New York: The Free Press.

Engel, Barbara Alpern, and Clifford Rosenthal. 1992, *Five Sisters—Women Against the Tsar: The Memoirs of Five Young Anarchist Women of the 1870s.* New York: Routledge.

Esposito, John. 2002. *Unholy War: Terror in the Name of Islam*. New York: Oxford University Press.

Al-Fadl, Jamal. 2001. *United States of America v. Usama bin Laden, et al*. U.S. District Court, Southern District of New York, S (7) 98 Cr. 1023, February 6–13, 2001: 162–392.

Faraj, Muhammad Abdel Salam. 1986. "Al-Faridah al Ghaibah." In Johannes Jansen, *The Neglected Duty: The Creed of Sadat's Assassins and Islamic Resurgence in the Middle East*. New York: Macmillan, 195–234.

Ferrarella, Luigi. 2004. "'Italians Are Enemies of God': 'No, There Is Only One God.'" *Corriere della Sera* (Milan), July 24, 2004, Open Source Center EUP20040712/000018.

Fetzer, Joel, and Christopher Soper. 2005. *Muslims and the State in Britain, France, and Germany*. Cambridge: Cambridge University Press.

Fielding, Nick. 2001. "Diary of a Terrorist: Inside the Mind of a Fanatic." *Sunday Times* (London), October 14, 2001.

———. 2002. "From a London Public School to the Shadow of the Noose." *Sunday Times* (London), April 21, 2002.

Finn, Peter. 2002. "Syria Interrogating Al Qaeda Recruiter; Sept. 11 Details Shared With U.S." *Washington Post*, June 19, 2002.

FISA. 1978. *Foreign Intelligence Surveillance Act, U.S. Code, Title 50, Chapter 36, Subchapter I*, available electronically at www.fas.org/irp/agency/doj/fisa/.

Gallagher, Tony. 1994. "We Were Sure They Were Digging a Grave for Us." *Daily Mail* (London), November 4, 1994.

Gerges, Fawaz. 2005. *The Far Enemy: Why Jihad Went Global*. New York: Cambridge University Press.

Gilmartin, Kevin. 1996. "The Lethal Triad: Understanding the Nature of Isolated Extremist Groups." *FBI Law Enforcement Bulletin*, September: 1–5.

Gladwell, Malcolm. 2002. *The Tipping Point: How Little Things Can Make a Big Difference*. New York: Back Bay Books.

Godfrey-Smith, Peter. 2003. *Theory and Reality: An Introduction to the Philosophy of Science*. Chicago: University of Chicago Press.

Groen, Janny, and Annieke Kranenberg. 2006. Strijdsters van Allah: Radicale moslima's en het Hofstadnetwerk. Amsterdam: J. M. Meulenhoff.

Gupta, Dipak. 2001. *Path to Collective Madness: A Study in Social Order and Political Pathology*. Westport, Conn.: Praeger.

Gurr, Ted Robert. 1970. *Why Men Rebel*. Princeton, N.J.: Princeton University Press.

Habeck, Mary. 2006. *Knowing the Enemy: Jihadist Ideology and the War on Terror*. New Haven: Yale University Press.

Hafez, Mohammed. 2003. *Why Muslims Rebel: Repression and Resistance in the Islamic World*. Boulder, Colo.: Lynne Rienner Publishers.

Hakim, Umar Abdal (a.k.a. Abu Musab al Suri, or Mustapha Setmariam Nasr). 2004. *The Call for Global Islamic Resistance*, published on various Internet Web sites.

Hannaford, Alex. 2005. "The Toughest Boy in School." *Guardian* (London), February 23, 2005.

Heffelfinger, Christopher, ed. 2005. *Unmasking Terror: A Global Review of Terrorist Activities*. Washington, D.C.: Jamestown Foundation.

Hoffman, Bruce. 2007. *Challenges for the U.S. Special Operations Command Posed by the Global Terrorist Threat: Al Qaeda on the Run or on the March?* Testimony Submitted to the House Armed Subcommittee on Terrorism, Unconventional Threats and Capabilities, February 14, 2007.

Hofstede, Geert. 1980. *Culture's Consequences.* Beverly Hills, Calif.: Sage.

———. 1991. *Culture and Organizations.* Berkshire, England: McGraw-Hill.

Horgan, John. 2005. *The Psychology of Terrorism.* London: Routledge.

Hudson, Rex. 1999. *Who Becomes a Terrorist and Why: The 1999 Government Report on Profiling Terrorists.* Guilford, Conn.: Lyons Press.

Hutzley, Jonathan, ed. 2007. *Unmasking Terror: A Global Review of Terrorist Activities.* Washington, D.C.: Jamestown Foundation.

Jehl, Douglas. 2002. "Death of a Reporter Puts Focus on Pakistan Intelligence Unit." *New York Times,* February 25, 2002.

Kaplan, David, and Andrew Marshall. 1996, *The Cult at the End of the World.* New York: Crown.

Katz, Elihu, and Paul Lazarsfeld. 1964. *Personal Influence: The Part Played by People in the Flow of Mass Communications.* New York: Free Press.

Kepel, Gilles. 2002. Jihad: *The Trail of Political Islam.* Cambridge, Mass.: Harvard University Press.

Khan, Kamran. 2002. "Sheikh Omar Makes Revelation About Terror Activities." *The News* (Islamabad), February 18, 2002.

Khosrokhavar, Farhad. 1997. *L'Islam des jeunes.* Paris: Flammarion.

———. 2002. *Les nouveaux martyrs d'Allah.* Paris: Flammarion.

Kohlmann, Evan. 2004. *Al-Qaida's Jihad in Europe: The Afghan-Bosnian Network.* Oxford: Berg.

Kucherov, Samuel. 1952. "The Case of Vera Zasulich." *Russian Review,* 11 (2): 86–96.

La Razon. 2002. "Al-Qa'idah Held 'Summit' in Spain Six Days Before 11 September." *La Razon,* June 26, 2002, Open Source Center EUP20020626000174.

Lee, Caroline, Rajeev Syal, and Anna Pukas. 1994. "The Charming Terrorist from the LSE." *Sunday Times* (London), December 11, 1994.

Lévy, Bernard-Henri. 2003. *Qui a tué Daniel Pearl?* Paris: Grasset.

Lewis, Bernard, 2002. *What Went Wrong? The Clash Between Islam and Modernity in the Middle East.* New York: Harper Perennial.

Linzer, Dafna. 2002. "Suspect in Pearl Killing Is College Dropout Who Was Radicalized by War in Bosnia." *Associated Press,* April 2, 2002.

Lipset, Seymour Martin. 1997. *American Exceptionalism.* New York: Norton.

Lustick, Ian. 2006. *Trapped in the War on Terror.* Philadelphia: University of Pennsylvania Press.

Mansour, Abdellatif. 2003. "Kamikazes à quatorze ans." *Maroc Hebdo International,* No. 574, October 3, 2003: 4–6.

McCants, William, and Jarret Brachman. 2006. *Militant Ideology Atlas: A Research Compendium.* West Point, N.Y.: Combating Terrorism Center.

McGinty, Stephen. 2002. "The English Islamic Terrorist." *The Scotsman,* July 16, 2002.

Milgram, Stanley. 1975. *Obedience to Authority.* New York: Harper Torchbooks.

Moaddel, Mansoor. 2005. *Islamic Modernism, Nationalism, and Fundamentalism.* Chicago: University of Chicago Press.

Najib, Abdelhak, and Karim Serraj. 2003a. "La mère d'Imane et de Sanae devoile tout." *La Gazette du Maroc,* September 8, 2003.

——. 2003b. "Kichk, des tracts, des butanes et . . . les jumelles." *La Gazette du Maroc*, September 15, 2003.

——. 2003c. "L'arrestation de Hassan Chaouni, alias Kichk." *La Gazette du Maroc*, September 15, 2003.

——. 2003d. "Le cas Mustapha Echatar." *La Gazette du Maroc*, September 22, 2003.

——. 2003e. "Fouad Al Gaz, le poissonnier." *La Gazette du Maroc*, September 29, 2003.

——. 2003f. "Jamais je ne me suis proposée pour voler une arme!" *La Gazette du Maroc*, October 6, 2003.

National Commission on Terrorist Attacks upon the United States. 2004. *The 9/11 Commission Report: Final Report of the National Commission on Terrorist Attacks upon the United States*, 2002. New York: Norton.

National Intelligence Council. 2006. *National Intelligence Estimate: Trends in Global Terrorism: Implications for the United States*. April 2006, found at www.dni.gov/nic/special_global_terrorism.html.

——. 2007. *National Intelligence Estimate: The Terrorist Threat to the U.S. Homeland*. July 2007 found at www.dni.gov/press_releases/20070717_release.pdf.

National Strategy for Combating Terrorism. 2006. www.whitehouse.gov/nsc/nsct/2006/.

Nilus, Sergius. 2003. *The Protocols of the Meetings of the Learned Elders of Zion*. Honolulu, Hawaii: University Press of the Pacific.

Olgun, Ahmet. 2006. "Lions of Tawheed Have Been Defeated This Time." *NRC Handelsblad* (Rotterdam), December 2, 2006, translated by the Open Source Center, EUP20061204024004.

O'Neill, Sean. 2001. "Britons Fall Victim to an Islamic Dream." *Daily Telegraph* (London), October 5, 2001.

——. 2002. "Public Schoolboy Who Turned to Terror." *Daily Telegraph* (London), July 7, 2002.

Pearlstein, Richard. 1991. *The Mind of the Political Terrorist*. Wilmington, Del.: Scholarly Resources.

Pew Research Center. 2006. *Europe's Muslims More Moderate: The Great Divide: How Westerners and Muslims View Each Other*, at http://pewglobal.org/reports/pdf/253.pdf.

——. 2007. *Muslim Americans: Middle Class and Mostly Mainstream*, at http://pewresearch.org/assets/pdf/muslim-americans.pdf.

Post, Jerrold. 1984. "Notes on a Psychodynamic Theory of Terrorist Behavior." *Terrorism: An International Journal*, 7 (3): 241–256.

——. 1986. "Hostilite, Conformite, Fraternite: The Group Dynamics of Terrorist Behavior." *International Journal of Group Psychotherapy*, 36 (2): 211–224.

——. 1990/1998. "Terrorist Psycho-logic: Terrorist Behavior as a Product of Psychological Forces." In Walter Reich, ed., *Origins of Terrorism: Psychologies, Ideologies, Theologies, States of Mind*. Washington, D.C.: Woodrow Wilson Center Press.

Quin, Mary. 2005. *Kidnapped in Yemen*. Guilford, Conn.: Lyons Press.

Qutb, Sayyid. n.d. *Milestones*. Cedar Rapids, Iowa: Mother Mosque Foundation.

Ramirez Sanchez, Ilich (Carlos). 2003. *L'Islam révolutionnaire*. Monaco: Editions du Rocher.

Reader, Ian. 2000. *Religious Violence in Contemporary Japan: The Case of Aum Shinrikyo*. Honolulu: University of Hawaii Press.

Rerhaye, Narjis. 2004. "Les jumelles mineures de la prison Zaki: Le cri d'une mère." *Le Matin* (Morocco), May 17, 2004.

Richardson, Louise. 2006. *What Terrorists Want: Understanding the Enemy, Containing the Threat.* New York: Random House.

Riedel, Bruce. 2007. "Al Qaeda Strikes Back." *Foreign Affairs,* 86, no. 3: 24–34.

Robins, Robert, and Jerrold Post. 1997. *Political Paranoia: The Psychopolitics of Hatred.* New Haven: Yale University Press.

Rousseau, Jean-Jacques. 1979. *Emile or On Education.* New York: Basic Books.

——. 1997. *The Social Contract and Other Later Political Writings.* Ed. Victor Gourevitch. Cambridge: Cambridge University Press.

Roy, Olivier. 1994. *The Failure of Political Islam.* Cambridge, Mass.: Harvard University Press.

——. 2004. *Globalized Islam: The Search for a New Ummah.* New York: Columbia University Press.

Sageman, Marc. 2004. *Understanding Terror Networks.* Philadelphia: University of Pennsylvania Press.

Scheuer, Michael. 2006. *Through Our Enemies' Eye: Osama bin Laden, Radical Islam, and the Future of America.* Revised edition. Washington, D.C.: Potomac Books.

Schmid, Alex. 1984. *Political Terrorism.* Amsterdam: SWIDOC.

Schmidt, Susan. 2007. "Trail of an Enemy Combatant: From Desert to U.S. Heartland." *Washington Post,* July 20, 2007.

Schmidtchen, Gerhard, et al. 1981. *Analysen zum Terrorismus—2: Lebenslaufanalysen.* Darmstadt: Deutscher Verlag.

Sheikh, Ahmed Omar. 2001. "Diary." *Indian Express,* October 11, 2001, found at www.indianexpress.com/res/web/pIe/ie20011010/top1.html, accessed February 14, 2007.

Silber, Mitchell, and Arvin Bhatt. 2007. *Radicalization in the West: The Homegrown Threat.* New York: New York Police Department Intelligence Division, found at www.nyc.gov/html/nypd/pdf/dcpi/NYPD_Report-Radicalization_in_the_West.pdf.

Silke, Andrew, ed. 2003. *Terrorists, Victims and Society.* Chichester, England: John Wiley & Sons.

Smith, Adam. 1776/1937. *An Inquiry into the Nature and Causes of the Wealth of Nations (The Cannan Edition).* New York: Modern Library.

Stern, Jessica. 2000. "Larry Wayne Harris." In Jonathan Tucker, ed., *Toxic Terror: Assessing Terrorist Use of Chemical and Biological Weapons,* 227–246. Cambridge, Mass.: MIT Press.

——. 2003. *Terror in the Name of God: Why Religious Militants Kill.* New York: HarperCollins.

Stock, Jon. 2002. "Inside the Mind of a Seductive Killer." *The Times* (London), August 21, 2002.

Thrasher, Frederic. 1927. *The Gang: A Study of 1,313 Gangs in Chicago.* Chicago: University of Chicago Press.

Tucker, Jonathan, ed. 2000. *Toxic Terror: Assessing Terrorist Use of Chemical and Biological Weapons.* Cambridge, Mass.: MIT Press.

Ulam, Adam. 1977. *In the Name of the People.* New York: Viking Press.

"U.S. Officials Have One of Bin Laden's Most Senior Operatives in Custody." 2002. *ABC World News Tonight,* June 18, 2002.

Videnieks, Monica, and Natalie O'Brien. 2000. "Nightmare Relived as 'Evil' Returns to Streets." *The Australian,* January, 4, 2000.

Vinido, Lorenzo. 2006. *Al Qaeda in Europe: The New Battleground of International Jihad.* Amherst, N.Y.: Prometheus Books.

Volkan, Vamik. 1997. *Blood Lines: From Ethnic Pride to Ethnic Terrorism*. Boulder, Colo.: Westview Press.

Weimann, Gabriel. 2006. *Terror on the Internet: The New Arena, the New Challenges*. Washington, D.C.: United States Institute for Peace Press.

Wiktorowicz, Quintan. 2005. *Radicalism Rising: Muslim Extremism in the West*. Lanham, Md.: Rowman & Littlefield.

Williams, David. 2002. "Kidnapper-Guy@hotmail.com." *Daily Mail* (UK), July 16, 2002.

Wright, Lawrence. 2006. *The Looming Tower: Al-Qaeda and the Road to 9/11*. New York: Knopf.

"X" [George Kennan]. 1947. "The Sources of Soviet Conduct." *Foreign Affairs*, 25 (July): 566–582.

Al-Zawahiri, Ayman. 2001. "Knights Under the Prophet's Banner, Part VI." Serialized in *al-Sharq al-Awsat* (London), December 7, 2001.

——. 2005. Letter from al-Zawahiri to al-Zarqawi. *Office of the Director of National Intelligence News Release No. 2-05*, October 11, 2005, accessed at www.dni.gov/press_releases/letter_in_english.pdf.

ACKNOWLEDGMENTS

Writing a book is always a collective effort. Most of the arguments in this work come from my interactions with other people involved in the field of terrorism research. I wish to thank them all, for they have wittingly or unwittingly contributed to this book. Interpretations are strictly my own, since these individuals did not have any input into the final product.

I want to start by thanking my collaborator Scott Atran and his team of University of Michigan students, especially Justin Magouirck and Dominick Wright. I want to thank all the scholars in the field whom it has been my privilege to meet: Gary Ackerman, Farhana Ali, Rogelio Alonso, Nicole Argo, Salwa El-Awa, Edwin Bakker, Daniel Benjamin, Peter Bergen, Mia Bloom, Albert Borowitz, Susan Brandon, Anthony Bubalo, Jason Burke, Seth Carus, Jocelyne Cesari, Steve Coll, Martha Crenshaw, Gerogi Derlugian, Jonathan Drummond, Greg Fealy, Boaz Ganor, Andrew Garfield, Fawaz Gerges, Anne Giudicelli, Janny Groen, Rohan Gunaratna, Dipak Gupta, Mohammed Hafez, Atef Hamdy, Mark Hamm, Bernard Haykal, Bruce Hoffman, John Horgan, Rexford Hudson, Sidney Jones, Michael Kenney, Gilles Kepel, Farhad Khosrokhavar, David Kilcullen, Katherina von Knop, Dirk Laabs, Gary LaFree, Robert Leiken, Ian Lustick, Clark McCauley, Ariel Merari, Kevin Murphy, Sally Neighbour, Brendan O'Leary, Robert Pape, Nikos Passas, Ami Pedazhur, Jerrold Post, David Rapoport, Fernando Reinares, Maria Ressa, Louise Richardson, Bernard Rougier, Olivier Roy, Michael Scheuer, Alex Schmid, Ronald Schouten, Mark Sedgwick, Steve Simon, Joshua Sinai, Anne Speckhard, Alisa Stack-O'Connor, Jessica Stern, Charles Strozier, Michael Taarnby, Maxwell Taylor, Ken Ward, Gabriel Weimann, Deborah Wheeler, Carrie Rosefsky Wickham, Quintan Wiktorowicz, Brian Glynn Williams, and Lawrence Wright. I have learned much from them, and even when we disagreed, their arguments forced me to sharpen mine. Without them, this book would not have been written.

I am indebted to many people who have supported my research through encouragements: Alexis Albion, Mustapha Javed Ali, George Backus, Jose Enrique Balbin, Richard Barrett, Daniel Beaudette, Arvin Bhatt, Steven Bongardt, Duncan Brown, Richard Burcham, Glenn Carle, Hsinchun Chen, Charles Chenoweth, Frank Ciluffo, David Cohen, Sarah Connolly, John Cummings, Richard Danzig, Richard Davis, Mirjam Dittrich, Irene Dubicka, Jacques Duchesneau, Rick Elias, James Ellis, Thelma Gillen, Edward Gistaro, Nathan Gray, Nancy Kay Hayden, Rick Howington, Larry Johnson, Rita Katz, Patrick Lang, Todd Leventhal, David Low, Brian Marcus, Philip Mudd, Neal Pollard, Joel Rodriguez, Lawrence Sanchez, Robert Sica, Mitchell Silber, Gary Strong, Donald Sutherland, Margaret Jo Velardo, John Voeller, Aaron Weisburd, Ira Weiss, Mark Weitekamp, Gerald Yonas, Michael Young, Hidemi Yuki, and Juan Zarate. Unfortunately, I cannot name dozens of analysts and government employees, who have discussed this topic with me and provided me with countless insights, which have enriched this book.

I must also express great appreciation of the journalists who have shared information with me and discussed some of these issues in "real time": Scott Baldauf, Paul Barrett, Nicolas Bourcier, Christophe Brule, Neil Docherty, Ernesto Ekaizer, Andrea Elliott, James Fallows, Al Goodman, Terrence Henry, David Ignatius, David Kaplan, Raffi Khatchdourian, Michel Moutot, Fabrice de Pierrebourg, Emmanuel Poncet, Sebastian Rotella, Henry Schuster, and Demetri Sevastopulo.

I also wish to thank the people at the University of Pennsylvania Press, who have encouraged me to write this book, namely Peter Agree, William Finan, and Noreen O'Connor-Abel.

Finally, my work is possible only because of the support and devotion of my wife, Jody, and son, Joseph, who had to put up with my absences and distraction throughout this time. I don't know how I can thank them both.